DATE DUE

1/12/13	
OCT 0 8 2015	

GAYLORD   PRINTED IN U.S.A.

Faith Finding Meaning

Faith Finding Meaning

A Theology of Judaism

BYRON L. SHERWIN

UNIVERSITY PRESS

2009

OXFORD
UNIVERSITY PRESS

Oxford University Press, Inc., publishes works that further
Oxford University's objective of excellence
in research, scholarship, and education.

Oxford   New York
Auckland   Cape Town   Dar es Salaam   Hong Kong   Karachi
Kuala Lumpur   Madrid   Melbourne   Mexico City   Nairobi
New Delhi   Shanghai   Taipei   Toronto

With offices in
Argentina   Austria   Brazil   Chile   Czech Republic   France   Greece
Guatemala   Hungary   Italy   Japan   Poland   Portugal   Singapore
South Korea   Switzerland   Thailand   Turkey   Ukraine   Vietnam

Published by Oxford University Press, Inc.
198 Madison Avenue, New York, New York 10016

www.oup.com

Oxford is a registered trademark of Oxford University Press

Sherwin, Byron L.
Faith finding meaning : a theology of Judaism / Byron L. Sherwin.
p. cm.
Includes bibliographical references.
ISBN 978–0–19–533623–8 1. Judaism. I.   Title.
BM562.S54   2009
296.3—dc22   2009002658

1 3 5 7 9 8 6 4 2

Printed in the United States of America
on acid-free paper

For JPG and KZF

I would rather have a good friend than all the possessions in the world.

—Plato

We seek the foundation of Judaism...in everything except religion....we...strive to make it [Judaism] so flexible that we can turn it
in every direction which it is our pleasure to follow....My object in this
sketch has been to make the reader *think* about Judaism....We usually
urge that in Judaism religion means life; but we forget that a life without
guiding principles and thoughts is a life not worth living. At least it was
so considered by the greatest Jewish thinkers.

—Solomon Schechter, *Studies in Judaism*

Preface

Ignored at best, deemed irrelevant or divisive at worst, theology is not a priority item on the Jewish communal or academic agenda. Whereas in medieval times, Jewish theologians felt compelled to demonstrate the existence of God and to defend Jewish theological presuppositions against claims made by other religions, contemporary Jewish theologians find themselves obliged to defend the very existence of Jewish theology against those who depict the theological enterprise as "the search by a blind person for a black cat in a dark room which is not even there."

From preschool to graduate school, the study of Jewish theology is either minimized or absent in Jewish education. Even in Jewish theological seminaries, theological training is sparse and elusive. Theology languishes as an excommunicate in the contemporary world of Jewish learning and communal existence. It is therefore astonishing but not surprising that theological illiteracy characterizes Jewish communal life.

It is the goal of the present work to demonstrate the existence and to portray the nature of Jewish theology, to affirm the poignancy of theological discourse in addressing existential problems such as the problem of life's meaning, to "make the case" for theology's ability to serve as an authentic and viable foundation for Jewish identity, to delineate theology's role in furthering Jewish continuity, and for rescuing contemporary Judaism from its tendencies toward inauthenticity and self-destruction.

The first two chapters provide a conceptual and historical analysis of why Jewish theology has been neglected or ignored, and how in the absence of theological discourse largely secular "substitute faiths" have been developed during the past few centuries that have displaced a theologically based foundation for Jewish identity. In addition, the findings of recent sociological and demographic studies of American Jewry are examined to indicate not only how these "substitute faiths" represent inauthentic foundations for Jewish identity but also how they have failed strategically to fulfill the "prime directive" of contemporary Jewish communal organizations and institutions: ensuring the continuity of Jews as Jews and the continuity of Judaism as a faith tradition.

Beginning with chapter 3, Jewish theology is presented as a means of providing an authentic and strategically viable vehicle for addressing the conceptual mistakes and strategic failures that have characterized modern Jewish communal life. Chapter 3 addresses the question, What is Jewish theology? by offering four criteria for a valid Jewish theology: authenticity, coherence, contemporaneity, and communal acceptance.

Throughout the Middle Ages, the theological endeavor was characterized as "faith seeking understanding." As such, theology was largely considered the provenance of philosophical theologians seeking to rationally justify that which was already believed. A consequence of this approach was the production of imposed dogmatic and systematized belief systems, often forcing scripturally based faith into the straitjacket of incompatible medieval philosophical concepts. Chapter 4 introduces an alternative view of the theological enterprise that is more conducive to our times and more correlative with classical Jewish teachings: "faith seeking meaning."

Beginning with the individual existential quest rather than with presumed theological concepts, "faith seeking meaning" places theology at the intersection of the individual's quest for meaning and the ongoing quest of theology to articulate the meaning of individual human existence within the parameters of a particular historical faith tradition—in this case, Judaism. In the chapters that follow, various fundamental features of Judaism are presented not in terms of imposed belief but rather in terms of how they can address the individual's quest for meaning. For example, one characteristic of meaningful living is participation in an intimate, committed love relationship. For Jewish theology, such a relationship is a covenantal one. In chapter 5, "living in the covenant" is portrayed as a means whereby faith finds meaning.

In the covenantal relationship, there is a meeting, a rendezvous, between God and the individual. Chapter 6 focuses on rendezvous points where the human being can encounter the divine: the self, the world, the sacred word, and the sacred deed.

Throughout the history of human experience, evil and absurdity have posed the most poignant challenges to goodness and meaning. The final two chapters (chapters 7and 8) deal with how these challenges might be addressed while keeping faith and meaning intact.

I am grateful for the following permissions to reprint in the present volume some short excerpts from my previous writings: *Sparks amidst the Ashes* (Oxford University Press, 1997); "Love and Law in Jewish Theology," *Anglican Theological Review* 64, no. 4 (October 1982); *Kabbalah: An Introduction to Jewish Mysticism* (Roman and Littlefield, 2006); "Judaism and the World to Come," *First Things*, no. 164 (June/July 2006); "Portrait of God as a Young Artist," *Judaism* 33, no. 4 (Fall 1984); "The Assimilation of Judaism," *Judaism* 55, nos. 3/4 (Fall/Winter 2006). Though a freestanding work, the present volume may be considered a companion volume to my *Studies in Jewish Theology: Reflections in the Mirror of Tradition* (Vallentine Mitchell, 2007).

I am grateful to Oxford University Press for publishing this work, and especially to editors Cynthia Read, Jennifer Kowing, and Justin Tackett. Authors are often asked: "How long did it take you to write this book?" With regard to the present work, the answer is: "a lifetime."

Contents

Faith Finding Meaning

From Crypto-Jews to Crypto-Judaism

In seventeenth-century Holland, an unprecedented phenomenon occurred in the long history of Judaism. Rabbis ministered to a Jewish community largely consisting of individuals who had been baptized and raised as Catholic Christians, or who were the children or grandchildren of Jews raised as Catholic Christians. This even included some of the rabbis and lay leaders of this community.[1]

Most of the members of the "Portuguese" Jewish congregation of seventeenth-century Amsterdam were Jews or the descendants of Jews who had converted to Christianity in Spain or Portugal. Known as *conversos* (converts), or by the derogatory term *marrano* (piglet), these descendants of the *cristianos nuevos* (New Christians) had now become "Renewed" Jews in their new home in Holland.

Many of the New Christians had lived publicly in Spain and Portugal as Christians while practicing remnants of the rituals of their Jewish forebears in secret, often in the privacy of their homes. As time progressed, they became increasingly detached from Jewish life and learning, holding on to a number of vestigial practices that offered a vague reminder of their ancestral legacy. For example, they would clean their chandeliers and put on a new shirt on Friday afternoons (in anticipation of the onset of the Jewish Sabbath), and at home they would refrain from eating pork (in compliance with Jewish dietary laws). As they gained prominence in the cultural, economic, religious, and political life of Spain and Portugal, various "establishments" in Iberia, representing the *cristianos viejos* (Old Christians) saw them as a threat to the integrity of existing social, cultural, political, economic, and religious institutions, and a backlash occurred. One expression of this was the persecution of the New Christians by the Spanish Inquisition.[2]

In 1492 when the Jews were expelled from Spain, and in 1495 when they were expelled from Portugal, Jews who decided at great personal risk and economic loss to leave Spain went to other lands to continue their lives as Jews. But, it is estimated, about one-third remained there as New Christians. Jews had lived in Spain for hundreds of years, some dating their residence back to the first century. Their expulsion by "the Catholic monarchs," Ferdinand and Isabella, who wanted Spain to be an exclusively Catholic nation, caused severe trauma to Spanish Jews who suddenly had to leave the ancestral land in which they and their forebears had flourished for centuries as Jews—religiously, culturally, and economically.[3] Because of the long-standing stability and creativity that had characterized Jewish life in Spain, the expulsion of the Jews from that land innerved Jews throughout Europe, where conditions of their continued residence were perpetually fragile. The earthquake of the trauma of the expulsion from the Iberian Peninsula sent aftershocks throughout the contemporary Jewish world, especially in Europe.

For Spanish Jewry, the expulsion precipitated intense problems of Jewish identity. Many families were split between those who had left Spain, refusing to surrender their Jewish faith, and those who remained New Christians either in Iberia or in other lands to which they later emigrated. Questions emerged: In what sense, if any, were the New Christians still Jews? Could they ever return to the Jewish faith? Was being a Jew a matter of inward belief, or did it also require outward expression? Was it only a matter of outward expression, with practices and observances that required no underlying theological beliefs? Was it merely an "ethnic" designation that required no specific beliefs or practices? Such questions confronted individual *converso* families and were addressed in the Jewish legal and theological treatises of the time.[4] Questions such as these also confront Jews today.

Those who continued their lives as Jews after the expulsion needed to reacculturate themselves to their new places of residence, such as Turkey, where Islam was the dominant religion. Yet their identity as Jews and the continuity of Jewish faith and practice remained intact. However, those who had become Christians, and whose children and grandchildren were raised as New Christians, and who had eventually left Spain and Portugal—mostly in the late sixteenth and early seventeenth centuries—faced a crisis of personal and religious identity. Either for opportunistic reasons or from conviction, they and their immediate forebears had accepted Christianity. Now, the Spanish establishment had called their identity as Spanish or Portuguese Catholics into question. They were now being persecuted by the very political, cultural, and religious institutions that had compelled their forebears to become Christians. They were considered neither true Catholics by the Catholics nor true Jews by the Jews. The Old Catholics considered them not to be really Catholic or really Spanish. And, they had severed their ties to their ancestral faith by accepting baptism and by living as Christians.

The Catholics in Spain and Portugal tended to consider the New Christians to be "old Jews," crypto-Jews, who could never fully divest themselves of Jewish faith or identity. Even the waters of the baptismal font were considered inadequate to transform a Jew into a Christian. Jews in the lands to which many fled—especially those whose ancestors had accepted expulsion rather than conversion to Christianity—considered these New Christians as apostate Jews and as traitors to their people, or as the descendants of apostate Jews.

Many *conversos* and their descendants sought to return to Judaism. The rabbis debated whether, and if so how, their return could occur. Some rabbinic authorities maintained that the sin of apostasy was so heinous that reconciliation was not possible, that accepting them, even as penitents, would be an affront to those who had sacrificed so much in the 1490s to retain their Jewish faith. But some of the rabbis, including those whose own ancestors had become Christians, accepted the *conversos* and established a process of penitence and education to bring them back into the Jewish fold. Among the New Christians, however, there were those who decided to remain Christian. There were also those who tried to simultaneously embrace both Judaism and Christianity. And there were those who embraced neither, rejecting religious doctrines and practices that their thinking and life experience had convinced them were false, and throwing their lot with the new skepticism and emergent "secularism" that had begun to emerge in seventeenth-century western Europe, which eventually led to the inception of the French and German Enlightenment in the eighteenth century.

Despite their sincere desire to return to the Jewish faith and the Jewish fold, *conversos* had many obstacles to overcome. Though they had left Spain and Portugal behind, though many had divested themselves of Christianity, though many had exchanged their Spanish names for Hebrew names, and though some had accepted harsh penances as the price of "return," most "new Jews" retained the culture and the language of Spain and Portugal. They not only remained influenced by Christian doctrines but also tended to understand the nature of Jewish identity and Judaism through the prism of Spanish-Catholic teachings. As one of them put it, "It is truly difficult to desert a religion which one has known from the cradle."[5]

Difficult as it was to abandon the Christian religion in which they had been raised, so was it difficult to embrace their ancestral faith in its fullness. The *conversos* found themselves returning to a home in which they had never resided, a faith that remained largely alien to them. They were mostly ignorant of Jewish religious practices and theological teachings. They knew little or no Hebrew—the language of Jewish learning and prayer. Though they were familiar with Hebrew scripture in translation, they tended to understand it through the prism of Christian interpretation, and, of the texts and traditions of rabbinic Judaism, they were largely uninformed. The doubts that had led many to reject Christianity now carried over to their endeavor to reaffirm Judaism. For example, many *conversos* who rejected Christian beliefs in an afterlife subsequently rejected Jewish beliefs in an afterlife.[6] Still immersed in Iberian Catholic culture and language, the *conversos* were semantically detached from Jewish concepts, practices, and culture. Many had been schooled not only in Iberian languages and literature but also in the classics of Greco-Roman culture, which influenced their (often initially negative) views of Jewish faith and practice.

Besides their geographic displacement from Iberia, the *conversos* experienced a feeling of "semantic displacement" in their new Dutch homes, and in the faith of their forebears. Though their rabbis and teachers usually could speak to them in their native Spanish or Portuguese about the doctrines, practices, and texts of the Jewish faith, it is likely that they could not divest certain terms or ideas of their Christian overlay of meaning, which were all too familiar to them. For example, references to God as "El Señor" (the Lord) or as "El Salvador" (the Savior) undoubtedly evoked Christian theological presuppositions, as these terms were readily identified in Spanish with Jesus Christ. It is not surprising, therefore, that legion efforts were made to teach Hebrew to the *conversos* as a way of addressing their semantic displacement.

The educational program of the rabbis of Amsterdam vis-à-vis the *conversos* aimed not only at conveying information about Jewish practices and sacred texts but also at acculturating the *conversos* into a way of life and thought compatible with traditional Jewish teachings. The goal was to enable the *conversos* to be able to think about their Jewish identity and their Jewish faith in "native" categories rather than in categories drawn from elsewhere, particularly from Christian or "secular" thought.[7]

One may draw a number of significant parallels between today's Jews and the *conversos* of seventeenth-century Amsterdam. Indeed, as we shall see, modern Jewry is, in some important ways, an ideological descendant of the *conversos*. Though most Jews today are not the descendants of baptized Christians, they are nonetheless like the *conversos* in that they are culturally, conceptually, and semantically displaced from the constitutive texts, ideas, and traditions of Judaism. If Judaism is the "first language" or "native" language of the Jewish people, then like the *conversos* of yesteryear, contemporary American Jews "speak Judaism" as a "second language" or speak it badly, if at all. As is further discussed later, modern Western Jews in general, and American Jews in particular, have tended to understand Jewish identity and Jewish faith in non-Jewish categories, often imported from liberal Protestantism and from secular Western thinking with roots in the French and German Enlightenment, and from the "secularism" of the *conversos* of the seventeenth century.

A major goal of the French and German Enlightenment was the subversion of religious authority and tradition. It is therefore singularly ironic that various forms of modern liberal religion embraced Enlightenment ideas to provide a foundation for their beliefs and practices. This is especially true of modern liberal forms of Judaism that were shaped by an ideology that aimed at the subversion of Judaism as well as of Christianity. Among other things, the Enlightenment wanted to replace religious obligations with individual autonomy, religious law and ritual with rational thought and a universalistic morality. Many ideas that characterized the Enlightenment were foreshadowed by the philosophy of Baruch Benedict Spinoza, the descendant of a *converso* family who lived in seventeenth-century Amsterdam, who was part of the community that the rabbis of Amsterdam, like Samuel ha-Levi Morteira and Menashe ben Israel attempted to return to the faith of their Jewish forebears.

Unlike many of his fellow *conversos* who reaffirmed Jewish faith and practice, Spinoza not only restated some of the ideas about Judaism that the *conversos* had acquired during their lives as Christians but took them some steps further. For example, before their reacculturation to the Jewish community, many *conversos* affirmed the authority and the sanctity of Hebrew scripture but refused to accept the authority of the rabbinic interpretations of scripture, considering them a perversion of the meaning and message of the scriptural text. These *conversos* denied the authority and the validity of many of the laws and theological teachings of the Talmudic rabbis, as well as the authority of the rabbinic leadership of their own Jewish community.[8] Spinoza not only affirmed this view but took it further by denying revelation and consequently rejecting the sacred nature of Scripture itself. Anticipating the views of the French Enlightenment, Spinoza sought to undermine the foundation of scripturally based religions—like Judaism and Christianity—by rejecting their supernatural foundation in revelation (now replaced with reason) and by denying the correlative claim regarding the sanctity and authority of scriptural traditions. For Spinoza, there is no supernatural, transcendent God to provide revelation but only the God of nature, God in nature, that is, pantheism.

As will be discussed further, Spinoza depicted Judaism primarily as a religion of law. However, like many *conversos*, he affirmed the Pauline doctrine that Jewish law (halakhah) is no longer binding. But, unlike Saint Paul, Spinoza did not consider the law as obsolete because it had been superseded by a new covenant initiated by the advent of Jesus and messianic redemption. Rather, Spinoza adapted a view popular in *converso* circles, according to which, with the destruction of the Second Jewish Commonwealth by the Romans in 70 C.E., the laws and commandments of the Torah became obsolete, with only universalistic moral laws having any continued validity or relevance.[9] Since, in this view, Jewish law was related to a condition of Jewish political sovereignty, once political sovereignty was eliminated, the need for these laws was also eliminated. Spinoza went further by rejecting the theological presuppositions upon which Jewish religious law is based, that is, a supernatural God, revelation and prophecy, divine providence, and the authority of the rabbinic interpretative tradition. For Spinoza, truth may only be obtained through reason. Both metaphysics and ethics are, in his view, rooted in reason rather than in revelation. In addition, like many of the *conversos*, Spinoza rejected traditional Jewish views of the afterlife by denying that the soul could survive the death of the body. Finally, while rejecting the binding character of Jewish law, Spinoza affirmed the binding quality of the laws of the state (in his case, Holland) as the primary object of his legal allegiance and obedience, and as the source of his protection from persecution—a view (discussed later) that was to resurface in American Jewry some centuries later.[10] These antinomian tendencies in the *converso* community would combine with the onset of a pervasive millenarian or messianic impulse in the late seventeenth century to move many *conversos* and their descendants to identify with the emergent Sabbatean movement, with its blatantly antinomian (i.e., anti-halakhic) features.

The trauma of the exile of the Jews from Spain and Portugal had given a new currency and urgency to the age-old problem of Jewish exile and suffering. One response was the emergence of heightened messianic expectation. The appearance of the "mystical messiah" (i.e., Shabbatai Zevi) from the ranks of the Sephardic community in the 1660s was enthusiastically greeted in many Jewish—especially Sephardic—communities. After Shabbatai Zevi's conversion to Islam under pressure from the Turkish sultan, many former *conversos* accepted the claim that Shabbatai Zevi was actually a crypto-Jew—like them, practicing Judaism in secret while practicing his adopted religion in public to avoid persecution and death. The notion of Shabbatai Zevi as a crypto-Jew not only resonated with them but also provided them with a framework for their own identity. For example, as Abraham Cardozo—a *converso* and a leading spokesperson of the Sabbateans—put it, "The Messiah was destined to be a Marrano like me!"[11]

Following an old tradition that taught that Jewish law would no longer be binding in the messianic age, Cardozo—like other Sabbateans—claimed that now that Shabbatai Zevi had ushered in the messianic era, Jewish law was no longer binding, including prohibitions against the eating of pork.[12]

Various studies have demonstrated the influence of Sabbateans and Sabbateanism on early Jewish reform in nineteenth-century central Europe. For example, many of the earliest Jewish reformers in Bohemia and Hungary came from well-known Sabbatean families. Like the Sabbateans, the early reformers—who identified the age of Jewish Emancipation as the onset of the messianic era—largely rejected the authority of rabbinic texts and traditions and denied the binding quality of Jewish religious law. It is not coincidental, for example, that Shabbatai Zevi anticipated the reformers' early action of the rejection of Jewish law by first abolishing the fast day of the Seventeenth of Tammuz.[13] As a leading historian of Reform Judaism succinctly put it, "The Sabbatean movement certainly played a role in preparing the ground for Reform."[14]

Many of the crypto-Jews and their immediate descendants were conversant with the arts and sciences, including the classics of Greco-Roman literature. Many had studied logic, physics, philosophy, and medicine, which was not the case with most Jews raised in a Jewish milieu at that time. In Holland, France, and Italy, groups of former crypto-Jews and their descendants had been deeply influenced by the rationalism and skepticism that were prevalent at the time. For example, some identify Francisco Sanchez, a son of *conversos*, as the father of modern philosophy. Sanchez was a physician whose 1581 treatise, *Quod nihil scitur* (*That Nothing Is Known*), is a groundbreaking work in the history of philosophical skepticism and epistemology.[15] It is not an exaggeration to claim, therefore, that "the secular culture of many Dutch and Italian Jews anticipated the Berlin Haskalah (Jewish Enlightenment) of the eighteenth century."[16] As will be discussed further, certain ideas characteristic of Jewish life and thought today can trace their roots directly to the Enlightenment, and to the thought of the *conversos* and their descendants, including Spinoza. Indeed, as Orobio de Castro—a prominent *converso* who returned to Judaism—observed, many of his fellow *conversos* were too assimilated into "secular" Western culture to enable them to reenter the orbit of Jewish life and thought.

Reflecting the Spanish concept of *honra* (personal honor), such *conversos*—according to de Castro—arrogantly considered it an affront to their "honor" to accept the teachings or the authority of the rabbis and teachers who tried to lead them back to Jewish faith and communal life. Their convictions regarding the superiority of Western cultural norms to Judaism and their assimilation of Christian prejudices against Jews and Judaism prevented them, psychologically, intellectually, and sociologically, from reintegration into Jewish communal and religious life.[17] As de Castro put it, "It seems to them that their reputation as learned men will diminish if they allow themselves to be taught by those who are truly learned in the Holy Law . . . [and they] fall into the abyss of apostasy and heresy."[18]

Immanuel Kant, the most prominent German Enlightenment philosopher of the eighteenth century, owed much of his knowledge of Judaism to the writings of two Jewish philosophers: Spinoza, and Kant's contemporary, Moses Mendelssohn. Whereas Spinoza considered Judaism a religion of legal bondage, Mendelssohn depicted it as "revealed legislation, laws, commandments and regulations."[19] Kant's understanding of Judaism as a religion dominated by a particularistic legal system led him to the conclusion that Judaism was at best an amoral and at worst an immoral religion. Consequently, in one of his lesser-known works, Kant called for "the euthanasia of Judaism." A religion of law, devoid of ethics, in his view, had no raison d'être. For Kant, Judaism is such a religion.[20]

In his philosophy of ethics, Kant identified basic criteria for ethical action. For Kant, ethical axioms must be universal and categorical (i.e., "the categorical imperative"), and they must express individual will and autonomy. As free autonomous acts, ethical actions cannot represent obedience to an externally imposed law.[21] As a religion demanding obedience to particularistic rather than universal legal imperatives, Judaism therefore could not, in this view, be moral.

In an essay entitled "What Is Enlightenment?" written in 1784, Kant stated:

> Enlightenment is man's relief from his self-incurred tutelage. Tutelage is man's inability to make use of his understanding without direction from another.... Have courage to use your own reason!—that is the motto of enlightenment.... If I have a book which understands for me, a pastor who has a conscience for me, a physician who decides my diet, and so forth, I need not trouble myself. I need not think, if I can only pay—others will readily undertake the irksome work for me.[22]

Kant's ideals for enlightenment and ethics: rationalism, individual autonomy, universal moral categories, the absence of external authority—especially religious tradition—became hallmarks of the early Jewish reform that emerged in nineteenth-century Germany. Despite the attempts of the Enlightenment to undermine religious authority and tradition, and despite Kant's pejorative views of Judaism, early Jewish reform presented Judaism, especially Jewish ethics, in Kantian terms.[23] By reducing Judaism to ethics and by presenting ethics in Kantian terms, early Jewish reform became an extension of Enlightenment thought, rather than being an extension of classical Jewish religious thought.

For the early Jewish reformers, "ethical monotheism" was depicted as the essence of Judaism. "Ethical" implied the affirmation of universalistic moral principles and the rejection of the binding quality of Jewish law—a view not dissimilar to that which emerged from *converso* circles. "Monotheism" entailed not belief in a caring, providential God but the affirmation of the existence of a Supreme Being, somewhat along the lines of Spinoza's affirmation of God as "a philosophical concept" or, as the 1885 American Reform Pittsburgh Platform put it, "a God-idea."[24] Defining Judaism as "ethical monotheism" also signifies the attempt of the early reformers to minimize, if not to eliminate, the notions of Jewish peoplehood and particularity. As part of their socio-political agenda to convince the civil authorities to grant Jews full rights of citizenship or "political emancipation," the early reformers empha-sized the commonalities of Judaism and Christianity, especially liberal Protestant Christianity. One result of these efforts was the notion of a "Judeo-Christian" tradition, a "Judeo-Christian ethic." This idea also has roots among the *conversos*, since—as was noted earlier—there were *conversos* who affirmed *both* Judaism and Christianity, that is, a Judeo-Christian tradition, a Judeo-Christian ethic.

In the nineteenth century, the notion of a Judeo-Christian ethic emerged from disparate sources of influence. One such source was bib-lical scholarship, especially as it was articulated by liberal Protestant theologians and biblical scholars, most prominently Julius Wellhausen and his school. Like many other Christian theologians of his times, Wellhausen sought to identify the essence of Christianity, just as his Jewish contemporaries endeavored to identify the essence of Judaism, in order to discern what was essential and what was tangential and dispensable in their particular religious traditions. Wellhausen—a lead-ing biblical scholar and prominent anti-Semite, sought the essence of Christianity, that is, the religion of Jesus. Because Jesus was a Jew, Wellhausen also found himself compelled to inquire into the essence of Judaism.

According to Wellhausen, the religion of biblical Israel was estab-lished by the "classical" or "literary" prophets such as Isaiah and Micah, who introduced the idea of universalistic ethical monotheism. In this view, these prophets were radical, revolutionary, religious individual-ists who rejected particularism, nationalism, legalism, and a focus on ritual observance. For Wellhausen, the essence of biblical Judaism, epitomized by the teachings of the classical prophets as he understood them, had been corrupted by the legalism, particularism, and ritualism of the biblical priesthood. It had been further distorted by the teachings of the Pharisees and subsequent rabbinic tradition. However, claimed Wellhausen, it was restored by Jesus and his teachings.[25] Thus, in Wellhausen's view, Jesus was the heir and the restorer of the authentic religion of biblical Israel. Just as the Talmudic rabbis had distorted the teachings of "prophetic Judaism," so later on did the church, particularly

the Catholic Church, distort the teachings of Judaism through legalism, faulty biblical exegesis, and ritualism. What was now required,
for Wellhausen, was a return to the religion of Jesus and the classical
prophets.

Like Wellhausen, modern liberal Judaism identified the essence
of Judaism with "prophetic Judaism." As such, it rejected the binding
nature of Jewish law and all "nonessential" theological ideas and religious practices. Claiming that universalistic ethics is the essence of
Judaism, Reform Jewish thinkers identified the ethics of "prophetic
Judaism" with Kantian ethics. Like Kantian ethics, it stressed individual moral autonomy, antinomianism, rationalism, and universalism.[26]
This approach led to the affirmation of a "Judeo-Christian" ethic.
Christians embraced this notion because they wanted to demonstrate
how Christian ethics emerged from the "prophetic ethics" of biblical
Judaism and to identify Christianity as the only legitimate and authentic heir to the "prophetic Judaism" of biblical Israel. Jews embraced this
notion because showing that Judaism and Christianity are essentially
the same when it comes to ethics—the essence of both religions—
would, they hoped, further the cause of Jewish political and social
emancipation by demonstrating that Jews had more in common with
Christians than they had differences. The problem, however, is that
there is Jewish ethics and there is Christian ethics, but they are not the
same. There is no Judeo-Christian ethic. The presuppositions and ethical postures of each differ from the other.[27]

In America, unlike Europe, Jews did not have to fight for fundamental civil and political rights, that is, for political "emancipation."
With the founding of the Republic, they were granted the same political
rights as other citizens, unlike their European brethren. They therefore
felt comfortable expanding their activities to include universalistic ethics in the fight for "social justice." In America, Jewish ethics was not
only theoretically universalistic but also programmatically universal,
moving beyond the boundaries of specifically Jewish social issues.[28]

The influx of east European Jews to America around the turn of
the twentieth century introduced European communistic and socialistic ideas that were also identified with the universalistic, cosmopolitan ideas of "prophetic Judaism." It is not surprising to find that by

the early 1980s, most "American Jews had been raised with the understanding that liberalism or political radicalism constituted the very essence of Judaism, that all the rest—the rituals, liturgy, communal organizations—were outdated, vestigial trappings for a religion with a great moral message embodied in liberalism."[29] As an astute observer of American Jewry has put it, for American Jews, "politics is our religion; our preferred denomination is liberalism."[30] Jewish political liberalism, as will be discussed further, derives from secular rather than Jewish religious traditions. It is discontinuous with Jewish religious teachings, rather than being a paradigmatic expression of them, as many American Jews believe them to be.

By the dawn of the twenty-first century, the Enlightenment idea of individual autonomy, coupled with American "rugged individualism," led to a "privatized Judaism." Jewish identity now became a matter of individually acquired taste that can change from person to person, and from week to week. In this approach, a major characteristic of American religion in general and of American Judaism in particular is that religious belief, observance, and identity became manifestations of "the sovereign self," that is, a contemporary version of Kant's individual autonomy. Judaism now became a matter of "whatever works for you" at any given episodic point in time.[31]

Whereas earlier generations of modern Jews consciously attempted to demonstrate that Jewish ideas and values are not incompatible with those of the dominant culture, striving to forge an uneasy, artificial synthesis between them, contemporary American Jews have attained what has been termed a state of "coalescence." "Coalescence" means that Jews are no longer even conscious of the possible differences between Jewish and non-Jewish values adapted from the general culture, such as American culture. Non-Jewish values are embraced as "Jewish" values without any awareness of their origin. However, various authentic Jewish values that do not coalesce with those imported from outside are considered "un-Jewish." Similarly, beliefs and values of other Americans (especially Protestant Evangelicals) that do not correlate with their worldview are considered "un-American." As one sociologist has put it,

When coalescence is complete, the resulting merged messages or texts are perceived not as being American and Jewish values side by side, but as being a unified text which is identified as authoritative Judaism. In coalescing American [liberal] values and Jewish values, many American Jews—including some who are very knowledgeable and active in Jewish life—no longer separate or are even conscious of the separation between the origin of these texts.[32]

As most contemporary Jewish sociologists have affirmed, "coalescence," "the sovereign self," and similar ideas pose an enormous threat to the future of the continuity of Judaism and of the Jewish people. As will be discussed later, recent demographic studies of American Jewry verify this claim.[33]

The metamorphosis of the Kantian notion of individual moral autonomy into the current notion of the "sovereign self" inevitably leads to Jewish discontinuity. Already in the Bible, the idea of "everyone doing what is right in their eyes"[34] was identified with moral and religious anarchy. According to a study of contemporary American Jewry: "The 'first language' that our subjects speak is by and large one of profound individualism. Their language is universalistic, liberal and personalist."[35] Such a view, this study concludes, is likely to "contribute to the dissolution of communal institutions and intergenerational commitment, thereby weakening the very sources of its own Jewish fulfillment and making them far less available to succeeding generations."[36]

The sovereign self champions radical autonomy and proclaims the modern dogma of individual choice. Consequently, the sovereign self is "condemned to freedom." However, without boundaries in which to exercise choice, the sovereign self often becomes paralyzed by the "insecurity of freedom." A heightened sense of doubt, anxiety, and boredom often characterizes the sovereign self.[37] The sovereign self is only able to embrace ideas, actions, and relationships that are the products of fleeting "feelings" and subjective intuition. Consequently, certitude and sustained relationships often remain elusive. The fluid, fleeting, temporary, and contingent nature of living within the fortress of the self cannot sustain lasting commitment. Obliged to nothing, often anxious about dealing with the continuous avalanche of choices available, the sovereign self has no roots to provide an anchor, no framework in which to discover or enact meaning, no boundaries for choice in which to exercise freedom. For philosopher Charles Taylor, such relativism conflicts with any ability to achieve authenticity. He writes, "Your feeling a certain way can never be sufficient grounds for respecting your position, because your feelings can't determine what is significant."[38] For Abraham Joshua Heschel, freedom is not merely the ability to choose; instead, "Freedom comes about in the moment of transcending the self, thus rising above the habit of regarding the self as an end. Freedom is an act of self-engagement of the spirit, a spiritual event."[39] We transcend bondage in acts of freedom, in creative actions.

From a sociological point of view, "prophetic Judaism" and its spin-offs, culminating in "coalescence," were developed to further Jewish integration in the post-Emancipation era. However, as sociologist Charles Liebman already wrote in the early 1970s, "More than ever before, the values of integration and survival are mutually contradictory."[40] With particular reference to universalistic ethics and political liberalism, Liebman observed that Jewish religious values are not unambiguously liberal; "they are folk-oriented rather than universalistic, ethnocentric rather than cosmopolitan."[41] Writing in the 1990s, he observed that liberalism "fails as a strategy for Jewish survival because it lacks the resources to justify Jewish cohesion and particularism."[42]

"Prophetic Judaism" was neither the Judaism of the prophets nor that of the rabbis. Wellhausen's views have been thoroughly discredited by subsequent biblical scholarship.[43] The prophets did not subvert biblical law and ritual but advocated its observance. The prophets were not revolutionary designers of Judaism, as Wellhausen claimed, but guardians of a tradition in which they served as a vital link between their predecessors and their successors—the rabbis. Rather than advocating a universalistic ethic, the prophets were fierce advocates and defenders of the national aspirations of the people of Israel.[44] The portrait of the prophets put forth by Wellhausen and adapted by huge segments of modern Jewry is neither "prophetic" nor "Judaism." Rather, it is an imposition of *converso*, Enlightenment, and liberal Protestant ideas upon Jewish theology and practice. Its denial of the binding nature of Jewish law, as Solomon Schechter observed, is reminiscent of Pauline Christianity, which rejected Jewish law in the name of a universalistic ethic. Schechter satirically called Jewish advocates of this position "amateur Christians."[45] As the early twentieth-century rabbi Alexander

Kohut put it, expressing his opposition to such views incorporated into American Reform Judaism's Pittsburgh Platform of 1885: anyone who denies "the binding nature of the Law writes his own epitaph: I am no longer a Jew," to which Kohut adds that such *reform* is to *deform* the very nature of Judaism.[46] In this view, a post-halakhic age is a post-Judaism age. Again to quote Schechter: "Our 'prophetic Jew': 'Bodily pilfers from the Pentateuch / And, undisturbed by conscious qualms/Perverts the prophets, and purloins the Psalms.'"[47]

Proclaiming that we live in a post-halakhic age, much of American Jewry has replaced Jewish legal ethics with a particular understanding of American constitutional law.[48] Following in the footsteps of Spinoza, most contemporary American Jews consider Jewish law obsolete, a function of long-gone political realities. Seeking the freedoms and the protections of the power of the republic in which they live, American Jews—like Spinoza—replaced Jewish law with secular law, the authority of the rabbinate with the legal authority of the state. For American Jews, the Constitution replaced the Torah as the ultimate authority over their lives, and lawyers replaced rabbis as communal leaders. Rejection of the binding quality of Jewish legal categories and teachings—a view with roots in *converso* thought, Spinoza's philosophy, Sabbatean theology, Kantian ethics, Wellhausen's biblical scholarship, and early Reform Judaism—was now articulated as the acceptance a particular interpretation of the American Constitution informed by liberal Enlightenment thought.

Prominent early twentieth-century American Jewish attorneys and jurists, like Louis Brandeis and Louis Marshall, identified a coalescence between the values embedded in the American Constitution with those of "prophetic Judaism." For Marshall, the Constitution was the new Temple of the Jews, "the holy of holies."[49] For these individuals and others, just as there is a Judeo-Christian ethic, there is a unitary "Judeo-American" legal tradition that made Jewish religious law both obsolete and irrelevant.[50]

It is not surprising that Jewish lawyers and jurists, such as Brandeis and Marshall, were catapulted into positions of leadership in the American Jewish community, despite their ignorance of Jewish tradition, thereby displacing the leadership and authority of the rabbinate. As

Brandeis, whose ancestors had been Sabbateans, once admitted, "I have been to a great extent separated from Jews. I am very ignorant of things Jewish."[51] Secular Jewish organizations with secular Jewish leaders now replaced religious ones as the self-appointed representatives of American Jewry and of American Judaism. For example, for many years, Marshall led the American Jewish Committee with what one observer characterized as "Marshall Law."[52] For Marshall, the task of the American rabbinate was no longer to adjudicate issues of Jewish law or morality but to further the acculturation of east European immigrant Jews to American lifestyles and values—or, using his word, to "civilize" them.

In *Masks Jews Wear: The Self-Deceptions of American Jewry*, the American Jewish theologian Eugene Borowitz described contemporary American Jews "as a new species of Marrano," that is, as crypto-Jews perpetuating a "Marrano inauthenticity."[53] According to Borowitz, while the crypto-Jews practiced a distorted form of Judaism in private while living publicly as non-Jews, American Jews publicly affirm their identity as Jews but live out their personal lives as non-Jews. For example, according to Borowitz, American Jewry has become a community where the sustaining of a variety of organizations and institutions has become an end in itself rather than a means toward realizing the purpose of Jewish religious and communal existence. As the early twentieth-century German Jewish philosopher Franz Rosenzweig had observed decades earlier, "We do not want to have organizations of Jews, but spiritually Jewish organizations. . . . what is the use of the most perfect organization of Jews if there are no Jews left to be 'organized'?"[54]

A significant feature of American "Marrano inauthenticity," according to Borowitz, is that God is not taken very seriously by American Jewry. For example, in his study of "the civil religion of American Jews," Jonathan Woocher pointed out that though belief in God plays a central role in "American civil religion," it plays a "thoroughly insignificant role in the civil religion of American Jews."[55] According to Woocher, American Jews largely consider belief in God as a cause for Jewish divisiveness rather than unity. Consequently, faith in God does not play a major role either in Jewish identity or in Jewish communal activity. As for Spinoza, so for most of American Jewry, God is only an abstract "philosophical concept" unrelated to human or Jewish existence.

Like the crypto-Jews of the seventeenth century, American Jews are largely well educated in secular studies and dismissive of rabbinic learning and authority, and they reject the binding quality of Jewish law and tradition. Like the *conversos* they are ignorant of and detached from the wellsprings of Jewish life and learning and are semantically displaced from their own religious heritage.

Sociological studies by Steven Cohen and others bear this out. Belief in God and (like many *conversos*) in an afterlife is lower among Jews than among other groups of Americans. The *2001 American Jewish Identity Survey* found that 73 percent of Jews surveyed identified themselves as "secular." Surprising to many was the increase (38 percent) over a decade of the number of Jewish adults, and even more the numbers of Jewish children (53 percent), who identified themselves as having no religion. Also startling was the substantial increase of the number of Jews practicing a religion other than Judaism.[56] As a consequence of these and similar findings, some demographers are predicting that if current trends are maintained or accelerate, within a few generations, most American Jews will be practicing a religion other than Judaism or no religion at all, and many of those who believe themselves to be practicing Judaism will actually be practicing and affirming something very different. In short, American Jewry already is, or soon will become, in many ways like the crypto-Jews who lived in seventeenth-century Amsterdam. As Solomon Schechter observed in the early twentieth century and as Abraham Heschel stated in the mid-twentieth century, Judaism remains an unknown religion among American Jews,[57] as it was an unknown religion among the crypto-Jews centuries ago.

Within 100 years of the arrival of the *conversos* in Amsterdam, that city emerged as a model Jewish community—a center of Jewish learning, observance, commitment, and authenticity. However, what will become of American Jewry is yet to be determined.

Substitute Faiths

The nineteenth-century Hasidic master Rabbi Mendel of Kotzk once said: "It is bad enough to be in galut [i.e., a state of exile, alienation], but it is even worse to be in galut, and not even to be aware of it."[1]

As was discussed in the previous chapter, like the crypto-Jews of centuries past, contemporary Jewry—especially American Jews—is largely alienated from Judaism, either by ignorance or by apathy. Ignorance here refers not only to an absence of knowledge regarding the fundamentals of Judaism but even more to the identification of Judaism and Jewish identity with ideas that are inimical, foreign, or incompatible with the constitutive teachings of Jewish religious tradition. As was also discussed earlier, a variety of ideas rooted in the thought of the crypto-Jews, and of the French and German Enlightenment of the eighteenth century, have come to dominate American Judaism, American Jewry, and the communal agenda of the American Jewish community. These include the "sovereign self," individual moral autonomy, secularism, a universalistic liberal morality, affirmation of a Judeo-Christian tradition, rejection of the binding quality of Jewish law, and the marginalization of fundamental theological issues such as belief in God. In addition, ideas allegedly rooted in biblical, rabbinic, and kabbalistic sources, although distorted beyond recognition in their meaning and message, now claim legitimacy as authentic and historically pivotal ideas of Jewish religion and as foundations for Jewish identity.

One example is indicated by the title of a 2008 exhibit at a number of major American Jewish museums: The New Authentics: Artists of the Post-Jewish Generation. The message here is that Jewish authenticity is a function of the obsolescence of Jewish identity and of Jewish belief. This is reminiscent of Spinoza's claim that the specious and obsolete nature of earlier Judaism necessitates the emergence of a post-Jewish Jew who now reflects the authentic nature of Jewish existence, that Jewish authenticity in our age demands the repudiation of Judaism in the past. In this view, the "new Jew," the "authentic Jew," is one who has repudiated and transcended his or her historical legacy; that authentic Jewish identity now entails the rejection of Jewish identity in a "post-Jewish" era.

Though "inclusivism" has been strongly embraced as a central value of postmodern Judaism, extreme inclusivism threatens the integrity and authenticity of Judaism and of the Jewish people. If Judaism and Jewish identity are whatever anyone wants them to be at a given time, if ideas and practices inimical to Judaism are readily integrated into Jewish thought and practice, if synagogue membership and positions of lay leadership are held by Jews and even by non-Jews practicing a faith other than Judaism or no faith at all, then what foundation is there for Jewish authenticity or integrity? If there are no boundaries or parameters for determining who is a Jew and what is Judaism, the doctrine of inclusivism becomes an inevitable threat to the continuity of Judaism as a religious tradition and to the Jews as a faith community.

A significant feature of American "Marrano inauthenticity," according to Eugene Borowitz, is that God is not taken very seriously by American Jewry.[2] As has been noted in chapter 1, in his study of "the civil religion of American Jews," Jonathan Woocher pointed out that though belief in God plays a central role in "American civil religion," it plays a "thoroughly insignificant role in the civil religion of American Jews."[3] According to Woocher, American Jews largely consider belief in God as a cause for Jewish divisiveness rather than unity. Consequently, faith in God does not play a major role either in Jewish identity or in Jewish communal activity. As for Spinoza, so for most of American Jewry, God is only an abstract "philosophical concept," a "God-idea," unrelated to human or Jewish existence. Sociological studies have consistently found that belief in God is lower among American Jews than among other groups of Americans, that American Jews predominantly identify themselves as secular. Sociological studies and opinion polls consistently reveal that American Jews are more tenuous in their belief in God than other Americans. There is a higher percentage of agnostics or atheists among American Jews than among other groups of Americans.[4] As sociologist Steven Cohen has written, "American Jews are among the most religiously inactive, the most theologically skeptical, in short, the most secular [group in America]."[5] The 1990 and 2001 Jewish population studies, as well as other demographic studies, revealed the inevitable dire consequences for the continuity of Judaism and the Jews of the shift to a community that defines itself primarily in secular rather than in religious terms.

Having rejected Jewish religious faith as a basis for their Jewish identity, many American Jews have embraced a variety of substitute secular "faiths." British Jewish theologian Louis Jacobs has identified the premises of a number such secular Jewish faiths: (1) the worship of the Jewish people rather than the exclusive worship of God, (2) making Jewish survival rather than the service of God the ultimate goal of Jewish existence, and (3) replacing Torah with Jewish culture.[6] With regard to these and other substitute faiths, Abraham Heschel has written, "We have not invented it [i.e., Judaism]. We may accept or reject, but should not distort it."[7]

The fallacies represented by these and other substitute faiths may be unmasked in a variety of ways. These include sociological investigation, theological discourse, and logical analysis. As will be discussed later, the premises and teachings of these substitute faiths express a variety of logical mistakes as well as logical and linguistic fallacies. Of these, three are paramount: the "reductionist fallacy," "conversion by redefinition," and the "category mistake."

The reductionist fallacy entails depicting an entire entity in terms of only one of its components; it reduces the whole to one of its parts. In the case of Judaism, the reductionist fallacy identifies the whole of Judaism with one of its parts. Conversion by redefinition is an attempt to represent an entity as something it is not, by redefining it. Such an endeavor also often commits the reductionist fallacy by redefining an entity by one of its parts. The British philosopher Gilbert Ryle coined the term "category mistake," which, according to Ryle, means committing a semantic or ontological error by ascribing to an entity features it could not properly have, features that are inappropriate to its essential nature.[8] From this perspective, contemporary American Jewry, like the *conversos*, tends to articulate its Judaism in semantic categories that are incompatible with or irrelevant to endemic categories of Jewish faith and practice. As will be further discussed later, framing Jewish theological issues or describing rubrics for Jewish identity drawn from secular, Enlightenment, or antinomian thought often is a category mistake. In what follows, examples will be identified.

One example of the reductionist fallacy is the popular claim that Judaism is a way of living but not also a way of thinking, that Judaism is only what one does but not also what one affirms. Where many contemporary Jews who take this view differ is on what kind of way of living Judaism is. Defining Judaism as a religion exclusively of "doing" is an example of the reductionist fallacy because it reduces the whole to one of its parts; it identifies the entirety of Judaism with a part of Judaism, albeit a significant feature of Judaism. This approach fails to recognize, as Heschel, Schechter, and others have asserted, that Judaism is a way of *thinking* as well as a way of living.[9]

The reduction of Judaism to secularly motivated "good deeds" will be dealt with later. Here it suffices to point out that certain segments of Jewish Orthodoxy also commit the reductionist fallacy by identifying all of Judaism with "doing," which for them means observance of Jewish religious law, halakhah. Though halakhah, as will be discussed later, is a crucial feature of Judaism, it does not represent its totality. Halakhah offers prescriptions as to how Jews should live their lives as Jews. Yet, the "pan-halakhic" approach (as Heschel calls it) is an attitude with roots in Spinoza's teachings, for Spinoza attempted to reduce Judaism to being only a system of laws.[10] A problem with this view is that it reduces Judaism to being only a legal system and fails to address vital questions such as what does Jewish belief affirm, what are the theological presuppositions upon which halakhah is based, why should halakhic norms be obeyed (*ta'amei ha-mitzvot*), and which are the theological norms that inform halakhic decision making? Reducing Judaism to halakhah or to

Jewish practice either rejects or marginalizes theology, when, in fact, a halakhic way of life is meaningless without a consideration of the theological presuppositions upon which the halakhah rests, such as a belief in revelation and in the authoritative role of rabbinic interpretive tradition.

Driven by expediency masquerading as pragmatism, the a-theological or antitheological predilection of American Jewry considers theology as an afterthought, if at all. As a prominent American Jewish leader put it, "We need to immerse ourselves in Jewish *doing*, guided always by our liberal principles, and if we do so, appropriate theological formulation will be developed afterwards."[11] Yet, a religion consists of what people do *because* of what they believe. Without a theological rubric serving as a foundation for the meaning of "Jewish" activities, such activities cannot necessarily claim authenticity. Authentic Jewish deeds can only flow from authentic Jewish religious thought. Action uninformed by prior thought is both uninformed and thoughtless. It was Ralph Waldo Emerson who reminded us that the ancestor of every action is a thought.

Another example of the reductionist fallacy has been the attempt to reduce Judaism to an ethical system. As was discussed in the previous chapter, early Jewish reformers attempted to reduce Judaism to a form of ethics influenced by certain Enlightenment and liberal Protestant ideas, claiming that Judaism is similar—if not identical—to forms of Kantian ethics, or to "prophetic Judaism" as Wellhausen and others defined it. But if all Judaism represents is a version of the universalistic ethics that emerged from the Enlightenment, then there is no longer a compelling response to the question, Why should Judaism continue as the distinct religion of a particular people?

When Judaism is reduced to politics, as various observers of American Judaism claim, then the accoutrements of Jewish religious faith—like belief in God, ritual observance, and religious education—become obsolete, vestigial inconveniences that only engender communal tension and disunity. If Judaism represents a particular political agenda, then it is no longer a religious faith tradition, that is, it is no longer what it is. Reducing Judaism to politics commits the reductionist fallacy as well as being an example of a category mistake.

When Judaism is reduced to nationalism, and the Jewish people is no longer considered "a unique people on the earth" (2 Sam. 7:23) but a nation like all others, even if it is amoral and mediocre, devoid of a particular mission and higher purpose, then what compelling reason is there for the sacrifices and the commitment required to help ensure its continuity? If the disappearance from the world of the people of Israel would be as insignificant to the world as the disappearance of the Carthaginians, would it constitute an irrevocable tragedy? Is the obsession with "Jewish survival" meaningful without a compelling response to the question of why Jewish existence has distinct purpose and meaning? Were an individual to stipulate the value of Jewish survival, the question would still remain: Survival for what?

During the last decades of the twentieth century, the prime directive, the central dogma of the Jewish civil religion became "Jewish survival," that is, the physical survival of Jews as Jews. Jewish theological concerns were considered irrelevant and "divisive" of communal solidarity. Theological issues as to *why* to be a Jew and *what* is Judaism were marginalized. A major feature of Jewish "survivalism" has been an "Israel-centric" understanding of Jewish identity, with the State of Israel becoming the symbolic incarnation of Jewish survival. "Israel" became the religion of the Jews with the old Zionist slogan "We are one," replacing the biblical claim that "God is one."[12] Judaism became reduced to Zionism, largely of a secular variety. As the Zionist ideologue Jacob Klatzkin put it, "Zionism began a new era...in order to establish a new definition of Jewish identity—a secular definition."[13] Secular Zionism became an example of a substitute form of Jewish faith, a new foundation for Jewish identity.

After the SixDay War in 1967, the "Holocaust-Israel" motif of "death/rebirth" became a central dogma of Jewish civil religion. This blatantly Christian motif of death and resurrection, death and salvation, proclaimed an indisputable nexus between the Holocaust and the State of Israel. In this view, the Holocaust demonstrated that without military and political power, Jewish survival becomes inevitably imperiled. Israel and political activity in the Diaspora on its behalf came to represent the epitome of Jewish military and political power, and the only viable tools to secure Jewish survival. As tools to power, politics and wealth to support it became the accoutrements of this substitute Jewish faith. The civil religion of both Israeli and American Jews emphasized the importance of military might in their attempts to express a conversion by redefinition of Judaism. For example, Jewish holidays were reinterpreted to accommodate the militaristic message that had been neutralized by the Talmudic rabbis. Hanukkah, for instance, was transformed from the rabbinic "festival of lights" to a militaristic "festival of fights," with the Israel Defense Forces becoming the modern reincarnation of the Maccabees and the Hasmoneans.[14] Reducing Judaism or Jewish identity to an attachment to Israel is an example of the reductionist fallacy. Historically, attachment to the Land of Israel has been a significant Jewish value, but it hardly represents the totality of Jewish religion or Jewish historical experience.

Ironically, and in contrast, many of the most prominent early Zionists in the early twentieth century did not embrace a Zionist identity that was linked to military power. Rather, they called for a coalescence between the Zionist program and prophetic Judaism as well as Enlightenment ideals. Theodore Herzl, the founder of Zionism, for example, defined the virtues of Jewish statehood as "justice, truth, liberty, progress, humanity and beauty." Ahad Ha-Am, founder of "cultural Zionism," implored others "to respect only the power of the spirit and not to worship material power." He insisted that "the Jewish state can only find peace when universal justice will ascend to the throne and rule the lives of the peoples and the states." Judah Magnes, a leading American Zionist and founding president of the Hebrew University of Jerusalem, expressed horror at the thought that Jews in the Holy Land might become "devotees of brute force and militarism as were some of the later Hasmoneans." His hope was that "the Jews of *Eretz Yisrael* [the Land of Israel] be true to the teachings of the Prophets of Israel."[15]

Early cultural Zionists in the early twentieth century, such as Ahad Ha-Am and the great Hebrew poet Hayyim Nahman Bialik, helped establish the foundation for the view, still very prevalent today, that represents the third substitute Jewish faith identified by Jacobs: replacing Torah with Jewish culture. By trying to reduce all of Judaism and Jewish historical experience to Jewish culture, this approach commits the reductionist fallacy. By defining the Torah in secular terms, it also

represents conversion by redefinition. By speaking of religious texts presumed to be rooted in revelation as secular cultural manifestations of
a national ethos, it also is an example of a category mistake. For example, in a speech delivered at the opening of the Hebrew University of
Jerusalem, Bialik said: "In the consciousness of the [Jewish] nation the
comprehensive human concept of 'culture' has, meanwhile, taken the
place of the theological one of 'Torah.'"[16] In this regard, it is relevant
to note that various medieval commentaries on the Talmudic accounts
of the apostasy of Elisha ben Abuya identified his apostasy with his
affirmation of Judaism as a national culture rather than as a religion.[17]
Though no one can deny the nationalistic or cultural impulses within
Jewish historical experience, neither represents the totality of that
experience. Jewish experience without Jewish religion is a distortion.
Judaism without God is a torso without a head.

Influenced by Zionist, socialistic, and other ideologies, Jewish communal life embraced the dogma of collectivism over individualism as
an integral feature of the civil religion of American Jewry. The individual's quest for meaning was replaced by the claim that the individual
could find meaning by subservience to the community. In this view,
meaning is no longer considered an individual matter, or a religious
one, but a collective one. The individual finds meaning only by serving
the community. In the words of Ahad Ha-Am, "This conception shifts
the center of gravity of the Ego...from the individual to the community; and concurrently with this shifting, the problem of life becomes a
problem not of individual but of social life. I live for the sake of the perpetuation and happiness of the community of which I am a member."[18]
However, as Heschel subsequently noted, "Human existence cannot
derive its ultimate meaning from society, because society itself is in
need of meaning." In addition, Heschel writes: "Life comprises not only
arable, productive land, but also mountains of dreams, an underground
of sorrow, towers of yearning, which can hardly be used for the good of
society, unless man be converted into a machine in which every screw
must serve a function or be removed. It is a profiteering state which trying to exploit the individual, asks all of man for itself."[19] In more recent
years, the collectivism embraced by the Jewish communal agenda eventually and inevitably came into sharp conflict with identity defined by

the sovereign self, and an impasse ensued in the quest for establishing a foundation for Jewish identity.

Yet, despite his affirmation of the collective as the source of individual meaning, Ahad Ha-Am was prudent enough to realize that vesting meaning and purpose in the collective rather than in the individual leads to the questions already noted: Why is the survival of the group significant? Why is it a source of meaning? Similarly, vesting Jewish identity and Jewish meaning in the survival of Jews as Jews inevitably leads to the question: Survival for what?

For Heschel, the dogma of Jewish survivalism is flawed. In his words:

> Preoccupation with the notion of survival is the result of a utilitarian philosophy, according to which Judaism is a means to an end, a device or contrivance to preserve the Jewish people.... However, a doctrine that regards Judaism as a contrivance is itself a contrivance and cannot therefore entertain the claim to be true. The significance of Judaism does not lie in its being conducive to the mere survival of a particular people but rather in its being a source of spiritual wealth, a source of meaning, relevant to all peoples.... Characteristic of humanity is concern with what to do with survival. "To be or not to be" is not the question. Of course, we are anxious to be. How to be and how not to be is the question.[20]

Similarly, as Louis Jacobs—who identified "making Jewish survival the ultimate goal of Jewish existence" as a substitute Jewish faith—observed:

> There is a tendency nowadays, even among religious Jews, to argue that Judaism is of value because it ensures Jewish survival. But this makes Jewish survival the ultimate instead of God and his service.... The religious believer will struggle as hard for the right of his people to survive...as the non-believing fellow Jew.... He will see the survival of the Jews as a means to an end and not the end in itself.... Religion is *sui generis*. It is not "for" something else. Its aim is the worship of God.[21]

The claim that Judaism is important only because it helps ensure Jewish survival is theologically problematic and sociologically spurious.

It maintains that the primary values of Judaism are not embodied in the spiritual message it bears, the ethical lifestyle it teaches, or the theological beliefs it affirms, but that the primary value of Jewish faith is to support Jewish group survival. Theologically speaking, such a view is idolatrous. Idolatry may be defined as treating that which is not absolute as if it were absolute. For Jewish faith, only God is absolute. Further, if (as will be discussed later) the meaning of Jewish existence derives from the claim that the Jewish people is a covenanted people, survival for survival's sake entails rejecting the very basis for the meaning of Jewish survival. In addition, survival for survival's sake is morally problematic. With survival as an end in itself, as an ultimate value, any deed that is perceived as furthering the cause of survival becomes permissible and justifiable. Such an approach can have morally and spiritually regrettable consequences. As with an individual, so with a community, the goal is not merely to survive but to live, and to imbue living with meaning, purpose, authenticity, and goodness. As Heschel notes, "'Jewish belonging' is no substitute for Jewish living."[22]

Physical survival is necessary but not sufficient. The fallacy of the strategy of Jewish survivalism as an end in itself has been unmasked by demographic and sociological studies. As such studies have consistently demonstrated, obsession with physical survival alone has not proved to be an effective strategy in providing Jews with a reason to survive *as* Jews. As has been noted earlier, statistics show that though the descendants of Jews are surviving as individuals, they and their children are not surviving in equal numbers *as* Jews. Survival for the sake of survival is a tautology that leads nowhere. It is a premise without a conclusion, a fallacy. Inevitably, the question of the meaning of being a Jew must be posed. The issue is: Survival for what?

With regard to Jewish survivalism, Leonard Fein has written:

> The Holocaust and Israel...give us both a motto—"Never Again!" [i.e., a response to the Holocaust] and a method—the nation state [i.e., Israel].... "Never Again!" tells us only what to avoid, not what to embrace.... And the nation state? Its defense points to politics, not to a value system.... I am inclined to think that most Jewish survivalists would be hard-pressed to name the Jewish value our survival is meant to ensure. Instead, the means have become the

end...preoccupation with survival for its own sake is...self-defeating...far from assuring the Jewish future, the survivalist obsession betrays it.[23]

Sociologically speaking, it is not coincidental that the Israel-centered nature of American Jewish communal life began to emerge in the late 1960s and early 1970s when Americans, including American Jews, began to identify themselves primarily in secular ethnic terms rather than in religious terms. As an ethnic group like other ethnic groups, American Jews sought identity with a "homeland," and Israel—after its great victory in the 1967 war—became the obvious candidate. With sad memories of persecution and poverty in the countries of their immigrant forebears' origins, American Jews sought to identify Israel as their homeland. A militarily strong nation, serving as a symbol of Jewish survival against all odds, Israel became a foundation for Jewish ethnic identity.

Though at the beginning of the twentieth century, no less of a figure than Theodore Roosevelt proclaimed that no real American could be a "hyphenated American," by the 1970s, identifying oneself as a hyphenated ethnic American became a way of articulating one's identity, and American Jews followed suit. Though ethnic identity implied group solidarity and a connection to a "homeland," it demanded neither religious belief nor observance. Secular institutions such as Jewish federations now replaced the synagogue, and their professional leadership replaced the rabbi as the center of Jewish communal life, authority, and power. This approach endorsed a form of Jewish identity based on a secular foundation where the affirmation of Judaism was no longer considered to be a necessary component of Jewish identity. Reducing Judaism and Jewish experience to a form of ethnicity not only represents an example of the reductionist fallacy but is problematic for other reasons as well, including sociological ones. For example, in what sense are Jews an ethnic group? Ethnic groups usually share the same ethnic features, such as food, language, customs, music, and appearance. Yet how can it be claimed that a Jew of Polish origin and a Jew of Yemenite origin, for example, share these ethnic features? What Jews of Polish, Yemenite, Russian, Algerian, and other origins share is not ethnicity but Jewish religion and the constitutive texts and traditions that characterize it.

As Eugene Borowitz predicted and as more recent demographic studies have confirmed, many of the ethnic and secular bases for Jewish identity have weakened. As Borowitz and others expected, with the dissipation of Jewish identity based on secular and ethnic rubrics, religion would once again become the foundation for Jewish identity. Rejecting many of the features of Jewish communal life and many of the dogmas of the civil religion, increasing numbers of Jews have embraced an amorphous form of "spirituality." "I'm spiritual, not religious," became a mantra for many individuals. Jews began to embrace a pastiche of beliefs and practices drawing upon elements of many religions and spiritual and New Age components as the basis of their personal and religious identity. A Judaism of the "sovereign self," a "boutique Judaism," where individuals decide on a sporadic basis which Jewish beliefs and practices they affirm or reject at a given time, has become increasingly common, thus threatening Jewish communal cohesion and the continuity of Judaism as a religion and the Jews as a people, according to sociologists. However, what eludes the attempt to equate Jewish identity with the sovereign self and with boutique Judaism is the awareness that establishing and identifying boundaries clarifies the nature of any authentic identity. Without such boundaries, Judaism becomes an amorphous anarchy rather than a historical faith in search of a future. Throughout Jewish historical experience, boundaries have served as a necessary component in helping to ensure the continuity of Judaism and the Jewish people. As will be discussed later, what is required is a basis for Jewish identity that affirms the individual without accepting the narcissism of the sovereign self, that affirms Jewish peoplehood without suppressing the spiritual yearnings of the individual, and that is authentic because it is rooted within the boundaries that characterize Jewish faith.

As Borowitz and others have observed, secular Jewish substitute faiths and other secular understandings of Judaism and Jewish identity have been unmasked by demographic data not as viable solutions to Jewish continuity or identity but rather as threats to the continuity of Judaism as a religion and to the Jews as a people. Consequently, the return to a Jewish identity grounded in Jewish religious thought becomes an urgent desideratum. As Borowitz and others also have observed, the horrors of recent history have cruelly revealed the naïveté of many of the claims of liberal, secular, and humanistic ideologies that were adapted by modern liberal Jewry in its attempt to redefine Judaism and Jewish identity. These include faith in human perfectibility, the conviction that history is automatically progressing toward a soon-to-be attained perfect world in which peace and universal prosperity would reign, and in which science and technology would solve all human problems such as poverty and disease. As Borowitz has observed, the collapse of many of the presuppositions of the secular Enlightenment and the weakening or dissolution of most modern attempts to redefine Judaism and Jewish identity, especially in secular terms, have created an existential crisis in the quest for meaning, identity, and purpose. An alternative for Jews, he contends, is to relocate their lost identity in Jewish religious faith, which is the task of theologians to define and to delineate for the contemporary Jew.[24]

A final example of the semantic displacement of American Jewry is its shibboleth: *Tikkun Olam*. Web sites of many American synagogues and Jewish communal organizations identify *Tikkun Olam* as *the* defining concept of authentic Judaism, and as a traditional Jewish teaching deeply rooted in Talmudic and medieval Jewish mystical teachings. Even American politicians try to appeal to Jewish voters by invoking *Tikkun Olam*. However, the current usage of this term represents a category mistake, is a blatant example of conversion by redefinition, and constitutes a paradigmatic example of the reductionist fallacy. In addition, it demonstrates the pitfalls of "coalescence."

The contemporary use of *Tikkun Olam* is a metamorphosed version of prophetic Judaism, which like prophetic Judaism has come to be understood as being synonymous with Judaism. The attempt by the early Jewish reformers to equate Judaism with prophetic Judaism is both an example of the reductionist fallacy and a category mistake. As in early American Jewish Reform, the contemporary use of *Tikkun Olam* commits the reductionist fallacy by equating Judaism with universalistic liberal ethics rooted in Enlightenment thought. The promiscuous use of the term *Tikkun Olam* identifies it with an enormous range of social programs, artistic projects, and a plethora of political causes. However, it is, in effect, little but a Jewish counterpart to Christian "liberation theology," although without the theology, thereby appealing to the largely secular nature of American Jewry.

In discussing the phenomena of "coalescence" and the sovereign self, the American sociologist Sylvia Barack-Fishman writes that most American Jews "tend to look to social action and universalistic principles of *Tikkun Olam* as the sustained mission of Jews and Judaism in modern times, selecting from traditional Jewish rituals and behaviors those elements which may contribute to a meaningful (but episodic) Jewish experience."[25]

The contemporary usage of *Tikkun Olam*, often translated as "mending the world," represents an example of conversion by redefinition. Though the term is found in classical Jewish literature, its meaning has been redefined in a manner that both distorts it and also commits a category mistake.

Although the term *Tikkun (ha-) Olam* appears in Talmudic and midrashic literature, no major study of early rabbinic thought recognizes it as a significant or central rabbinic concept.[26] Ironically, some Jewish advocates of "abortion on demand" have described the "right to choose" as an example of *Tikkun Olam*; yet the earliest uses of the term in rabbinic literature relate it to the human obligation to populate the world. The replacement of Jewish law with American civil law has made religious divorce (i.e., the *get*) an unnecessary anachronism, according to post-halakhic Judaism. Yet early references to *Tikkun Olam* in the Talmud specifically identify the *get* as an instrument for achieving *Tikkun Olam*.[27] In a study of the uses of this term in Talmudic and midrashic literature, the following conclusion is reached: "It seems to me that in the Talmud, *Tikkun Olam* means 'for the proper order of the Jewish community.' It is a long way from that definition to 'build a better world.'"[28] In sum, the current universalistic and random use of *Tikkun Olam* is a distortion of the meaning of the term as it emerges in classical Jewish religious literature.[29]

The use of the term *Tikkun Olam* in the *Aleinu* prayer, for example, calls for "*Tikkun Olam* in the Kingdom of Heaven." According to rabbinic interpretations, this entails *Tikkun Olam* through observance of the commandments of the Torah and halakhah. Therefore, to employ *Tikkun Olam* for secular pursuits is a blatant distortion of the meaning of the term. Indeed, early versions of the *Aleinu* prayer are unabashedly particularistic, distinguishing the Jews from the moral depravity and religious heresies of other peoples.[30] A universalistic reading of this text cannot be supported. This prayer expresses the desire to see idolatry uprooted from the world. There is no mention of "social justice."

In Lurianic kabbalah, *Tikkun Olam* relates not to the "repair" of the sociopolitical conditions of our world but to that of the upper worlds, particularly to the world of the Godhead, the *sefirot*. For the kabbalists, *Tikkun Olam* is a theocentric concern, not an anthropocentric, political, or social one. For the Lurianic mystics, *Tikkun* refers either to the repair of the upper worlds, especially the Godhead, or to *Tikkun ha-nefesh*, that is, repair of the individual soul, spiritually debilitated by sin, and requiring repentance—often by means of extreme ascetic practices—for the violation or neglect of Jewish law.[31] The emergence of Jewish-mystical-ethical literature in the sixteenth and seventeenth centuries focuses on the cultivation of moral virtues and the dispelling of moral vices as the path to *Tikkun ha-nefesh*. This is a discipline for moral and spiritual rehabilitation, not a program for social or political action.[32]

If various substitute Jewish faiths are flawed—strategically, sociologically, historically, and logically—as has been discussed earlier, where is one to look for an authentic, viable, and valid foundation for Jewish identity? How can American Jews today—like many of the *conversos* in the seventeenth century—find their way back to their spiritual home in Judaism? The German Jewish philosopher Franz Rosenzweig characterized this as a process of "groping their way home."[33] Rosenzweig depicts this process of return as one that begins with alienation and moves from the "periphery to the center." For Rosenzweig, the "new Jewish learning" moves "from a world that knows nothing of the Law [Torah], back to the Torah," that is, back to Judaism.[34] And, as Rosenzweig further observed, the place to begin is with the study and teaching of Jewish theology.[35]

One function that Jewish theological discourse can serve is as a corrective in determining which ideas are authentic to Judaism and which are not. Jewish theology can therefore play a critical role not only in clarifying what Judaism believes but also in critiquing the authenticity

and integrity of features of Jewish communal life. Though sociological discourse can clarify and analyze what certain groups of Jews may
believe about Judaism at a given juncture of space and time, Jewish
theological discourse can clarify what Judaism is, that is, what its constitutive beliefs and practices are Consequently, theology can serve a
"subversive" role in determining whether the Jewish communal agenda
and the beliefs and actions of Jews at a given time and place are correlative with or disparate from those of the religion they identify with, and
allegedly espouse.

Though the cultural assimilation of Jews has been a constant concern in the American Jewish community, little attention has been paid
to the assimilation of Judaism, to what Solomon Schechter called "the
Galut [exile] of Judaism...the *Galut* of the Jewish soul wasting away
before our very eyes."[36] Not only have Jews become secularized, but
so—to a significant degree—has the Judaism they espouse. "Secular
Judaism" is an oxymoron, a contradiction in terms. How can a religion
and a faith community be secular? As demographic data reveal, the
assimilation and secularization of Judaism inevitably lead to the assimilation of Jews, to the endangerment of the continuity of the Jewish
people, as well as the Jewish faith.

Already in 1903, in a lengthy paper presented to the Central
Conference of American Rabbis, Professor Max Margolis identified
theological discourse as an urgent desideratum for American Jewry,
noting that "no religion can be without a theology."[37] Without a theology, the nature of a religion remains obscure even to its own adherents.
The continuity of a religion depends upon the continuity and continuous clarification of its beliefs. Theology focuses upon the beliefs that
make a religion worth living, living for, and perpetuating. Without the
continuity of Jewish belief, of Judaism, the continuity of Jews as a faith
community becomes imperiled. As the American Jewish theologian
Arthur Green has written, "The Jewish people is ready for theology,
needs it urgently. . . . Indeed, thinking about our Jewishness is precisely
what Jews need most to do. . . . We need to define our goals for the continuity of Jewish life. What do we mean by a Jewish future in America?"[38]
Like the *conversos* of seventeenth-century Amsterdam, contemporary
American Jews need to "grope their way home," and the place to begin,

as Rosenzweig observed, is with the beliefs that characterize Judaism, that is, with Jewish theology. In the words of Zalman Schachter, a leading figure in the contemporary "Jewish Renewal" movement, "That is why, having survived the persecution of two thousand years, we need to survive also the danger of dissolving into mere secularism or into a vaguely spiritual New Age soup in which the distinctive contributions of the various religions would be wiped out. That is why our instinctive reluctance to be the last link in the chain is a healthy one."[39]

Despite the role that Jewish theological discourse can play in helping Jews who are "groping their way home," despite the "subversive" role Jewish theology can play in helping to determine the authenticity of various beliefs and practices that dominate the Jewish communal agenda; and despite its role in helping to answer the visceral question, What is Judaism?, Jewish theology has not been taken very seriously by American Jewry. All of which leads to the questions posed by Jakob Petuchowski decades ago: "Does Judaism need a theology? Is Jewish theology possible today?"[40] We might now rephrase these questions as: Does Jewish theology exist, and if so, what is it? These questions are addressed in the chapter that follows.

THREE

The Nature of Jewish Theology

Abraham Joshua Heschel wrote:

> It was in the spirit of Spinoza that the slogan was created: Judaism
> has no theology. As a result...Jewish thought has been kept a
> well-guarded secret....We have lost the sense for the relevance of
> Judaism, and we run for refuge to all sorts of substitutes. Judaism
> today is an unknown religion. The vital issues it raises, the sublime
> views it discloses, the noble goals it points to are forgotten. We have
> failed to learn how much Judaism has to say to the mind, to the soul.
> Judaism is not a mood, a feeling, a sentimental attachment to cus-
> toms and ceremonies. Judaism is a source of cognitive insight, a way
> of thinking, not only an order of living.[1]

There is an old quip that compares the theological quest to a blind
person entering a darkened room to look for a black cat that is not even
there. Throughout most of its history, American Jewry has adapted a
similar attitude toward Jewish theology. Ignored at best, deemed irrelevant or divisive at worst, theological thinking has never been a priority item on the American Jewish communal agenda. American Jewry
has expressed its largesse in many ways, but the training and support of
Jewish theologians has not been one of them. Even Jewish theological
seminaries in the United States are exceedingly lax in teaching Jewish
theology or in training Jewish theologians. While the medieval Jewish
theologians felt obliged to adduce "proofs" for the existence of God,

today's Jewish theologians find themselves challenged to prove the existence of Jewish theology.

In the previous chapter, various attempts to reduce Judaism and Jewish historical experience to cultural, national, and sociological and various other categories were examined and critiqued. However, no attempt was made—or could be made—to deny the cultural, national, legal, or social dimensions of Jewish historical experience. One of the implications of reducing Judaism to one or more of these categories is the rejection of either the existence, the significance, or the relevance of Jewish theology to understanding Judaism and Jewish identity. Certainly, reducing Judaism to secular categories would eliminate the presence of and the need for theological discourse. The denial of the existence of Jewish theology and its marginalization neglect the fact that even a cursory survey of Jewish life and literature would adduce massive evidence to affirm the existence and persistence of Jewish theological discourse throughout the long history of Judaism. To deny the existence of Jewish theology is to disregard the huge body of classical Jewish religious literature that deals explicitly and implicitly with issues of overt theological concern. To reject or marginalize theology is to dismiss, among other things, the theological teachings of the Hebrew Bible, the Talmud, midrash, Jewish philosophy, and Jewish mysticism. It is to disenfranchise from Judaism its most revered expositors and practitioners, including the prophet Jeremiah, the psalmist, Hillel, Rabbi Akiva, Saadya Gaon, Judah Halevi, Maimonides, Abraham Abulafia, Isaac Luria, the Ba'al Shem Tov, a wide variety of modern Jewish thinkers, and many others. It is to neglect the yearnings for God in the Psalms, Job's struggles with the problem of evil, the preciousness of the prayer book, the theosophy of the *Zohar*, the spiritual legacy of east European Jewry brought to a cruel end by the Holocaust. It is to reject and to neglect a source of wisdom that the world needs to hear, a source for life's meaning of which individuals throughout history have constantly been in search. Jewish theological discourse is an attempt to provide Judaism, individual existence, and Jewish identity with meaning. To neglect or to marginalize Jewish theology threatens to make Judaism and Jewish existence meaningless.

According to Louis Jacobs, Jewish theology may be defined as "an attempt to think through consistently the implications of the Jewish religion."[2] Yet American Jewry has resisted such attempts for many reasons. One reason is because Americans tend to embrace activism and pragmatism, often neglecting and opposing doctrinal or ideological discourse. If Americans are basically activists, pragmatic, and a-theological, then American Jews are such, even more so. Indeed, as was discussed in the previous chapter, American Jews tend to understand Judaism as a religion primarily concerned with *doing* things rather than *thinking* things, as a religion of action that rejects doctrine, as an ethnic commitment rather than adherence to a transcendent faith.

As was noted earlier, Jonathan Woocher found that belief in God plays a "thoroughly insignificant role in the civil religion of American Jews," and that it is perceived as a divisive force insofar as Jewish communal solidarity is concerned.[3] Woocher characterizes the "civil religion of American Jews" as being "a-theological," an insight Woocher may have adapted from Norman Frimer's article "A-theological Judaism of the American Community" (1962). Frimer locates the source of this a-theological view in the adoption by American Jewry of paradigmatically American attitudes that are "basically activistic and pragmatic with an overtone of distrust for doctrine or ideology." Yet, as Frimer also observes, such activism and pragmatism are informed not by a "sacred theology" but by sociological and political rationales, that is, by secular rather than religious motivations, with the amorphous "good deed" replacing religious laws and commandments.[4]

Yet, despite the historically a-theological and even antitheological nature of American Jewry, a stream of Jewish theological works has consistently been produced, especially throughout the twentieth century.[5] As early as 1904, the (Reform) Central Conference of American Rabbis established a committee, chaired by Kaufmann Kohler, then president of Hebrew Union College, to formulate, in Kohler's words, "not [only] the principles of reform Judaism, but of Judaism."[6] The articulation of the nature and parameters of Jewish religious belief was deemed necessary as a way of responding to the questions, What is Judaism? and What is the meaning of Judaism for our times? Not simply an exercise in abstract theological speculation, the goal was to convey the products of these efforts to a Jewish laity, confused and uncertain as to which beliefs Judaism affirms and which it rejects. Attempts by Kohler, Schechter, and others to delineate the fundamental claims and boundaries of Judaism were efforts at responding to the perceived need to clarify for themselves and members of the movements they led the nature and meaning of Jewish belief and identity for their times.[7] That need continues today. Jewish theological discourse is a way of addressing that need.

A second reason American Jewry has resisted attempts to develop an American Jewish theology is because American Jews tend to be secular. Indeed, as has been noted, studies consistently indicate that they tend to be more secular than other Americans. Obviously, the more secular a community, the less likely it is to be concerned with theological thinking. It is not surprising, as Heschel noted, that the antitheological tendency of modern Jewry has its roots in the views of a seventeenth-century Dutch *converso* who was excommunicated by the Jewish community of Amsterdam, namely, Spinoza.

Like the *conversos* of times past, Jews today need to know the nature of their faith. Jewish adults need to know it not in the simplistic terms that may have been learned in their childhood but in a manner that is correlative with their level of education and intellectual sophistication. The simplistic theological platitudes many Jews learned as children in religious school may be appropriate for children but not for thinking, educated Jewish adults.

Both consciously and subconsciously, increasing numbers of Jewish adults are thinking about theological issues as they are "groping their way home." They are trying to "think Judaism through," but they are being provided with neither the tools nor the intellectual resources to do so. American Jews are inundated and "educated" about Israeli affairs, sociopolitical issues, and fund-raising needs, but precious little time, effort, or resources is being expended to inform them about the nature of the faith they espouse.

More American Jews are thinking about theological issues than many rabbis, academicians, and educators suspect. They are searching for the meaning of life, the meaning of Judaism, and other primary issues addressed by Jewish theological discourse. For example, as they confront the inevitability of human mortality, increasing numbers of Jewish senior citizens and baby boomers are interested in what Jewish thought has to say about an afterlife. Increasing numbers of Jewish parents are seeking "Jewish" responses to their children's theological questions, such as questions about God. With growing popular interest in kabbalah (i.e., the Jewish mystical tradition), increasing numbers of Jews are wondering why they have never learned about the theological teachings or meditative practices of the Jewish mystics. With the current emphasis on "spirituality," more and more Jews want to know why they have not been taught "Jewish spirituality," with its wealth of wisdom and insight into what Heschel called the "inner life." Not finding answers to their questions, many either give up the search, search for answers outside of Judaism, or accept superficial and uninformed teachings as "authentic" responses to the questions that confront them.

Jewish theology is a necessary vehicle for Jews who need and want to know the nature of the religion that they espouse: what it affirms, what it rejects, how it differs from other religions, how its beliefs developed, which of these beliefs can be asserted today with intellectual honesty, and what Judaism teaches about such visceral existential issues as the meaning of life. In order to understand the prayers they recite, the religious practices they observe, the holidays they celebrate, Jews need to be aware of the theological presuppositions that these assume. For example, can one appreciate the meaning of the High Holidays without exposure to Jewish theological conceptions of repentance? When Jews recite Shema, can they remain oblivious to the theological implications of the claim that God is one? Should the meaning of terms like "Torah," "revelation," "covenant," *mitzvot* (commandments), *olam ha-ba* (the world to come), that are sprinkled throughout classical Jewish literature and liturgy, remain obscure? Should issues such as why the good suffer, the meaning of Jewish peoplehood, rationales for religious observance (*ta'amei ha-mitzvot*), and other ongoing issues in Jewish theological discourse be neglected? Is the question of the "boundaries" of Jewish belief not relevant to the question of whether a Jew can also be a Christian, a Buddhist? Does the preoccupation of Jewish theology with meaning, including the meaning of human existence, have nothing to convey to Jews searching for meaning in their lives?

From a theological point of view, the products of sociological and demographic studies are relevant not because they provide an understanding of Judaism but because they demonstrate how alienated and detached contemporary Jews are from their own religious and intellectual heritage. They demonstrate how "coalescence" has led contemporary Jewry to understand both Judaism and their own identity as Jews in categories both foreign and inimical to those that emerge from Judaism itself. They demonstrate why we urgently need Jewish theological discourse to clarify and convey what Judaism is: which beliefs it embraces, which insights it offers in the ongoing quest to identify and enact the meaning of human existence, the meaning and nature of Jewish existence, and how to formulate a foundation for Jewish identity and for the continuity of Judaism in our rapidly changing, challenging, and increasingly dangerous world. In so doing, the nature of an authentic Judaism and Jewish identity needs to emerge from the framework of the constitutive ideas and texts that have shaped Judaism as a religious faith.

The question of Jewish identity—or "Who is a Jew?" as Maimonides already claimed—is not a function of sociological data or variables but is primarily determined by the affirmation of certain *beliefs*. In this regard, it should be noted that Maimonides begins his legal code, the *Mishneh Torah*, with a section called "Principles of the Foundations of Judaism" ("Hilkhot Yesodei ha-Torah") that sets down the theological presuppositions of Jewish faith. In his view, it is meaningless to discuss Jewish actions unless one has first established the theological presuppositions from which they flow, and which they presume.

In his earlier *Commentary to the Mishnah*, Maimonides comments on the word "Israel" (i.e., Israelite, Jew) in a Mishnaic text. Here, Maimonides presents his famous thirteen principles upon which "our religion is based" for those "with no training in theology." Having done so, Maimonides concludes:

> When a person believes in all these fundamental principles, and their faith is thereby clarified, an individual is then part of that "Israel" whom we are to love, have compassion for, and treat as God commanded with love and fellowship. Even if a Jew commits every possible sin, out of lust or mastery by their lower nature, that individual... is one of the "sinners in Israel." But, should a person give up any one of those fundamental principles, that individual

has removed himself or herself from the Jewish community. Such a person is an atheist, a heretic, an unbeliever.[8]

In this text and elsewhere, Maimonides makes clear that Jewish identity is *primarily* determined not by what a Jew does but by what a Jew believes. For Maimonides, because actions articulate beliefs, beliefs must first be clarified; actions are meaningless unless they emerge from a framework of conviction, meaning, and purpose. From this perspective, a Jew is a person who affirms certain beliefs and rejects others. Theological inquiry as to the nature of Jewish religious belief can serve a crucial role in helping to clarify the nature of Jewish identity, precisely today when many previously—and often secular—entrenched forms of modern Jewish identity are both dissipating and disappearing.

In the centuries after Maimonides, many Jewish thinkers accepted his view that Judaism is characterized by the affirmation of certain beliefs and the rejection of others. Where they disagreed was about which specific beliefs these were, which are primary and which are secondary, which are the products of passing polemical concerns, and which are critical to Judaism as a historical religious faith.[9] As will be discussed further, certain theological beliefs may be considered to be critical to Judaism, and without them Judaism would no longer be Judaism, but something else. In this regard, a blatant attempt to replace Jewish theological beliefs with secular beliefs and with affirmation of institutional commitment as a way of ensuring "Jewish continuity" may be cited as a further example of how the Jewish communal agenda offers substitute Jewish faiths to theologically based beliefs. A leading Jewish communal organization advertised its own creedal statement, apparently meant to supplant that of Maimonides. Under the title "I Believe," it lists a series of institutional creedal statements. For example, while Maimonides lists belief in the immortality of the soul as a basic Jewish theological presupposition, this document reads: "I believe that, after I have departed this earth our [name of organization deleted here] must continue my vision of a better world through their [i.e., the organization's various agencies] life-transforming programs and services.... I believe in making my mark on this [Jewish] Community through [donating to] the Centennial Campaign."

Solomon Schechter reminded us, "We usually urge that in Judaism religion means life; but we forget that life without guiding principles and thoughts is a life not worth living."[10] In response to Moses Mendelssohn's view that Judaism has no dogmas, Schechter said that Mendelssohn had made the dogma-less doctrine of Judaism into a dogma itself.[11] For Schechter, though Judaism does not embrace a dogmatic creed in the same sense as do various Christian denominations, there are nonetheless certain ideas and principles that underpin Jewish religious thought and practice. As Schechter puts it, "It is true that every great religion is 'a concentration of many ideas and ideals,' which make the religion able to adopt itself to various modes of thinking and living. But these must always be a point round which all these ideas concentrate themselves. This center is Dogma."[12] As Jakob Petuchowski wrote, "We need a Jewish theology which will make clear that Judaism does not mean 'everything' or 'nothing in particular.'"[13]

From this perspective, dogmas in Judaism are not meant to be a litmus test distinguishing between orthodox faith or heresy, salvation or heresy, but are rather meant to establish boundary markers and guidelines "beyond which one could not go in discussing Judaism."[14] According to the eminent historian of Jewish philosophy Julius Guttmann, "It is possible to speak of the fundamentals or principles of Judaism and not merely of the Judaism of this or that particular generation. . . . These concepts, beliefs and principles are truly fundamental to a unified Jewish belief, and also [are] the groundwork for future developments. This is not to say that in such a rich and variegated development there were not differences of opinion." In addition, Guttmann observes that foreign elements that "did not distort these fundamentals" were sometimes "domesticated or integrated into the spirit of Judaism, and received a form which then rendered them congruent with the inner motives of Judaism." Yet there were also inimical foreign elements that either were rejected outright or had some sway for a short time. Guttmann continues, "It was never in the power of these deviations to distort or upset the fundamental pattern of belief of Judaism. This fundamental spirit has never flagged and has indeed formed the life-pattern of generations."[15]

Even medieval Jewish philosophical formulations of principles of faith aimed not at creating a catechism but at setting limits to the ongoing process of interpretation. As a consequence, such "principles" are to an extent dynamic, allowing for flexibility, difference of opinion, and even ambiguity.[16] For example, according to the Talmud:

> The disciples of the wise sit in manifold assemblies and occupy themselves with the Torah, some pronouncing unclean and others pronouncing clean, some disqualifying and others declaring fit. How in these circumstances shall I learn Torah? Therefore, the text says: All of them are given from one shepherd. One God gave them; one leader uttered them, from the mouth of the Lord of creation, as it is written (Exod. 20:1): "And God spoke *all* these words."[17]

According to the Talmud, "Just as each blow of a hammer strikes forth many sparks, so a single verse [of the Torah] unfolds into many meanings."[18] However multivalent these interpretations are, they are not without limit. The rabbinic view that the Torah is a "multifaceted mirror" with "seventy faces" indicates that the interpretation and exposition of Judaism embrace a wide yet finite range.[19] The tradition itself defines these limits. Those who go beyond them forfeit their place within the ongoing development and growth of Jewish tradition. In this regard, *The Ethics of the Fathers* condemns even one who is "learned in the Torah and virtuous" when he or she "reveals faces of the Torah that contradict tradition [*halakhah*]."[20] *Peshat* (the literal or contextual meaning of a text) that cannot be legitimately assimilated into the corpus of tradition should not be incorporated into the corpus of Jewish theology because the boundaries of Jewish theology—though broad—have limits.[21]

Though an expansive diversity of views characterizes Judaism, there are boundaries nonetheless. Just as the Jewish dietary laws permit a wide variety of foods to be eaten and proscribe that certain foods may not be eaten, the ideas that constitute an authentic Jewish theology and the texts that may be utilized in its formulation are diverse, but not without limits. Certain ideas, certain worldviews, cannot legitimately appear on the menu of Jewish theology. Jewish theology embraces a broad but finite range.

The wide range of ideas present in the enormous mass of texts that constitute classical Jewish religious tradition might be compared to a Jewish theological smorgasbord. The assortment of dishes served would be vast, though limited. As individuals partake of the repast, each takes an empty plate and proceeds along the table, creating a combination of foods particular to their own taste and appetite. Choices can be made only from those dishes that are on the table. Similarly, a theologian constructs his or her collage of Judaism or of a particular issue or problem of Jewish theology, ethics, or law from the menu at hand.

An immense repast is set out in the banquet hall of tradition; staple dishes as well as exotic offerings grace the banquet table. A variety of available foods, unusual delicacies, and rich seasonings and garnishments are represented on the menu of tradition. But despite this cornucopia, the bill of fare is not without limits; the banquet table has its borders, its perimeters. Rabbinic literature compares the Torah to a "multifaceted mirror," but the number of faces that may be reflected in the mirror, though widely diverse, nevertheless has its limits.

In order for a meal to be complete, certain courses must be eaten and certain types of foods consumed. As no meal can be considered complete without the consumption of certain foods, no theology of Judaism can be considered complete without the incorporation of certain basic ideas such as God, revelation, Messiah, providence, afterlife, and so forth.

As each person who is invited to partake of the offerings of an immense smorgasbord would emerge with a plate of food configured differently from that of another person, so each formulation of a theology of Judaism would be different from that of one's fellow. Though in the final analysis, the choices of literary resources are identical, the form and presentation of each theology of Judaism will nonetheless differ. This is precisely why each Jewish theologian is free to compose *a* Jewish theology while no Jewish theologian can offer *the* Jewish theology. To be authentic, each theology of Judaism must derive from the same diverse menu; nevertheless, each Jewish theology bears the stamp of its composer. Just as every symphony is composed of identical notes though the organization and presentation of these notes differ from composer to composer and from symphony to symphony, so is each authentic theology of Judaism a distinct aria of ideas. Thus, each authentic theology of Judaism simultaneously reflects the resources of a shared tradition and the particularity of an individual Jewish theologian and of the theology of Judaism he or she has elicited from that commonly affirmed tradition. As Louis Jacobs so well put it, "The whole question of whether one can choose within Judaism only arises if one has first chosen Judaism."[22]

A central task of Jewish theology is to establish the nature and parameters of Jewish religious thought, to articulate coherently authentic views of Judaism, and to demonstrate how the wisdom of the Jewish religious teachings of the past can address the perplexities of contemporary Jewish existence. The four criteria that characterize a valid Jewish theology are identical to those of any valid theology. These are authenticity, coherence, contemporaneity, and communal acceptance.[23]

Authenticity depends on the nature and use of sources consulted, and on the faith commitment of the individual consulting them. Coherence relates to the cohesion, clarity, and communicability of a formulated theological perspective. Contemporaneity pertains to the successful application of past traditions to present situations. Communal acceptance refers to the ratification of a theological posture by committed members of a specific faith community.

Should a theological stance not achieve communal acceptance, then it proves barren. When not contemporaneous, it becomes anachronistic. If it lacks coherence, a theological position invites unintelligibility and hence proves unavailing. When a theology cannot claim authenticity, it is demonstrably spurious. Though these four criteria for theological validity apply to theology in general, what follows addresses how and why they particularly relate to the formulation of a valid *Jewish* theology.[24]

Due to the scarcity of parchment in medieval times, scribes would often write new texts on top of earlier ones, producing a form of writing called "palimpsest." Theological discourse may be considered a form of palimpsest. Theology is always a posteriori, never a priori. Theology is not a *creatio ex nihilo*. Authentic theological discourse always rests upon who and what has gone before—texts, people, experiences.

On a verse in Exodus (17:6), "I [God] will be standing there before you," a midrash explains, "God said to Moses: Everywhere that you find a human footprint, I have been there before you."[25] Just as theology may be characterized as thinking God's thoughts after God does, the theologian may be characterized as walking in God's footsteps. The theologian also walks in the footsteps of a specific faith tradition. Consequently, before theologians can blaze a new path down a well-trodden road of a particular faith, they must walk in the footsteps of those who came before. Before becoming a pioneer, the theologian must first become an heir. A historical tradition, an extant canon of sacred literature, and a living faith community precede each attempt to formulate a theology of Judaism. Recognition of the existence of Judaism as an objectively and historically existing religious faith precedes any attempt to formulate a theology of Judaism. The challenge is not to create but to re-create that tradition.

To use a medieval analogy, the theologian is like a "dwarf riding on the shoulders of a giant."[26] The giant represents the cumulative corpus of the tradition that precedes the individual. This analogy indicates that the wisdom of the past represented by the giant makes the stature of the giant necessarily higher, and his vista broader, than that of the dwarf who represents only his own wisdom and that of his particular generation. The giant represents the summation and quintessence of tradition, but when perched on the giant's shoulders, the dwarf is provided an opportunity to see more, to exceed that which is attainable by the giant alone. Together, the giant and the dwarf guarantee the continuity and development of tradition. Without the giant, there is no viable foundation for such development. Without the dwarf, the giant might become simply a relic of bygone days.

In his commentary to the Mishnah, the late sixteenth-century Talmudist Abraham Azulai discussed this analogy of the dwarf and the giant:

> For the modern is like a dwarf and the ancients are like giants but because the modern is later, he is like a dwarf riding the shoulder of a giant who can see at a distance farther than the giant. And so it is with the modern who may be unable to attain what the ancient had attained, but being later and having had the benefit of the knowledge and great wisdom of the ancients, then, if he himself should discover something new, be it but a trifle, he will certainly with that trifle contribute more wisdom than they; even though his own wisdom would have been naught had he not the benefit of their wisdom.[27]

Tradition is a living force that animates and informs the present. Tradition is that which assures the continuity of creativity. Without the dwarf, tradition is like a giant, a relic of bygone days. However, without the giant, there is no viable foundation for future creativity, development, and growth. Without the giant, the dwarf either stands tied close to the ground or is transfixed in midair, waiting to fall into the abyss.

The giant would be unwise to be threatened by what the dwarf might achieve. Indeed, he should be grateful to the dwarf for expanding his purview. The dwarf should be grateful to the giant, for without the giant the vision of the dwarf would remain severely limited. Once perched on the giant's shoulders, the dwarf must overcome the temptation of forgetting that he is not a giant, but a dwarf riding on the shoulders of a giant. It is further incumbent upon the dwarf to know the giant well. What the dwarf will be able to see depends upon the nature of the giant and where the giant will carry the dwarf.

Represented in this analogy by the giant, tradition is a bequest of the ages. It is a trust vouchsafed only to those who labor on its behalf. To be received, tradition must first be acquired. Study of the bibliographic menu of sacred texts is necessary but not sufficient. Like food, the tradition must become incorporated. It is not enough to know sacred texts. One must also absorb and become absorbed by them. As Schneur Zalman of Liady wrote:

> Seeing that through the knowledge of the Torah man's soul and mind encompass the Torah and are in turn encompassed by it, the Torah is called food and the sustenance of the soul. For just as material food sustains the body and enters it and is transformed in the body into flesh and blood, by virtue of which a man lives and endures, so it is with regard to knowledge of the Torah and its comprehension by he who studies with concentration until the Torah is grasped by the mind and becomes united with it.[28]

In this view, one must consume and be consumed by the Torah, the tradition. Study of the Torah is but a means, becoming Torah is the goal. Commenting on the phrase "ve-zot torat ha-Adam" [literally: "and this is the Torah of man"] (2 Sam. 7:19), the Hasidic master Mordecai of Chernobyl explained it to mean that "the man himself *becomes* the Torah."[29] The Torah becomes incarnated in him.

The theologian cannot be a passive voyeur, a casual tourist surveying the landscape of tradition. The philosopher or the historian of religion can stand outside the arena of his or her inquiry as a disinterested observer. For the theologian, however, commitment precedes inquiry. Experience of the life of faith and participation in a faith community anticipates theological investigation.[30] Only the wellsprings of individual religious commitment can generate a viable theology. Only from the passion of faith can theology emanate.

Theology is not an intellectual parlor game but the articulation of a prior commitment. Observance of the commandments is an expression of that commitment. Jewish theologians are obliged not only to *do* what they *believe* but to *believe* what they *do*. Halakhah is faith in the form of deeds. Performance of the commandments represents belief articulated as action. In a sense, halakhah may be considered the "practical theology" of Judaism, that is, Jewish theological ideas expressed as specific concrete acts. As a midrash observes, "If a person studies [Torah] without the intention to observe it, it is better that he had not been born ... it would have been better that he had been strangled by the placenta at birth, and had never ventured forth into the world."[31] Another midrashic text describes the scholar who refuses to apply what he or she knows to ameliorating social problems within the community as a destructive individual. "'But the person of separation overthrows it' (Prov. 29:4)—this refers to the sage who knows halakhah, midrash, and Haggadah to whom widows and orphans go to plead their case, but who excuses himself with the plea: I am engaged with my studies and have no leisure. To him God says: I regard you as if you have destroyed the world."[32]

The rabbis read the verse describing the Torah as an inheritance (*morashah*) of Israel (Deut. 33:4) as denoting the betrothal (*me-orashah*) of the people of Israel and of each individual Jew to the Torah.[33] As Samuel of Uceda observed, commenting upon this rabbinic text, betrothal infers commitment, and commitment grants a license for intimacy with the Torah, with the tradition.[34]

The person committed to the Torah, to the tradition, is granted entrée into her inner domain. According to the *Zohar*, the true scholar is a lover of the Torah, invited by the Torah to penetrate her private precincts, to gain access through intimacy into her deepest mysteries, to uncover secrets she otherwise cloaks.[35] As Moses Hayyim Ephraim of Sudlykow wrote, "When one studies the Torah for its own sake, to keep it and to perform it, then he brings all his limbs close to their source whence they originated and were generated, namely the Torah,...and he becomes identical to the Torah like the unification of man and woman."[36] Speculating further on a rabbinic text that compares the Torah to Israel's spouse, a commentator explains this analogy to mean that the Torah is caused to conceive by the sages of Israel, thereby assuring the continuous rebirth and development of the tradition.[37]

To a lover, his or her beloved is unique. Jewish theology focuses upon the specifically unique rather than upon the scientific tendency toward generalization.[38] Jewish theology posits its own sui generis nature. The formative events that concern it (such as the revelation at Sinai), the corpus of sacred literature that informs it, the people of Israel who live it, and the historical experience of the Jewish people that helps to shape it are held to be unique. Consequently, a task of the theologian is to discern the particular categories of faith and thought that characterize and are native to Judaism.

The historian of Judaism focuses dispassionately upon the anatomy of Jewish sacred literature and historical experience, scrutinizing individual limbs. But a minute examination of individual parts tends to eclipse the vision of the whole. The theologian seeks a total gestalt, unencumbered by historical considerations: "There is neither earlier nor later in the Torah."[39] For theologians, the corpus of tradition is like the body of their beloved. The theologian strives to know the personality of the beloved in ways unavailable to the historian of religion. The variety of knowledge available through anatomical research is not the kind of knowledge available through an act of love.

The historian of Judaism has access to Judaism on a surface level. But license to penetrate the deeper meaning of Judaism is vouchsafed only to one who already has received and accepted it. As a lover of the Torah, one is given an access code to the text denied to the historian of religion, to the social scientist examining Judaism, and to the historian of Jewish experience. As the Torah is sui generis, its knowledge by its lovers is also sui generis. According to Samuel of Uceda, on the semantic level the Torah is only truly given and only truly gives herself to her lovers.[40]

As lovers embarks upon a never-ending quest for the knowledge and experience of their beloved, the Jewish theologian embarks on the never-ending journey toward knowledge and experience of the Torah. Though lust may be satisfied, deep abiding passionate love cannot ever truly be quenched.[41] In this regard, Samuel of Uceda noted, "Even if people would live two-thousand years, they could not grasp its [the Torah's] totality."[42]

A blessing praises God for allowing us to be "preoccupied with the words of Torah" (*la-asok be-divrei Torah*).[43] Perpetual preoccupation with the Torah is required. Like any love relationship, a modicum of mystery must prevail to stimulate the further pursuit of knowledge of the beloved. Through continuous penetration of and preoccupation with the Torah, one inevitably acquires erudition and understanding.

To make love to the Torah it is necessary to disrobe it. In Hebrew, the word *peshat* comes from the root *P-Sh-T*, which also means to "strip" or to "divest." According to Jewish mystics, the true *peshat* of the text is not its literal, plain, or contextual meaning but its divested, unclad, hidden spiritual meaning.[44] The true meaning of the text must always elude the scholar who identifies the text with its appearance, who seeks the apparent rather than the concealed *peshat*. Only in the act of making love to the Torah by one committed to it can its true meaning and nature be elicited and discerned. Love of the Torah grants license to become engaged with its meaning and message.

The Ethics of the Fathers states: "Beloved are Israel, for they were given a precious object [the Torah]. A special love was shown them in that they were given a precious object. As it is written (Prov. 4:2): 'I have given you good doctrine, forsake not My Torah.'"[45] In his commentary to this passage, Samuel of Uceda observed:

> Only to Israel it [the Torah] was given as a gift and not to others.... The intention [of the text under discussion] is that to the sages and to [the people of] Israel was given [the license] to interpret [the Torah] and to explain it, and that is evident from the verse: I have given you good doctrine.... I gave it to you to interpret.... I have given this gift to Israel alone.... [It is] an inheritance [*morashah*] [through which I (God)] became betrothed [*me'urasah*] to you. No other man can be involved with a woman once she has become betrothed.... This may have been the intention of the men of the Great Assembly who established the blessing of the Torah which reads "who has chosen

us from among all peoples and gave us the Torah," meaning that an unconditional gift was given to us to explain and to interpret as we desire. It was given to us alone, and not to any other people.[46]

The task of Jewish self-understanding is never-ending, perpetual. As Judah Loew reminds us, a blessing describes God as "one who gives the Torah" (*notein ha-Torah*). As Loew observes, "That is to say, you [God] give the Torah each day." As Loew further reminds us, another blessing praises God for allowing us to be "preoccupied with the words of the Torah" (*la-asok be-divrei Torah*).[47] Theology requires perpetual personal involvement; it requires enduring individual commitment.

Knowledge of and preoccupation with the Torah, coupled with the quest to understand Judaism in its own terms, grant license to the attempt to formulate a theology of Judaism. Here "Torah" is meant in its most generic and expansive sense: the teachings of Judaism as embodied in the literary works and oral traditions that have been held sacred by Jewish tradition.[48] In this sense, "Torah" is the entire canon of sacred Jewish literature. At its inner core is the corpus of biblical and rabbinic literature. At its periphery are the teachings of today's Torah scholars: "Everything an erudite student will expound in the presence of his master, was already spoken to Moses at Sinai."[49] The Torah is a single corpus, one organic conceptual unit. Consequently, one cannot approach the Torah as if it were an archaeological dig requiring stratification and identification of its individual historical layers; that is the problem of the historian of religion. Rather, a theologian apprehends the Torah as a single organism, as if all of the texts that constitute it "were uttered in a single statement."[50]

As was noted earlier, a criterion of a valid Jewish theology is coherence. Some make the mistake of equating coherence with systematization. Indeed, some claim that Jewish theology does not exist because theology is a Christian enterprise characterized by a form of systematic thinking alien to Judaism, that only systematic theology is theology. However, this claim fails to realize that not all theology, not even all Christian theology, is systematic theology, that theological discourse exists in many forms, that systematization is not endemic to theological discourse. What is endemic to theology is a concern with fundamental existential problems like the meaning of life, and with the meaning of certain claims of a religious tradition about God, revelation, faith, evil, and so on—all of which have been addressed over the centuries in Jewish religious thought. The history of Judaism is saturated with theological concerns, and Jewish theology need not be systematic to be theology. Coherence does not necessarily entail systematization. To be authentic, a theology of Judaism must emerge from the constitutive sacred and significant texts of Jewish religious tradition, where Judaism is understood in its own native categories; yet, to be theology, it need only be coherent and not systematic.[51] As Samuel S. Cohon observed, "Attempts to cram Judaism into categories derived from other religions and theologies can only lead to grotesque results."[52]

As part of a religious minority in a predominantly Islamic or Christian culture, inevitably influenced by Western philosophical tradition, both the medieval and the modern Jewish thinker become tempted to assimilate Judaism into alien and even inimical philosophies and theologies. Jewish thinkers may remain oblivious to the "cultural conditioning" absorbed from their geographic environment and may be led to articulate a theology of Judaism in a manner that does not cohere with authentic Jewish thought or with the inherent vocabulary of Jewish theological discourse.[53] In this regard, Solomon Schechter made a distinction between assimilating and being assimilated. An organism is able to assimilate and should assimilate that which strengthens and enriches it. However, an organism is always endangered by being assimilated into that which is inimical to it, into that which distorts its very nature.[54] Or, as Heschel put it, "This I surely know—the source of Jewish thinking cannot be found in the desire to reconcile Judaism with a current doctrine."[55]

Three notions characteristic of medieval philosophical theology are the demand for a systematic formulation of theological ideas, the perceived need to reconcile religious and philosophical truth, and the rational demonstration of the convictions that theology asserts (i.e., "natural theology").[56] Following Aristotle, who considered the validity of a system of thought as being affirmed by its logical consistency, "systematic theology" has often been embraced as the only valid variety of theological discourse. From this perspective, if logical consistency is a requirement for theological validity, then for a Jewish theology to be valid, it has to be systematic and internally logically consistent. Based upon these assumptions, numerous Jewish thinkers, particularly during the Middle Ages, attempted to impose the rubric of Aristotelian systematic thinking upon Judaism in the attempt to articulate a valid theology of Judaism.

The history of Western theology, beginning with Philo of Alexandria more than 2,000 years ago, is based on the mistaken presumption that classical Jewish thinking rooted in biblical literature and philosophy rooted in ancient Greco-Roman thought say the same things and make the same claims, albeit in a different idiom. For Heschel, creating a hybrid of the two—a major goal of medieval philosophical theology—distorts the authenticity of both classical Jewish thought and philosophy. As Heschel reminds us, "The categories in which Biblical man conceived of God, man and the world are so different from the presuppositions of metaphysics upon which most of Western philosophy is based that certain insights that are meaningful within the Biblical mind seem meaningless to the Greek mind."[57] Seen from this perspective, authentic Jewish theology is an endeavor to think Judaism through utilizing native Jewish categories. In this view, Jewish theology is self-reflective. It is a perpetual exercise in self-examination, self-clarification, and self-understanding.[58]

Though it may be described as a religious way of thinking or as a coherent "worldview," Jewish theology need not be systematic in order to be valid. Classical Jewish religious literature, that is, biblical and rabbinic literature, for example, did not consider the systematization of ideas either necessary or desirable. System offers structure and focus but not necessarily theological validity. System provides a finality that can prove inimical to creative theological development.

Imposing a contrived system upon reality or upon Judaism would be like trying to lay a flat grid upon the Alps. Jewish thought, especially Jewish mystical thought, perceives reality as being characterized by polarity, contradiction, creative tension (see chapter 7). Without one entity, its polar opposite is bereft of meaning. Jewish theological discourse is at home with "polar" thinking. Logic and system may be vehicles to clarity, but they are not necessarily indicative either of coherence or of truth.

Because Judaism is not wedded to Western philosophy, it has no endemic need to correlate or identify its claims with those of philosophical discourse. The assumption, made by so many medieval and modern religious philosophers, that philosophy and religion are one mouth that speaks two languages that mean the same thing, that contradictions between philosophy and religion are merely apparent, is simply a fantasy. In this regard, Emil Fackenheim has written that:

> the attempted fusion of theology with either philosophy or science is a confusion. As regards the specific tasks of Jewish theology, it is *a priori* evident, not only that this is a confusion, but that it is a confusion fatal to the tasks of Jewish theology. For the categories of philosophy and science are, one and all, universal, but from such universal categories no conclusions can be derived which must be a theological justification of the particular existence of the Jewish people.[59]

Once philosophical truth is affirmed, and religious teaching is required to become consistent with it, the perversion of religious teachings becomes inevitable, and the assimilation of religion into philosophy unavoidably ensues. Religious teachings are compelled to speak a foreign language. Gersonides, for example, insisted that any "apparent" contradiction between the Torah and philosophy can be resolved through interpreting religious doctrine according to philosophical doctrine without "destroying the tenets of revealed religion."[60] Gersonides failed to appreciate, however, that conflicts between religious and philosophical doctrine can be actual and not merely apparent. He further failed to grasp how religious teachings can become distorted by requiring them to conform to already affirmed philosophical doctrine.

Bahya ibn Pakudah expressed a typical formulation of the medieval philosophical approach when he described one who has faith only on the basis of tradition as the blind leading the blind, whereas the believer through reason is like a blind person who has learned how to see.[61] However, he neglects to consider the possibility that one who believes through reason can also be blind to truth.

While always encouraging the application of the divine gift of human reason to the quest for true belief, one nevertheless senses a hesitancy in classical Jewish thought automatically to equate the products of rationality with truth. That which is rational may be neither reasonable nor true. In the quest for religious truth, rationality may become a "dead end," or a faulty directional signal. Reason can offer acuity of vision, but it cannot grant sight itself. Reason is a necessary but not a sufficient aspect of the theological endeavor. It cannot demonstrate the validity of the convictions of theology, though it may clarify their meaning once they enter the purview of our vision. In theology, reason is a tool, a vehicle to be utilized for the clarification of what is already believed, but it is not truth personified. Like any tool, it can either improve or damage the entity to which it is applied.[62] Theology deals with the meaning of faith, and as Emil Fackenheim observes, "Faith may be defined as the sole positive answer to questions of ultimate importance, the asking of which is reason's prerogative but which reason is no longer able to answer."[63]

Though a Jewish theology need not be systematic, correlative with philosophy, or rationalistic to be valid, it does require coherence. A lack of coherence is a danger to the formulation of a valid theology. As Louis Jacobs observes, "Loose and wooly thinking in the area of religion can lead to a glorification of the absurd. . . . Holy nonsense is still nonsense."[64] Though a theology can be personal and reflective of the particular style and approach of the individual theologian, it cannot become an exercise in abstract expressionism, comprehensible only to its author.

A major purpose of theological discourse is to communicate a vision, a stance, a perspective out of the collision between traditional wisdom and contemporary situations and events. A theology of Judaism that does not communicate is like a messenger who is unable to deliver the message. Such a theology proves mute and unavailing.

According to scripture, Bezalel, who built the Tabernacle, was the first Jewish artist. The Talmud observes that Bezalel "knew how to combine the letters by which the heavens and the earth were created."[65] In other words, theological creativity derives from the ability to create new meanings from old texts. Out of the raw materials of tradition, the theologian must produce a narrative portrait of Judaism that is authentic, coherent, contemporaneous, and communicable.[66]

The individual human being is perpetually engaged in a process of self-understanding and self-discovery. The Jewish theologian is a person continuously engaged in the endeavor to understand his or her existence as a Jew. A critical component of this process is continuous self-understanding, discovery and rediscovery of the Torah, and of that which is rooted in the initial revelation at Sinai. Study of the Torah aims not merely at a conveyance of information to its reader but at the transformation of its reader. The transformed and re-created reader can engender a re-created and reimagined theology of Judaism.

Once the Torah has been incorporated and assimilated into the self, the Jewish theologians' quest for understanding the Torah and their quest for self merge into a single endeavor. Since, as the Jewish mystics teach us, "God, Torah, and Israel are one," the quest for self and for Torah is inextricably related to the quest for the divine.[67] Thus, the Jewish theologian is engaged in the perpetual task of self-understanding within the context of the Torah—the tradition—as well as within the context of a specific moment in time and space. The theologian is charged with realizing the challenge posed by a midrash, "Let the Torah never be for you an antiquated decree . . . but as a decree issued this very day."[68] Theologians take inherited notes and recompose them into a new song for their own age. A goal of Jewish theology is to make our ancestors our contemporaries. In so doing, the theologian heeds the words of the psalmist: "Sing unto the Lord a new song" (Ps. 96:1). Creativity, innovation, and contemporaneity are features of any valid Jewish theology.

To reduce aesthetics to subjectivity would be a mistake. Like the aesthetic dimension, the religious dimension is objectively present in the world. Like art, it requires a certain sensitivity to be appreciated and understood. It is objective and subjective at the same time.[69] One must invest something of oneself to understand a great work of art. However, though one need not be an artist to be inspired by great art, one must become an artist in order to produce great art. Similarly, one need not be a theologian to study or to understand the teachings of the Torah, but one must become a theologian in order to re-create Torah.

Though theologians are not charged with the initial creation of tradition, they are required to re-create the tradition from the raw materials bequeathed by the past. According to a midrashic analogy, one is obliged "to derive flour from wheat, a garment from flax."[70] The theologian is challenged with vesting the bequest of tradition with new meaning, with liberating meanings implicit in pregnant sacred texts. The theologian is a midwife whose vocation is to bring forth new life from the womb of tradition.[71] For the Jewish theologian, erudition is a vestibule, not a final destination. Medieval Jewish writers compared the erudite scholar who had amassed much learning but who had not completely grasped its meaning or its implications to a "donkey carrying books."[72]

In medieval Jewish literature, the consonants of the Hebrew alphabet are compared to a body and the vowels to a soul.[73] Yet a Torah scroll is written only with consonants. Indeed, a vocalized Torah scroll is unfit for ritual use.[74] The Torah requires a *person* to supply the vowels, the vocalization, the soul, in order for it to become animate, alive, heard.[75] Without the person, the sacred text remains mute. Without the person to animate it, to provide it with a voice, tradition might otherwise remain inert. By giving vocalization to the text, the reader animates and interprets the text, giving it life, allowing it to be spoken, heard, and understood.

Once the human process of acceptance, transmission, and "publication" commences, the Torah that we have "is no longer in Heaven" (Deut. 30:12) but falls under the provenance of the continuous process of human interpretation and even misinterpretation.[76] Once surrendered into human hands and accepted by them, the Torah takes on a life of its own. Now its readers become its coauthors and its interpreters. Its readers become writers who convey its meaning. By providing the Torah with a voice, with animation, the theologian thereby becomes a coauthor of the Torah, a collaborator with God in perpetuating and helping to augment and amplify in the present the voice once heard at Sinai.[77] As Meir Ibn Gabbai wrote, "Even the sages who arise in each generation receive that which is granted from Sinai.... If new teachings [regarding the understanding of the Torah] are produced daily, this proves that the foundation [of revelation] ever gushes forth and that the great voice [from Sinai] sounds forth without interruption."[78]

According to a midrash quoted by ibn Gabbai, "Not only did all the prophets receive their prophecy at Sinai, but also each of the sages who arose in each generation received his wisdom from Sinai."[79] As a Hasidic master put it:

> Everything depends upon the interpretations of the rabbis. . . . Until they had interpreted it, the Torah was not considered complete, but only half finished; it was the rabbis, through their interpretations, who made the Torah whole. Such is the case for each generation and its leaders; they complete the Torah. The Torah is interpreted in each generation according to that generation's needs, and according to the soul-root of those who live at that time. God thus enlightens the sages of the generation in [the interpretation of] God's holy Torah. A person who denies this is as one who denies the Torah itself.[80]

As has been noted earlier, Judah Loew observed that in the blessing over the Torah, God is described not as having *given* the Torah but as *giving* the Torah (*notein ha-Torah*) because the Torah is continuously being given, is perpetually being revealed and received.[81] Judah Loew's brother, Hayyim ben Betzalel of Friedberg, said further that "this blessing is stated all in the present tense because God is *still* giving us the Torah each day, since each person is able to introduce new meanings into it, provided they are correlative with the roots of observance and faith."[82] As Isaiah Horowitz wrote:

> The scholar produces new words [in the understanding of the Torah] or derives them through the power of their insight. But all of it was contained in the power of that voice that was heard at the revelation; and now the time has come for them to bring it from potentiality to actuality through the efforts of their mediation. . . . It thus follows that though we say of God that "God has *given* the Torah," God can also be designated in every present time as "the One who *gives* the Torah."[83]

According to some of the Jewish mystics, though the Torah that God gives is the same Torah for all, each individual may understand it in their own particular way, according to the manner peculiar to their individual "soul-root."[84] From this perspective, the process of the rediscovery and re-creation of the initial revelation rooted at Sinai is a profoundly personal and individual endeavor. As Louis Jacobs observes,

"Every writer on the subject [of Jewish theology] can only repeat what the Jewish preachers of old were fond of saying when they faced the question: Who am I to preach to others? They protested: I am speaking to myself. If others wish to overhear what I say, I cannot object." As Jacobs further puts it, "While the historian asks what has happened in the Jewish past, the theologian asks the more personal question: what in traditional Jewish religion continues to shape my life as a Jew in the here and now... the task [of the theologian is] discovering what is it that a Jew can believe in the present."[85]

Experience of the life of faith precedes theological speculation. The faith commitment and the experience of faith of the individual theologian ultimately derive from participation in a living faith community. In the final analysis, it is that faith community that will either incorporate or veto the theological views of a given theologian. Unless it acquires some form of communal acceptance, a theology of Judaism may prove to be authentic, coherent, and contemporaneous but will nonetheless remain barren and ineffectual. Acceptance by the faith community means inclusion within the ever-expanding canon of tradition.

"Communal acceptance" does not infer acceptance by a consensus of the Jewish community as a social unit. In the biblical period, the consensus among Jews to worship the idol Baal did not mean that the authentic religion of biblical Israel was, or could ever be, Baalism, for idolatry is outside the boundaries of possible Jewish theological options. Rather, communal acceptance relates to acceptance not simply by Jews who are "Jewish" by birth but by those who constitute the believing community, the *faith* community, that is, those committed to the vocation of the people of Israel. The vocation of the Jewish people as a faith community is divine service as understood by the Torah. As Arthur Cohen put it, "Theology, of necessity, addresses the supernatural vocation of the Jew. When the Jewish vocation is abandoned, not theology but religious sociology takes over."[86]

Acceptance or rejection by the majority of Jews, or by the "organized" secular Jewish community that formulates "Jewish" views and policies by group consensus, is irrelevant to the Jewish theologian. Such acceptance or rejection is not germane to the validity of a theology of Judaism he or she may formulate. The communal role of the Jewish theologian today is more likely to be subversive than supportive of the Jewish communal agenda. The commitment of the Jewish theologian is not organizational but theological. When theologians perceive Jewish communal existence to be out of sync with Jewish theological conviction, their subversive role becomes activated.

Faith Finding Meaning

The previous chapter offered a portrait of the nature of and the criteria for a valid Jewish theology. But that portrait is incomplete. Theology is an enterprise that proceeds on three levels: "depth-theology," "descriptive" or "constructive" theology, and "philosophical theology." The preceding chapter focused on only one of these levels of Jewish theology, that is, descriptive or constructive theology, where the primary goal is to construct from the resources of tradition an authentic and coherent formulation of Jewish religious belief, in an attempt to respond to the questions, What is Judaism and what Judaism is not? Descriptive theology is like the creation of a work of art out of the raw materials of the tradition and out of the faith commitment of the theologian. Descriptive theology portrays what Judaism believes.

From descriptive theology, a third level emerges that is derivative from it, that is, philosophical theology, which seeks to rationally understand that which is already believed. Philosophical theology aims at refining, further clarifying, and sharpening the focus of faith claims, utilizing the tools of philosophy and logic. Philosophical theology seeks to offer "proofs" and "demonstrations" for what is already believed. For example, faith in God's existence is not adequate for the philosophical theologian who feels compelled to "demonstrate" through reasoned argument that which is already believed, for example, the existence of God. For the philosophical theologian, unreflective faith is necessary but not sufficient. Rather, for faith to be complete, it needs to be justified, defended, distinguished from falsity and doubt. For the philosophical theologian, theology is "faith seeking understanding."[1] Faith is incomplete without rational understanding and analysis.

In a sense, the descriptive theologian is like an artist while the philosophical theologian is like an art critic. For the philosophical theologian, the true believer is a person who not only has fervent faith but also understands rationally that which is already believed. Yet, by itself, philosophical theology is a conclusion without a premise. Without descriptive theology, philosophical theology remains like a roof hanging in the air without a foundation. The medieval Jewish philosophers made the mistake of equating philosophical theology with all of theology, rather than realizing that philosophical theology is a theological "afterthought," that is, an attempt to justify and to systematically formulate the teachings and claims of an existing faith tradition that may elude systematic expression. Historically, a major function of philosophical theology has consisted of polemical and "apologetic" attempts to clarify and defend a particular position of faith from external ideological onslaughts and internal conflicts. As members of a minority religion in both the Christian and Muslim worlds, Jewish philosophers sought the "level playing field" of philosophical discourse and logical method as a way of defending and rationally justifying Jewish religious belief. In addition, they felt obliged to address the concerns of their contemporary fellow Jews who had become influenced by the philosophical teachings of Western culture that had permeated the societies in which they lived.

Though descriptive theology would constitute the main form of Jewish theological discourse, philosophical theology also plays a significant role. Among the tasks of philosophical theology is to continuously refine, clarify, and sharpen the focus of what is seen in the lens of descriptive theology. However, underlying descriptive theology is a primary level that may be called "depth-theology."[2]

Depth-theology is rooted in individual experience. Descriptive theology is defined by the ideas, texts, and historical experiences that have shaped Judaism as a historical faith. Philosophical theology aims at justifying and defending the established beliefs of the faith tradition.

Depth-theology emerges from the deepest existential questions that per-colate in the antechambers of individual hearts and souls. Descriptive theology derives from Jewish thinking about Judaism. Philosophical Jewish theology emerges from the attempt to justify, defend, and clarify that which is already believed.

Without depth-theology, theology is like a house without a founda-tion. Without descriptive theology, theological discourse is like a house without living space, that is, a living room, a kitchen, bedrooms. Without philosophical theology, it is like a house without an attic. Consequently, depth-theology is necessary but not sufficient. Descriptive theol-ogy is sufficient but not necessary unless depth-theology precedes it. Philosophical theology is neither necessary nor sufficient but can serve as a desirable accoutrement. Depth-theology is rooted in the individual spiritual quest. Descriptive theology is rooted in the spiritual life and legacy of a faith community.

Both descriptive and philosophical Jewish theology begin with ideas, texts, and an existing faith tradition. However, depth-theology precedes all attempts to identify, formulate, and clarify doctrines of faith. Rather than beginning with Judaism as an objectively existing religious tradition, as a way of thinking and living, it begins with the individual; depth-theology focuses on the ultimate questions of individ-ual human existence. Rather than asking, What is Judaism?, it poses questions such as, Who am I? Where am I? Why am I? Unlike descrip-tive theology, which aims at elucidating the nature and the content of faith, depth-theology aims at elucidating the nature and meaning of personal, individual existence.[3]

Any theology that neglects depth-theology is incomplete. Only once depth-theology has been addressed can descriptive theology come into play. A descriptive theology of Judaism can and should provide a framework for meaning, but only once the quest for meaning has been initiated. Descriptive theology can describe the characteristics and implications of faith only once they have been experienced. But such experience takes place on the level of depth-theology. A descriptive the-ology of Judaism can only begin to speak once the ineffable, prearticu-lated encounter with meaning, faith, and God has been experienced. A descriptive theology of Judaism can only begin to speak to individuals after they have first confronted the most visceral human problems such as, What is my life's meaning? Depth-theology begins with individual introspection, with an intense inward gaze. According to scripture, Judaism begins with God's words to Abraham: "Lekh L'kha" (You, go out; Gen. 12:1). A Hasidic master, Judah Aryeh Leib of Ger, interpreted these words literally: *Lekh*—"Go;" *L'kha*—"into yourself."[4]

The quest for the meaning of one's own life is at the foundation of theology and proceeds on the level of depth-theology. Descriptive theology entails the quest for meaning in the framework of a particular faith tradition. Descriptive Jewish theology entails the quest for meaning out of the framework and the constitutive teachings of Judaism. Descriptive Jewish theology can depict the nature and the boundaries of Judaism. Though its responses to the most visceral existential questions emerge from a particular tradition, the problems it confronts are universal, relevant to all human persons. Descriptive theology begins with a journey into the resources of a tradition. Depth-theology begins with a journey into the depths of one's own self, one's own soul. Though "theology" literally means "discourse about God," depth-theology commences at the intersection between meaning and the individual self, between God and the individual person. According to a Hasidic story: "The Rabbi of Kotzk once confronted a young man who had come to his court. 'Why have you come here?,' he asked. 'I have come to find God,' the young man replied. 'Too bad you wasted your time and money,' the Rabbi of Kotzk said. 'God is everywhere. You could have found God as well had you remained at home.' 'Then for what purpose should I have come here?,' the young man asked. 'To find yourself,' said the rabbi."[5]

All too often, theological discourse and religious institutions concentrate upon the meaning of beliefs, rituals, community, and public policies while neglecting the spiritual meaning of the life of the individual. Philosophical theology begins with *faith seeking understanding*, while depth-theology begins with *the individual seeking meaning*. The spiritual quest begins not with presumed faith or with the existence of an established historical tradition but with the individual in search of meaning.

It is singularly ironic that in our age of the "sovereign self," when the spiritual quest is popularly viewed as an individuated journey, religious communities and theologies tend to reduce religious life into the furthering of a social agenda, into social action, into debates about issues of social policies, into providing "workshops" on ritual or liturgy, or on teaching a catechism. As a result, religious institutions and educational institutions and theologians tend to neglect the innermost existential and spiritual needs of those seeking insight regarding fundamental existential issues. As Heschel put it, "The moment we become oblivious to ultimate questions, religion becomes irrelevant, and its crisis sets in."[6]

Descriptive theology deals with recorded answers. Depth-theology begins with questions. Though descriptive theology attempts to provide answers to questions like, What does Judaism believe about God? and though philosophical theology attempts to provide answers to questions like, How can we demonstrate the existence of God?, depth-theology begins with personal questions such as, Why am I here? This is not an abstract problem but a profoundly personal one. The particular issue that personally confronts each of us is not so much the meaning of the universe or the meaning of life in general but, What is the meaning of *my* life? Why am *I* here? How we respond to this problem reveals what matters most to us, what our values are, what our beliefs are, to what and to whom we are most committed, what we choose to do with the gift of life. How a person responds to the problem of life's meaning reveals the plot, the perceived purpose, of who a person is and why individuals do what they do.

"Lamah zeh anokhi?" asks Rebecca of God. Literally, this means "Why is this me?" but it may be translated as, "Why do I exist?" (Gen. 25:22). This is the problem that has confronted each human person throughout the ages. In dealing with this problem, the problem of the meaning of life, three issues must be addressed: (1) the nature of the problem, (2) our response to the problem, (3) our enactment of that response.

For some, the quest for meaning is aborted at conception. Ironically, individuals whom we would describe as having led eminently meaningful lives found life to be devoid of meaning. This includes the great trial lawyer Clarence Darrow, who described life as "an awful joke" and who wrote, "Life is like a ship on a sea, tossed by every wave and by every wind, a ship headed for no port and no harbor, with no rudder, no compass, no pilot; simply floating for a time, then lost in the waves."[7] Similarly, Steven Weinberg, a Nobel laureate in physics, has been cited as saying that the more the universe seems comprehensible, the more it seems pointless. The great scholar of myth Joseph Campbell once said, "I don't believe life has a purpose. Life is a lot of protoplasm with an urge to reproduce itself and continue in being."[8] Sigmund Freud wrote in a letter to Marie Bonaparte: "The moment a person questions the meaning and value of life . . . he is sick. By asking this question one is merely admitting to a store of unsatisfied libido to which something else must have happened, a kind of fermentation leading to sadness and depression"[9] Yet, throughout the centuries, human beings have embarked on a spiritual pilgrimage to locate and exact life's meaning. Already in the 1930s, Carl Jung described the emptiness and the absence of meaning that many people experience in their lives as "the general neurosis of our time. . . . The least of things with meaning is worth more in life than the greatest of things without it."[10] The quest for meaning is a response to the call of a spiritual emergency.

Ask most people if they would prefer a meaningless or a meaningful life, and they will tell you that a meaningless life horrifies them. But if you then ask most people why their lives are meaningful, they tend to fumble for an answer. As Herman Hesse wrote, "Even a superficial person disinclined to thought feels the age-old need of finding meaning in his life. When he ceases to find one, private life falls prey to frenzied self-seeking and deadly fear."[11] Or, as Rabbi Harold Kushner has written, "I'm convinced that it is not the fear of death, of our lives ending, that haunts our sleep so much as the fear that our lives will not have mattered, that as far as the world is concerned, we might as well never have lived. What we miss in our lives, no matter how much we have, is that sense of meaning."[12] And, on the quest for meaning, John Paul II wrote:

> The truth comes to the human being as a question: Does life have a meaning? Where is it going? At first sight, personal existence may seem completely meaningless. . . . The daily experience of suffering—in one's own life and in the lives of others—and the array of facts which seem inexplicable to reason are enough to ensure that a question as dramatic as the question of meaning cannot be evaded. . . . The need

for a foundation for personal and communal life becomes all the more pressing at a time when we are faced with the patent inadequacy of perspectives in which the ephemeral is affirmed as a value and the possibility of discovering the real meaning of life is cast into doubt. This is why many people stumble through life to the very edge of the abyss without knowing where they are going. At times, this happens because those whose vocation it is to give cultural expression to their thinking no longer look to truth, preferring quick success to the toil of patient enquiry into what makes life worth living.[13]

Since meaning must be personal, it must be subjective. Yet if it is completely subjective, it can be morally problematic. For example, Hitler's life was meaningful to him and to his followers, but it certainly was not moral. A person may find meaning in implementing genocide, in being a serial murderer, in being a pedophile, but we should not consider such a life as being valuable, moral, or exemplary. As a contemporary American philosopher suggests, to be truly meaningful, or as he calls it "robustly meaningful," a life must be exemplary. It must embody values that articulate "interests, projects, purposes, and commitments" that produce significance and that leave "footprints."[14] It must be of value. It must matter. It must be a life of commitment and of active engagement in articulating that commitment through valuable and moral deeds. Finding a locus of meaning in one's life reveals what and whom we value most.[15]

To attempt to locate the meaning of one's own life within the finitude and the fragility of one's own life is a tautology. To say, "I am the source of the meaning of my life" begs the question and, as such, is a fallacy. For if I am attempting to locate a source for the meaning of my life, my life—which is in search of meaning—cannot also be the source of its meaning.

In the quest for meaning, seeing the sovereign self as one's own savior is to accept a false messiah. From the Enlightenment onward, the attainment of meaning and self-fulfillment became a mantra of secular humanism. Yet despite its emphasis on the self-sufficient self searching for meaning, modern thought has provided little guidance as to how to attain it. Only once a source of meaning has been identified can the individual self attempt to actualize and articulate it. However, the self in quest of meaning cannot generate its own meaning. Meaning derives from that which is beyond the self, from that which transcends the self. An objective transcendent source of meaning has to be individually chosen in order to be subjectively meaningful. For the person of faith, God is that transcendent source of meaning. As the philosopher Ludwig Wittgenstein put it, "To believe in God means to understand the question about the meaning of life. To believe in God means to see that the facts of the world are not the end of the matter. To believe in God means that life has meaning."[16] The affirmation of individual human meaning is a conclusion when faith in God is a premise. What we do with the gift of life is our response to the Giver of life, the source of meaning.

Judaism is a theistic faith, grounded in the claim that God is; that the world is because God is; that there is evidence of design, purpose, and meaning in the world and in human existence; that this design and purpose are compositions of a Designer, and that moral norms that provide human life with meaning, goodness and purpose inhere in the Designer, that is, in God (see also chapter 7).[17]

Judaism affirms a partisan view of reality while tenaciously rejecting alternative views that deny the existence of God, that disclaim a purposeful creation, and that rebuff the affirmation that human existence has intrinsic meaning. A prominent alternative to the theistic view is to affirm the existence of the universe as a sheer, unexplained brute fact, to posit either that the universe and human life have no intrinsic purpose or that such purpose is either merely apparent or a human contrivance, that moral norms inhere only in the morally precarious realm of human invention, and that the religious experience of humankind throughout the ages is but one grand delusion. In the final analysis, the theist and the nontheist disagree about more than the issue of whether or not God exists. They are divided by fundamentally different philosophies of existence.

For the theist, a reasonable means of explaining how and why we are here and what we ought to do here is available. For the nontheist, *how* and *why* we are here, and *what* the purpose of our being here is, remain open questions. The theist affirms intrinsic meaning and purpose, while nontheists must discover and build a life upon their own fabrications.

Neither the theist nor the nontheist can "prove" the truth of his position. But the theist offers a way of explaining the universe and the human place in it. The nontheist may discard the theist's position, may reject the theist's premises and conclusions. Nevertheless, the nontheist must do more than simply debunk the theist's view. The nontheist must establish a basis for explaining how the universe came to be, from where human purpose may be derived, and how moral norms might be discerned. For the theist, the ultimate question is how to live a life consistent with the Creator's purpose, how to create an artful existence from the life entrusted into his or her care. The nontheist, on the other hand, might be led to affirming with the French existentialist Albert Camus that "there is but one major philosophical problem and that is whether or not to commit suicide."[18] The nontheist might be led to Macbeth's view that "Life's but a walking shadow, a poor player that struts and frets his hour upon the stage and then is heard no more. It is a tale told by an idiot, full of sound and fury, signifying nothing."[19]

For the theist, there is intrinsic meaning in human existence precisely because there is a God who created the world with purpose and meaning. For the nontheist, human meaning, like human life, indeed, like the universe itself, may be the product of chance, an accident waiting to happen. In this regard, Bahya ibn Pakudah observes that if we read a beautifully written poem, we cannot assume that it came to be as the result of ink spilled by accident onto a sheet of paper, conveniently situated nearby. Instead, we conclude that the poem has an author, that its composition expresses the author, and that the author had a purpose in composing it. Similarly, claims Bahya, creation is not by chance. The universe has a creator, and the creator had a purpose in creating the world and humankind.[20] The alternative view that claims that the universe is the product of randomness and fortuitous chance implies that ultimately there is no purpose to existence, no meaning to meaning. The fundamental question that divides the theist and the nontheist is not whether God exists, not how the universe came to be, but whether the search for meaning has meaning.

For the nontheist, an autonomous basis for morality must be affirmed for moral behavior to be justified. For the theist, the existence of God serves as the ultimate source of and justification for moral behavior. For example, a rabbinic text interprets the well-known verse from Leviticus (19:18)—"You should love your neighbor as yourself, I am the Lord"—to mean "You should love your neighbor as yourself *because* I am the Lord, because I [God] have created him."[21] As Heschel has written, "Man is meaningless without God, and any attempt to establish a system of values on the basis of the dogma of man's self-sufficiency is doomed to failure."[22]

For Solomon ibn Gabirol, asking why we were created presumes a creator who created the world and each of us with a purpose, and with meaning. At the beginning of ibn Gabirol's *Fountain of Life*, which is written in the form of a dialogue between a teacher and his disciple, the teacher says to the student: "Now that by your nobility of character and your zeal for learning you have progressed to this point, you may now ask questions about what has most impressed you in our inquiry. But in doing so, please approach the ultimate question of why humans have been created."[23] Similarly, it is told that the Hasidic master Israel Friedman of Rhyzen once offered this prayer to God: "I do not want to know why you created the world, or why you permit the good to suffer and the evil to prosper. Only, please tell me, dear God: What am I doing in this world of yours?"[24]

Another Hasidic master, Nahman of Bratzlav, once said that a question is half an answer. By asking the question in the manner in which he does—"why humans were created"—ibn Gabirol provides part of an answer. By asking "why were humans created," rather than, for example, "why do humans exist," ibn Gabirol discloses his view that the existence of the world and of human beings in it is not a matter of simple cause and effect but (as he says elsewhere) a matter of divine will. Neither is creation a matter of chance. In this view, by its very nature, creation is purposeful, meaningful. Creation is distinct from brute existence, and it presumes purpose and meaning. To the claim that existence can occur by chance, ibn Gabirol counters that creation occurs to articulate that purpose and meaning; meaning has to be meant, intended, willed. If the universe were not created, if (as Aristotle claimed) it were eternal, it would be meaningless. And if it were meaningless, we could not know about meaning. Consequently, for ibn Gabirol, the question is not whether there is meaning but rather how might it be elicited.

Elsewhere, ibn Gabirol writes, "If I left the world as I entered it, and returned to my home as I emerged from it, for what should I then have been created?"[25] Like many of the medieval Jewish philosophers such as Bahya ibn Pakudah, ibn Gabirol identifies human meaning and purpose with the individual's quest for bliss. This quest entails raising ourselves to a higher level of consciousness; realizing our intellectual, spiritual, and moral potentialities; overcoming the foibles of moral vice; developing the moral virtues; and contending with the obstacles, evils, and challenges that punctuate daily existence.

Ibn Gabirol's philosophical treatise is called *The Source of Life*. For him, God is that source of life, the source of all. As for many other Jewish philosophers and mystics, so for ibn Gabirol, the ultimate goal of human existence is cohesion with that source of life both in this life and in the life to come, that is, the afterlife. For ibn Gabirol, like many of the medievals, the human intellect, the rational faulty of the soul (i.e., cognitive intelligence), is the primary attribute that humans share with God. It is the primary vehicle through which human individuals can realize their purpose for having been created. For ibn Gabirol, self-knowledge, knowledge of the world, and intellectual contemplation of God propel the individual toward the performance of deeds aimed at the attainment of bliss. The development of cognitive intelligence offers a higher level of moral awareness that leads to purpose-driven actions, especially moral action. The cultivated intellect is better equipped to penetrate the veils of illusion, to discern truth, and to apprehend the meaning and purpose of one's existence without distraction or diversion. For ibn Gabirol, it is precisely because the human mind—like the world—has been purposefully created, and is not the product of randomness and chance, that we are able to use our minds to discover design in the universe and meaning to our existence.

For the medievals, like Maimonides, the human mind is a vehicle not only for attaining awareness of the presence and the nature of meaning but also for realizing meaning through how life is lived. In Maimonides' view, individual self-realization and actualization are the purpose of human existence. This entails a movement from potentiality to actuality, whereby an individual moves from being potentially human to being an actualized, authentic human person. For Maimonides,

Joseph Albo, and others, the Torah offers a blueprint for how—by combining wisdom and deed, intellect and action—human beings may realize their purpose, elicit meaning, acquire human and individual authenticity, and bind their intellects with their source, that is, God.[26] For Maimonides, human meaning and purpose are attained by the activation and development of the attribute humans share with God, that is, the intellect. For Maimonides, being created in the image of God refers to our having been created as intellectual, thinking beings.

Maimonides taught that despite the capacities of the human intellect, knowing the purpose and meaning of creation nonetheless eludes our intellectual grasp.[27] Knowing why everything that is here is here is beyond the ken of our understanding. To claim that we understand why God created the universe would be an act of intellectual vulgarity. To claim that the universe or even our world was created to provide the human species with meaning and purpose (as does Judah Loew, for example) would be an exercise in arrogance, a gross overestimation of the cosmic importance of the human species. Rather, Maimonides claims that whatever the purpose of the creation of the universe might be, each species and each individual member of that species was created to actualize it own particular potential. In this view, rather than focus on the question of the purpose of the universe, each human person should focus on the purpose of his or her own individual life. Human existence becomes meaningful when each individual actualizes his human potential according to her own particular abilities.

For Maimonides, the focus of the quest for meaning is the individual human person. Each person is on a divinely ordained mission to actualize his potential as a human being and as a particular person by doing and thinking the right things, that is, by observing the commandments of the Torah, by cultivating the moral virtues, by developing the intellect, and by seeking intellectual cohesion with God. By climbing the ladder toward what he calls "human perfection," the individual can realize his or her purpose in having been created and can transition into becoming an actualized human being.[28] In his regard, Maimonides interprets Hillel's well-known statement, "If I am not for myself, who will be for me?" to mean that no one but one's own self can create the work of art that is one's own self.[29]

According to the biblical narrative, Judaism begins with God's call to an individual, to Abraham (Gen. 12); according to rabbinic legend, however, Judaism begins with Abraham's intellectual quest to encounter the creator of the universe, the source of creation, meaning, and truth.[30] The rabbis read the biblical account of God's call to Abraham, and they asked, How did Abraham know who was calling to him? Until this point in the biblical narrative, little had been said about Abraham. No prior relationship with God had been reported of Abraham. Abraham lived in an idolatrous culture. How, then, did he come to recognize God who the rabbis called "the One who spoke and the world came into being"? The rabbis, therefore, amplified the biblical narrative with a series of legends that describe how Abraham acquired intellectual and existential awareness of God, the creator. In the sixteenth century, Eliezer Ashkenazi portrayed Abraham's quest for God as the first attempt at using philosophical inquiry to discover truth and meaning.[31]

According to rabbinic legends, Judaism began not with God's call to Abraham but with Abraham's intellectual and existential quest for God. Living in an idolatrous world, Abraham began his quest as a child, questioning the theological presuppositions of the then dominant idolatrous religion. According to one legend, Abraham's father, Terah, was a manufacturer of idols. Abraham could not believe that the idols he saw his father make from sticks and stones were actually gods, that they created the world. In an act of defiance, Abraham shattered the idols in his father's shop, thereby setting a precedent for the religion he founded of shattering idols—entities worshiped as gods that were, in fact, not God.[32] Having rejected idolatry, Abraham—according to another legend—continued his quest by trying to identify an entity in the natural world that might be God.

Abraham then gazes upward and sees the sun shining brightly in the sky, bringing the warmth of its power to the world, and he concludes that the sun must be God. So, Abraham worships the sun. But, then, night falls, and the moon rises in the heavens. Abraham concludes that if the moon is powerful enough to dislodge the sun from the heavens, it must be God, so he worships the moon. But, in the morning, the sun dislodges the moon and again reigns in the heavens. Now Abraham concludes that neither the sun nor the moon can be God, but that God must be the creator of the sun, the moon, and the world, that God transcends everything in nature, that nature is not divine but is rather a creation of God.[33] Here, a third midrash continues the narrative: "Abraham may be compared to a man who is traveling from place to place when suddenly he saw a radiant palace. 'Is it possible that there is no master who cares for this palace?,' the man wondered. Then, the master of the palace appeared and said, 'I am the master of this palace.'"[34] It is only at this point, say the rabbis, that Abraham was able to recognize the source of the voice that called to him. God then reveals his presence and his word to Abraham.

Only once Abraham becomes aware of God's relationship to the world as its creator can he enter into relationship with God. Once such awareness has been attained, the individual can experience what Martin Buber calls "an inexpressible confirmation of meaning." Buber writes further, "Meaning is assured. Nothing can any longer be meaningless. The question about the meaning of life is no longer there.... [This] meaning that has been received can be proven true by each [hu] man only in the singleness of his being and the singleness of his life."[35] In this view, meaning need not be discovered, but uncovered. Secreted in the mystery and marvel of creation, implanted within the world and in our own selves by God, meaning awaits recognition engendered by an expression of awareness. Once meaning is perceived as being intrinsic, endemic to existence, the challenge is no longer to discover its source, but rather to enact it. Meaning is no longer an abstract philosophical problem to be verified by logic but a personal challenge to be verified by how one lives one's life. The task now is no longer finding the meaning *of* life, but evoking meaning *from* life. Meaning can become manifest by expressing that which the human creature has in common with the Creator, by articulating the "image" of creativity they share. Human meaning may be articulated by living one's life "in the image of God," the image of the Creator, by living in a manner compatible with our having been created in "the image of God."

The Ten Commandments forbid making anything in the image of God. Yet, in the biblical story of creation we are told that God broke his own commandment. God made a being in the image of God, that is, the human being. Of all God's creatures, only the human creature is described by scripture as having been created in "the image and likeness of God" (Gen. 1:26–27; see also Gen. 5:1, 9:6). As Rabbi Joshua ben Levi said, "A procession of angels pass before a human being wherever he or she goes, proclaiming—Make way for the image of God."[36]

Rabbi Akiva taught that not only have human beings been created in the divine image but that divine grace allows them to become aware of it: "Beloved are human beings for they were created in the [divine] image. Even more beloved are they, because they can be aware of having been created in the [divine] image. As it is written, 'For in the image of God, God made human beings'" (Gen. 9:6).[37]

The enigmatic Hebrew phrase *tzelem elohim*—"the image of God"—appears in the first chapter of Genesis (1:27), in the account of the creation of the first human being. What do we know about God to this point in the biblical narrative (Gen. 1:26–27)? All we know is that God is the supremely creative being. And, of all the creatures that God is described as having created, only the human creature is depicted as having been created in the image of God. We can therefore interpret the phrase "image of God" to mean that human beings share the creative ability with God; that, like God, human beings are creative beings. As Leo Baeck wrote:

> In the knowledge of having been created by God there is however only the beginning of human consciousness. With that knowledge Judaism unites the awareness of being able to create and of being called upon to create. To be both created and yet creator is the heart of Jewish religious consciousness.... If the feeling of having been created by God is the first fundamental feeling of Judaism, then the awareness of man's own creative power for doing good is its second fundamental experience....for only the two together give the full meaning of life. The unity of both is religion as Judaism teaches it.[38]

Neither the world nor the human person is created in a complete form. Completing the task of creation is the challenge posed by God. It is precisely this task of completing creation that bestows meaning and purpose upon human life. In acting as God's "partner in the work of creation," the individual can activate and articulate being created in the image of God, the image of the creator. For the Jew, the covenant provides the framework in which this partnership ensues. As Abraham Heschel put it,

"There is only one way to define Jewish religion.... Life is *a partnership* of God and man."[39]

Human creativity, which serves as the vehicle to express human meaning, relates to the world, the word, and the self. Judah Loew of Prague considered creativity to be the crucial component of human nature by means of which the human being can transcend nature by manifesting an attribute that human beings share with God. For Loew, in augmenting God's initial creation, human creativity becomes a natural way of transcending the natural world and of allowing nature to expand beyond its original limitations. In Loew's words: "Human creativity transcends nature. When God created the laws of nature in the six days of creation, the simple and the complex, and finished creating the world, there remained additional power to create anew.... Human beings bring to fruition things that were not previously found in nature; nonetheless, since these are activities that occur through nature, it is as if they entered the world to be created."[40] From this perspective, human beings are not only part of nature, but through science, technology, and art, they can be agents for creating nature as well.

A midrash reminds us that "whatever was created in the first six days of creation needs further preparation."[41] Furthermore, according to Loew, "When we contemplate the works of God, [we realize that] everything God created requires repair and action."[42] The human task is to work toward completing God's creation, but this task relates to God's word as well as God's world. As the repository of God's word, the Torah requires human "repair" (*tikkun*) and completion (*hashlamah*).[43] In pursuing this task, an individual can become a cocreator of the world, a coauthor of the Torah, God's partner in covenant and in creativity. In this regard, the *Zohar* comments upon a verse in Isaiah (51:16), which contains the Hebrew word *ami*—"my people." Says the *Zohar*, "The word *'ami'*—may be read as *'imi'*—'with me,' meaning 'to be a partner with me' [i.e., with God], for just as I [God] made heaven and earth by a word...so did you [i.e., through study of the Torah]."[44]

The goal is to live a life aimed at revealing the "image of God" encrypted in human nature. The challenge to live in the creative "image of God" also entails crafting a unique and exquisite work of art during our life—and that work of art is our life, our own self. How we express our life's meaning is how we meet God's challenge to create our life as a work of art. Through action, through the performance of sacred, significant, and ethical deeds, the image of God that has been implanted in each person can become manifested, articulated. From this perspective, God's most superlative artwork is the human being. It is the human task to complete God's unfinished masterpiece—the human person. Each of us is an unfinished masterpiece of God. Like a master artist, God leaves completion of his works to his apprentices—to each of us. In one of his poems, the ninth-century Italian Jewish poet Ammitai ben Shephatiah writes of God, the ultimate, "awesome artist."[45]

A biblical verse reads: "There is none holy as the Lord, for there is none besides You, neither is there any rock [*tzur*] like our God" (1 Sam. 2.2). The Talmudic rabbis suggested reading *tzur* (rock) as *tzayar* (artist). They would then translate the phrase as "there is no artist like our God."[46] In other words, God is a creative artist, and our being created in the image of God means that we, like God, can become creative artists. This is the way in which we articulate our creative freedom, our having been created in the image of God.

For Jewish tradition, the encounter with the tenuous nature of human life, with the reality of our own mortality, is meant to be not an invitation to morbidity but a collision with realities that can serve as catalysts for human self-development. Being conscious of human finitude when set against the infinite plentitude of creation causes one to pause to consider how to infuse meaning into the blink of eternity that is each human life. At birth, each human person is issued a passport to transcendence, an invitation to develop one's own life as a work of art. The disposition of each human life depends on whether one chooses to accept this invitation, to make use of this passport.

Hillel said, "If not now, when?" Commenting on this statement, a medieval Jewish writer observed that Hillel did not say, "If not *today*, when?" but "If not *now*, when?" because "even today is in doubt whether one will survive or not, for any instant one can die."[47] Consequently, "One cannot wait even a day or two to exert oneself in the pursuit of human fulfillment" through the creation of one's life as a work of art.[48]

The Talmudic rabbis asked why God began the creation of human beings with only one human being. Surely, it would have been more efficient for God to initially have populated the world with a million human beings. According to the Talmud, God began with one human being to teach us that each human being is like Adam, whose name means "human being" in Hebrew—that each person, like Adam, is singular and unique. The Talmud further observes that though there are countless numbers of human beings, nonetheless, no two human voices, no two human faces, no two human persons, are exactly alike. And, precisely because each person is unique, each human life is unprecedented and intrinsically sacred. Each person has aspirations and potentialities that belong to her alone. From the claim that each person is unique, the Talmud concludes that each person is justified in saying, "For my sake was the world created."[49] This bold statement may be taken to mean that the purpose of each individual human creature is to explicate, to articulate, to fashion her uniqueness, to create his life as a unique work of art.

What for many centuries was called the "soul" is currently often referred to as the "self." The soul, the self, is not a ghost that possesses the body during life. It is the *principium individuationis*; it is that which makes each person who he uniquely is; it is the organizing principle of each person's life. However, the tragedy of many lives, according to the British poet Edward Young, is that though people are born as originals, they often die as copies. Creating life as a work of art is a way of affirming that we want to be originals and not copies.

Unlike the laws of nature that already exist but await human discovery, great works of art are unprecedented and unique products of individual creativity. In this regard, the great physicist Heisenberg once said that if he did not discover the indeterminacy principle in physics, someone else would have. But if Beethoven had not written his Ninth Symphony, no one else could have. Similarly, a great violinist once said that before God could create a Stradivarius violin, God had to first create Stradivarius.

The divine image implanted in human beings is not a gratuitous gift but a challenge to be met.[50] That challenge can be met through certain types of human creativity. As Joseph B. Soloveichik put it, "The peak of religious ethical perfection to which Judaism aspires is man as creator."[51] Ethics is a way in which individuals can create their life as a work of art. According to the Talmudic rabbis, this entails ethical actions in emulation of God's actions. For example, "just as God clothes the dead, attends the sick, comforts the mourners and buries the dead, so you do likewise."[52] Just as God performs acts of love, mercy, compassion, righteousness, holiness, and truth, so should we do likewise.[53] Behavioral analogies identify *imago Dei* with *imitatio Dei* and ask us "to walk in God's ways." The phrase *imitatio Dei* may denote both the ways in which God acts and the ways in which God has commanded us to act.[54]

For Jewish religious literature, human existence is too precarious, life is too fragile, not to be taken with the utmost seriousness. In painting the portrait that is one's own life, a single reckless stroke can mar the entire work. Commenting on the verse in Ecclesiastes (9:8), "Let your garments be always white; let not oil be lacking on your head," a Hasidic master observed: "A person should view themselves as being dressed in a silken white garment with a pitcher of oil on their head, walking a tightrope. A single wrong step and they become soiled; a single irretrievable step and they fall into the abyss below."[55]

In the art of living, each individual is an apprentice. As Maimonides said, "It is impossible for a person to be endowed by nature from birth with either virtue or vice, just as it is impossible that a person should be skilled by nature in a particular art."[56] Life is an apprenticeship during which one has the opportunity to create the ultimate art form—one's own life.

The expectation of moral action presumes the availability of moral volition. Unlike other ancient Near Eastern religions, for biblical religion human action is not rooted in tragic necessity or predetermined by fate, but in the free exercise of the God-given and God-like experience of expressing the moral will. Human beings are like God in that they have the capacity to create. But, without will, without choice, creativity cannot occur. According to Soloveichik, "Choice forms the base of creation."[57] Human beings share the divine capacity to create because they share the divine attribute of will. However, creativity entails not only volition but imagination. Nahman of Bratzlav interprets the claim that human beings are created in the image and likeness of God to mean that, like God, human beings are endowed with an imagination.[58]

For Judah Loew of Prague, moral volition is both the primary divine attribute that human beings share with God and that which distinguishes human beings from both the angels and the animals.[59] Though angels have higher intellects than human beings, according to Loew, angels lack the ability to make choices. In Loew's words:

> In this way, human beings resemble God, in that they were created in the divine image. But, this is not the case with angels who have no choice. They only do what God appoints them to do, and they are incapable of altering their mission. But humans who were created in God's image enjoy the benefit of making determinations for themselves, like God who does what God desires. And thus, humans control their own selves to do what they will, and are masters of their ability to choose.[60]

Although Loew and Maimonides disagreed on the interpretation of the biblical phrase "image of God," they nonetheless agreed that moral choice is a vital and unique characteristic of human nature. For Loew, moral volition is a shared attribute of humans and God, whereas for Maimonides it is a divine gift bestowed upon humankind. In Maimonides' words:

> The human species is unique in the world—there being no other species like it in the following respect, that a person by himself, and by the exercise of intelligence and reason knows what is good and what is evil, and there is none who can prevent the human person from doing what is good or that which is evil....This doctrine [of moral free will] is an important principle, the pillar of the Torah and the commandments....If a person's destiny had been decreed, and his innate constitution drew him to that which he could not set himself free, then what purpose would there be for the whole of the Torah?[61]

In other words, the Torah is a guide to a life of goodness and meaning, and without free will, there would be no possibility of realizing that goodness or meaning. However, while ethical behavior is a crucial component in the life of meaning, it is necessary but not sufficient. Meaning requires more than morality. Goodness is a necessary but not a sufficient component for a life of meaning.

The soul is a seed implanted within each person. Each individual is like a tree that may choose whether to bring forth its own fruit. At life's end, one may return a diminished form of what one received, or more than one received, at life's beginning. One has the choice to corrode or to create, to pollute or to improve, what one initially has been granted.[62] Unlike an oak that becomes a tree or a kitten that becomes a cat, a human being only can become a fulfilled human being through deliberate action and choice. In crafting the soul, the individual moves from potentiality to actuality, from human being to being human. Crafting the soul cannot be acquired by proxy. Self-potential may only be realized by means of what the Hasidic master Mendel of Kotzk called *arbiten auf zich*, "working on oneself."[63]

While little Jewish genius was invested throughout the ages to create works of fine art, much Jewish genius and effort were expended on the endeavor to create lives that were works of art. Rather than concentrating on *things* of beauty, Jewish teachings focused on the creation of *people* of beauty. The primary goal was not physical prowess, or comely appearance, or even commercial success. Rather, the goal was to create one's own life as a work of art.[64] The Jewish people produced no edifices to rival Notre Dame, no paintings like those of Michelangelo or Raphael. The particular art form cultivated by the Jews was not architecture, painting, or sculpture but human existence. For much of secular Western aesthetics, *art* was a way of *life*. For Jewish thought, *life* is a way of *art*.

Great art is not simply the product of momentary inspiration. The apprentice artist who wishes to create a masterpiece of his or her own cannot rest content with a dazzled gaze at the masterpieces of the past. Similarly, standing awestruck by the spiritual, intellectual, and moral achievements of the great personalities of the past will not suffice for one who desires to shape one's life as a work of art. Like the novice artist, each individual must proceed to study the masterpieces produced in the past in order to distill from them insight and information, wisdom and inspiration, that can be incorporated into the creation of one's own work of art, which, in this case, is one's own self. And, as in the case of the aspiring artist, the individual committed to cultivating the art of living cannot be satisfied with a terminal course of study. For such a person, each completion is the prelude to a new beginning; each graduation is a commencement. Continuous study, perpetual practice, and relentless self-development are the necessary ingredients toward the goal of artful living.

As was noted earlier, human creatures articulate their having been created in the image of God by how they act. The meaning and purpose of human existence are manifested through action within relationship: the relationship of the individual person to themselves, the relationship of the individual toward God, and the relationship of the individual toward others. As Judah Loew put it:

> One must achieve the good which is one's purpose, thereby justifying one's existence, and when one's existence has been justified, the whole of the universe has been justified, since all hinges on human beings. . . . Therefore, a person should endeavor to cultivate good qualities. And what makes a person "good" so that one might say of him: What a fine creature he is? The first requirement is that one must be good in relation to one's own self. . . . The second category of good is that one be good toward the Lord who created the human being to serve God and to do God's will. The third category is that one be good to others. For a person does not exist by himself. He exists in fellowship with other people. . . . A person is not complete until he is completely pious vis-à-vis these three varieties of [human] perfection: with his Creator, with other people, with his own self as well.[65]

Meaning becomes manifest through relationships, particularly love relationships. Life cannot be meaningless to anyone who loves. In Judaism, a person is commanded to love God, to love oneself, and to love others. These three kinds of love coalesce in the covenant. For Judaism, as will be discussed in the next chapter, meaning may be attained and articulated by living in the covenant.

Living in the Covenant

Questions are not posed in a void. They are asked from within a particular framework. To appropriately answer a question requires that we know the framework in which both the question and the answer make sense. Offering an answer to a question from a different framework than that of the question often leads to "a category mistake."[1] If, for example, in response to the question, "Did you listen to music last night?" I say, "Last night I listened to five pounds of Mozart," my statement may be factually correct, but it commits a category mistake by quantifying Mozart's music by the weight of the composition books from which his music has been played. Similarly, a response to the question of the meaning of life has to be made within a particular framework.[2] For a Jewish person in search of meaning, Judaism provides such a framework.

Though the quest for meaning begins with a journey into our deepest selves, Jews are not asked to make this journey alone. The cumulative wisdom and experience of Jewish tradition can accompany them, forging a link between the past and the present, ancestor and descendant, individuals and their inherited spiritual legacy. Just as an individual word gains its meaning from the context and syntax in which it is employed in a particular language, a person's life can derive meaning from the context of his or her religious tradition.

Each day, at the beginning of the traditional Jewish morning liturgy, the problem of the meaning of life is posed as follows:

> What are we? What is our life; what is our kindliness, our upright-
> ness, our helpfulness, our strength before you, O God? The heroes
> [we extol] are as nothing before you. People of fame and renown are
> as though they never have lived. Those we consider wise are as if
> without wisdom. Those known for their discernment are as if devoid
> of knowledge. In comparison to you, the deeds of mortals are vanity
> and their years on earth are as nothing. Indeed, the preeminence of
> humans over animals is naught, for everything is so trivial.

And this is the text's response: "But we are your people, the people of
your covenant, the descendants of the patriarchs."[3]

Here we have the claim that the key to meaning is relationship,
that the meaning of the life of each Jewish person can be actualized by
living in a covenantal relationship with God. In this view, the individual
self gains its inestimable worth, and realizes its intrinsic meaning, by
being covenanted with God. By entering into a covenantal relationship
with us, God enables us to realize the meaning and purpose of our
lives.

According to the Talmud, the covenant compacted between God
and Israel at Sinai is the raison d'être, the source of meaning, not only
for the existence of the people of Israel but also for the existence of
the world. The Talmud reports that "the Holy One, stipulated with the
Works of Creation and said thereto: If Israel accepts the Torah [at Sinai]
you shall continue to exist, but if not, I shall revert you back to chaos
and to void."[4] Without the revelation of the Torah at Sinai, creation is
revealed to be a purposeless venture. Without the covenant, Jewish existence is a non sequitur, a fallacy. As a committed love relationship, the
covenant is a pact, a sacred partnership. At Sinai, the covenant is made.
The Torah is the content of the covenant, God's blueprint for meaning,
for living in the image of God, for creating life as a work of art.[5]

According to a midrash, "The Holy One said: When you stood at
Mount Sinai and received the Torah, I wrote that I loved you, as it is
written, 'It was because the Lord loved you.' (Deut. 7:8)."[6] The covenant
is initiated by God as an act of love, of divine grace. Living in the covenant means living with love. The word in biblical Hebrew for "grace" or

"love" is *hesed*, which denotes committed, steadfast love.[7] Not a passing fancy, covenantal love is an enduring commitment: "My love will never depart from you, neither shall my covenant be removed" (Isa. 54:10). To be complete, love requires reciprocity. Because God loves us, we are to "love the Lord our God with all our heart, our soul, our might" (Deut. 6:5). Love is covenantal, reciprocal. Love is a passionate partnership, a declaration of interdependence. From committed love, meaning ensues.

Love indicates what and who matters most to us, what and who we find most meaningful. Love is the queen of the virtues precisely because it reveals to us those relationships, convictions, and commitments that we most highly value. As philosopher Irving Singer has written, "For a person in love, life is never without meaning. For love is not merely a contributor to a meaningful life. In its own way, it may underlie all other forms of meaning."[8] In the *Zohar* we read: "Everything is called love, and everything is established for the sake of love."[9] In this view, a coercion to love lives in the depths of every human soul. Whereas truth is an answer to how to think, love is an answer to how to live.

For the person who loves, life is never devoid of meaning. For a person without love, life is an empty shell, a hollow vessel, a lonely journey. For this reason, it is difficult, if not impossible, to find a person who could say without the most profound regret: "I cannot love." Nothing demonstrates the centrality of love more than the absence of love in life. Saint Paul understood this well when he said, "I may ... know every hidden truth; I may have faith strong enough to move mountains, but if I have no love, I am nothing" (1 Cor. 13: 2). For the individual in search of meaning, love is a path that guides us out of the inner jungle of the soul into the meadow of meaning.

According to Singer, "We live during a period in which large numbers of people have renounced their faith in love."[10] Though many are afraid of not being loved, it may well be that they are also afraid of loving. Because love requires commitment without guarantees, giving without the assurance of receiving, intimacy with the exposure of vulnerability, love demands faith and courage—the ability to take a risk. Consequently, for those fettered by the restraints of the "sovereign self," who are "relationship challenged," love and meaning are often elusive.

To attain meaning rooted in faith, one must risk relationship by transcending the self. For the person of faith, all love, like all things, has its source in God. For Judah Loew, we love God with the love God has given us with which to love.[11] For the person of faith, human meaning derives from the assurance that God loves us unconditionally. This claim that God loves us unconditionally provides a source for meaning and a context for the articulation of meaning through living in the covenant.

The corollary of God's love for us is our love for God. According to Loew, the human love of God expresses a striving for meaning, for fulfillment. In his words, "God sustains human life.... It is therefore appropriate to love God because everything that one loves should be that which brings fulfillment and completion, and God can provide this for human beings."[12] Loving God entails the awareness and the recognition of the fact that precisely because God loves us, God helps us to attain meaning and fulfillment. Love, in this view, can never be possessive, obsessive, or an exercise in the control of the other. Rather, love means wanting the one we love to have the opportunity to realize his or her potential. For Judaism, the Torah is a gift of God, given out of love that provides a guidebook toward human realization.

By serving as God's partners and collaborators in helping to complete the creation of the world, by acting as coauthors of the Torah, and by crafting life as a work of art, human beings express their love of God and help God realize God's own potential as a creative being. In love, through love, both God and human beings can help each other "grow."[13]

Litanies of love celebrate the uniqueness of the beloved. Love entails recognizing the distinctive uniqueness of an other. Unlike science, which tends to subsume individual creatures and events into universal categories such as species and laws of nature, religion tends to emphasize the unique. For example, the event of the theophany at Sinai at which the covenant is forged is considered significant because it is unprecedented, singular, unique. God, who initiates the covenant, is one, that is, unique, one of a kind. In logic, one would say that God is a member of a class of beings of which God is the only member. The people of Israel, the recipients of the covenant, are called "one people," that is, a unique people (2 Sam. 7:23). According to the Talmud, each individual is unique and is therefore unprecedented and irreplaceable.[14] Like great works of art, no two human beings are identical; each is unique. Love is the recognition of the uniqueness, the singularity of an other.

For a bride and groom solemnizing their love in marriage, the other is unique. It is not surprising, therefore, that rabbinic tradition analogizes the theophany at Sinai to a wedding. According to one tradition, at Sinai, God, the bridegroom, is wedded to Israel, the bride: "'On the day of his espousals' (Song of Songs 3:11). This alludes to the revelation at Sinai which was as it were, a wedding ceremony [between God and Israel], as is borne out by the text 'Betroth them today and tomorrow'" (Exod. 19:10).[15]

Love entails not only passion but also commitment and responsibility. To be actualized, love must be articulated in deeds that transcend the self. Though love originates within the recesses of the self, if it remains there, it will be stillborn. Love that remains within is like a bachelor dancing with himself at his own wedding.

The covenant embraces a polarity between passion and responsibility, love and obligation, emotion and action, awe and intimacy. A covenant is a partnership, a pact. For this reason, the rabbis compare the Torah given at Sinai—at the day of "espousal"—to a *ketubah*, a marriage contract. According to this analogy, the Torah serves as the marriage contract that binds the bridegroom and the bride together. As a *contract*, the Torah is a legal document that states the mutually accepted duties and responsibilities of the two parties to the agreement. However, as a *marriage* contract, the Torah is a document attesting to the love that obtains between God and Israel.

To the dispassionate reader a marriage contract might appear to be a dry legalistic document, but to the bridegroom and the bride it represents an expression of their love, a concretization of their commitment. To those who attend a wedding, the liturgy may sound unduly encumbered by legalistic jargon. However, the bridegroom and the bride hear the legal wording of the marriage service as a song echoing their mutual love. At Sinai, the Torah—the marriage contract between God and Israel—was presented. Some read it and hear its melody of love; others, however, see only law but remain deaf to its message of love.[16] Commenting on the biblical account of the giving of the Torah at Sinai, the Ba'al Shem Tov offered the following analogy in the form of a story:

> A musician was playing at a wedding celebration at a local inn. His music so enraptured the people that they were driven to dance. Then a deaf man who could not hear the music happened to pass the inn. As the fiddler stood in the corner, the man did not see him. As he was deaf, he did not hear the music. Looking through the window, all he saw were people jumping up and down. "Madmen, all madmen," he muttered and went his way.[17]

Those who have identified the Torah with law alone, those who portray Judaism as a religion obsessed with law to the exclusion of love and emotion, fail to hear the music. Like the deaf man in this tale, they perceive rituals of celebration as acts of madness. But to those who hear the music, observance of the laws of the Torah is an expression not simply of obedience to God but also of love for the Giver of the Torah. Observance of the teachings of the Torah is a free expression of joy and not a spiritually crippling manifestation of servitude. Observance of the commandments is not a curse from which the Jew needs to be redeemed, as Saint Paul suggested, but a blessing that bestows meaning.

Though made at one time, at one place, the covenant is binding upon all Jews for all time, at all places. As a husband and wife must perpetually renew their love, must continually recommit themselves to the pledge made on their wedding day, as love must be continually revitalized lest it be taken for granted, lest it dissolve into habit, so must the original covenant between God and Israel continually be reaffirmed both in the life of the people of Israel and in the life of each member of the people of Israel.

Scripture reports occasions at which Israel renewed the covenant with God originally made at Sinai.[18] The liturgies of various Jewish festivals of the year offer opportunities for the renewal of the commitment to the covenant.[19] For example, events in the life cycle of the individual Jew such as circumcision (Hebrew: *brit*, i.e., covenant), bar or bat mitzvah, marriage, and so on, offer opportunities for the individual Jew to renew the pledge their ancestors had made long before. Each day, with each prayer service, an opportunity for reaffirmation is offered. In this vein, Mendel of Kotzk once said that the liturgy refers to the Pentecost festival (Shavuot) as "the time of the giving of the Torah." "Why," he asked, "is it not called 'the festival of the receiving of the Torah'?" For if Israel had not accepted the Torah, there would be no occasion to celebrate. And, as is the wont of Hasidic masters, he answered his own question, saying: "The reason is because the Torah was given only once—at Sinai. But, it cannot be received only once; otherwise it would be forgotten. It must be received continuously, daily."[20]

Describing the arrival of Israel at Sinai for its "wedding" with God, scripture records, "'In the third month after Israel has departed Egypt, on *this* day they came to the wilderness of Sinai'" (Exod. 19:1). The rabbis asked: "Should not the verse read 'on *that* day' rather than 'on *this* day?' This is [to teach] you that the words of the Torah should be new to you, as if God gave them to you today."[21] Similarly, the Hasidic master Abraham Joshua Heschel of Apt said: "Everyone is told to consider themselves as standing at Mount Sinai, receiving the Torah. To human beings, there are past and future events, but not for God; day in and day out God gives the Torah, and day in and day out a person may receive the Torah."[22]

Before beginning to recite the daily morning prayer, the observant Jew dons the prayer shawl and phylacteries (tefillin). As one does so, one recites a verse from Hosea (2:21:22) that recalls the espousal of Israel to God at Sinai:

I betroth you to me forever
I betroth you to me in righteousness, with justice,
With loving-kindness and with mercy.
I betroth you to me with faithfulness and you shall love the Lord.

The liturgy of the daily morning service commences with an assurance of God's endless love. The liturgy of the evening service confirms that theme while providing a reminder of the nexus between law and love. God's law is a token of God's love. The evening liturgy reads: "With great love have you loved the people of Israel, teaching us your Torah and your commandments, your statues and your judgments.... Blessed are you, Lord, who loves your people Israel."[23]

Each act the observant Jew performs in the course of the day—such as rising from sleep or eating—is accompanied by a blessing. Many of these blessings take the following form: "Blessed are you, our God, King of the universe, who has sanctified us [*kideshanu*] with his commandments and commanded us to..." A long-standing tradition maintains that the Hebrew word *kideshanu*—"who has sanctified us"—can also be translated as "who betroths us to himself." Thus, by observing the commandments, by obeying God's laws, each person, in each act, may become betrothed to God. By observing the commandments, an individual's love for God is continuously renewed, for love that is not renewed becomes stale, routine.

Observance of the laws and commandments of the Torah is an essential way of manifesting love for God. The words "religion" and "legal" both derive from the identical Latin root *ligo*, which means "to be bound ." Observance of the commandments binds us to God. One of these commandments is "You shall love the Lord your God" (Deut. 6:5). "How does a person love God?" asks a midrash. The answer: "Perform [God's commandments] out of love."[24] In other words, performing the commandments is not a means *toward* love of God; it *is* love of God. Loving is doing. Love is not a prelude to action but action itself. Love is expressed *as* deed. How we love and whom we love can be expressed and verified only by how we act in relationship to the one we love. Love is not simply an attitude but an act; not only an emotional disposition but also a deed; not a prelude but a commitment. In this view, a lover is delighted with the opportunity to carry out the wishes of the beloved. The commandments of the Torah express the will of God, and consequently the command to love means that we behave toward God as a lover behaves toward a beloved.

Love entails choice, risk, and faith. Without love, faith is false, faithfulness superfluous, commitment meaningless. Though faith can generate meaning, meaning must first flow from committed love. Without faith and love of God, a person cannot expect to find meaning in religious experience, in ritual observance. Love, faith, and living in the covenant provide a framework not only for individual meaning but also for how we understand the experiences that punctuate our lives. Though faith may derive from an intense personal experience, faith also provides a foundation and a framework for how we perceive our experiences.

Faith is the product of effort and is the articulation of a chosen commitment. As Kierkegaard reminds us, a person must take a "leap of faith." According to Mendel of Kotzk, the angels that Jacob saw descending and ascending in a dream (Gen. 28:12) were human souls. Once on earth, these souls look for a ladder by which to ascend once more to God. However, during life, some souls give up, having not found a ladder. Others try to ascend, even without a ladder, so they take a leap. Faith is an upward leap. The choice of whether or not to strive to move upward is our own. Like love, faith means taking a risk, taking a leap.[25] Faith entails the courage to cast off the bonds of the ego in order to leap upward toward that which transcends us.[26]

Awe precedes faith. Awe is "an act of insight into a meaning greater than ourselves."[27] Only once that insight has been attained can faith offer a framework for a meaningful life. The beliefs, virtues, commandments, and lifestyle that characterize the life of faith fill out the details of this framework. To have faith means to bear witness by how we live in the presence of God, by how we live in partnership with God. We articulate our beliefs through the lifestyle we elect to follow. Faith in action is how we articulate meaning in life, how we make explicit the implicit meaning implanted in each human life by the Giver of life. That there is intrinsic meaning in each human life rests upon the theological claim that each human life is intrinsically sacred, unique, and irreplaceable. Faith in action is how we translate this claim into a lifestyle.

Deeds articulate commitments; sacred deeds express faith and engender communion with God. According to Judah Loew, faith is communion with God.[28] Through faith, a person is elevated beyond the realm of the senses. Faith allows us to perceive the light buried in the darkness, to see the truth behind the veils of illusion. Faith thereby becomes an act of liberation, of redemption, of revelation. Faith means revealing the concealed.

On Exodus 14:31—"And Israel saw the great work that God did upon the Egyptians, and the people feared God, and they had faith in God and God's servant Moses"—Rabbi Isaac Meir of Ger commented: "Although they saw the miracles of God with their own eyes, they were still in need of faith, because faith is superior to sight; with faith you see more than with your eyes."[29] In one sense, to see is to believe. For Rabbi Isaac Meir, to believe is truly to see.

Faith embraces a polarity between words and deeds, beliefs and actions. Faith also combines mind and emotion, intellectual assent and existential commitment. Faith never demands an abrogation of the intellect, a surrendering of the mind. Intellectual affirmation is a necessary but not a sufficient feature of faith. Psalms 14:2 reads: "Is there a man of reason who seeks God?" The Rabbi of Kotzk took it to mean: "A person who has nothing but their own reason is incapable of seeking God."[30] Faith is not only something a person believes but something a person does. Observing the will of God is how a person verifies what one claims to believe.

We might consider the word "faith" as a verb rather than as an abstract noun. Doing godly deeds is how individuals verify what they claim to believe in. Faith is verified not by logic but by life, that is, by living a life compatible with our stated beliefs. For example, when someone says, "I love you" to another person, the proof of the truth of the statement is not its logical validity but is demonstrated in the performance of deeds that are consistent with that claim. In prayer, we state our faith commitment. How we act, how we live, demonstrates whether we are what we pray, whether we do what we say.

Faith is an inheritance, a legacy given to the present from the past. But to be complete, faith must be renewed. It must be reaffirmed by each person, in each generation. The Jewish liturgy often uses the phrase "our God and God of our ancestors, the God of Abraham, the God of Isaac, the God of Jacob." It was asked, Why is it necessary to specify each name after already saying "the God of our ancestors"? The reason given is that neither Isaac nor Jacob relied entirely upon their father's faith. Each sought God, each expressed faith in his own particular way. Of Deuteronomy 6:5, "You shall love the Lord your God with all your heart," a modern commentator took it to mean: "You must love God with all your *own* heart, and not only with the heart of your ancestors."[31]

Faith is a gift of God's grace, but it requires human effort to be whole. There is no faith at first sight. Authentic faith is never a matter of "immaculate perception." As the Talmud puts it:

> If someone says to you: "I have labored but have not found," do not believe him.
>
> If someone says, "I have not labored but have found," do not believe him.
>
> But if someone says: "I have labored and have found," then believe him.[32]

Faith means living in partnership with God. Faith assures us that our lives have meaning, that we are needed, loved, by God. As Pascal reminded us, a life of faith is a wager, a risk, a game of "you bet your life." In a real sense, people bet their lives on the beliefs they embrace, the relationships they nurture, and the outcomes of the actions they perform. But, suppose that faith were an illusion, a mistake, and that God is a human fantasy. Nonetheless, says Pascal, betting on faith is a wager that the believer cannot lose, for even if the believer is wrong, what has the believer lost? But if a person rejects and denies faith as the foundation of meaning and goodness, what has one gained?[33]

Faith is also "hide and seek":

> The grandson of Rabbi Baruch was playing hide-and-seek with a friend. He stayed in his hiding place for a long time, waiting for his friend to come and to look for him. When he realized that his friend was not looking for him, he became very sad and disappointed. He ran into the study of his grandfather, crying and complaining about his friend. Upon hearing the story, Rabbi Baruch also began to cry. "Why are you crying, grandpa?" asked the boy. "Because," said Rabbi Baruch, "God, too says 'I hide. Will no one come to look for me?'"[34]

Faith is how we search for God. It is how we respond to God's question to Adam, Where are you?; and it is how we attempt to encounter the divine presence in the world, how we invite God into our lives. It is how we respond to the prophet's query, "What does the Lord, your God, require of you?" (Mic. 6:8). Faith shapes what we do with the gift of life that God has entrusted into our care.

As with regard to the quest for meaning, so in the quest for faith, the individual Jew need not embark on this quest alone. Once the leap of faith has been taken, once the commitment to faith has been made, the nature of that faith needs to be ascertained. Moving from depth-theology to descriptive theology, the content of faith requires clarification and elucidation. Living in the covenant entails a connection between the individual and the faith community, between past and present, between ancestor and descendant, between the legacy of faith from tradition and the challenges to faith in the present. Though the quest for faith may begin with the individual, it does not end there. Authentic faith within a religious tradition in the present entails continuity with faith developed in the past. Consequently, for Judaism, authentic faith is rooted in memory.

Recall of the past is a call to faith in the present. As Heschel has written:

> When we want to understand ourselves, to find out what is most precious in our lives, we search our memory.... That only is valuable in our experience which is worth remembering. Remembrance is the touchstone of all actions. Memory is a source of faith. To have faith is to remember. Jewish faith is a recollection of that which happened to Israel in the past.... Recollection is a holy act: we sanctify the present by remembering the past.[35]

Losing one's memory means losing one's mind. To remember is to re-mind. Bereft of certain remembrances, a person becomes *dis*membered from the divine, from one's own self, from one's past, from one's faith community.[36] In his classic work *Kuzari*, the medieval poet and philosopher Judah Halevi observed that the Ten Commandments begin not with a creedal proposition but with a memory of an experienced event: "I am the Lord your God who brought you out of the land of Egypt, out of the house of bondage" (Exod. 20:1). For Halevi, faith is rooted in the memory of events.[37] Tradition's task is to transmit experience as memory. Memory makes the past present, the future possible. The foundation for faith in the present is forged by the perpetuation of certain memories of the past. As Deuteronomy tells us: "Remember the days of old, consider the years of ages past; ask your father, he will inform you, your elders, they will tell you" (32:7).

No command to believe is stated in Hebrew scripture. Rather, memory of events, of experiences, is prescribed. The transmission of the faith tradition from generation to generation is vested in the conveyance through memory of experienced events. For example, a verse in Deuteronomy (4:9) reads: "Take heed to yourself diligently, lest you forget the things your eyes saw, and lest they depart from your heart all the days of your life, make them known to your children and your children's children."

The prophets of Israel did not formulate creedal propositions. Rather, they offered memories of moments illuminated by the divine presence. They did not enjoin the people to define God but to witness the divine presence in history. God asked Israel to be a people of witnesses to God (Isa. 43:10), not a committee of definers of God.

Reflection upon the role of remembrance in the Jewish liturgical year yields a variety of insights into the nature of Jewish faith. Because faith is articulated as memory, and because memories of certain formative events of ancient Jewish history are identified with the Jewish holy days, it should not be surprising to find that central concepts of Jewish theological concern are associated with the religious festivals. Thus, the underpinnings of Jewish theology are not systematic but liturgical. As the nineteenth-century rabbi Samson Raphael Hirsch put it, the Jewish liturgy is Judaism's catechism. Celebration of the Jewish festivals conveys the Jewish theological agenda. For example, Passover relates to redemption, Pentecost to revelation, Sukkot (the Feast of Booths) to divine providence, Sabbath to creation, Tisha B'Av to theodicy.[38]

Theological concepts and concerns are not permitted to remain abstract propositions. Rather, they are communicated as specific memories through festivals of celebration and remembrance. For Judaism, theological concepts never atrophy into abstract creeds because they are continuously being articulated through sacred deeds. The function of rituals associated with the various Jewish holy days is to internalize in the life of each member of the people the memory of an event in the life of the people. Consider, for example, this citation from the Passover Haggadah:

> In each generation, each individual should consider himself or herself as if he or she was redeemed from Egypt, as it is said, "It is because of what God did for *me* when *I* went free from Egypt" (Exod. 13:8). For the Holy One redeemed not only our ancestors, but *us with them*, as it is said, "God took *us* out of there to bring us to the land

promised to our ancestors' (Deut. 6:23). Therefore, we must... praise
God who... took *us* from slavery to freedom."[39]

The liturgy for the Seder, the Passover meal, is called Haggadah,
"telling." This relates to the biblical injunction to pass down memories
of experiences to one's children: "You shall tell your child on that day.
It is because of what the Lord did for me when I went free from Egypt"
(Exod. 13:8). The goal of Jewish ritual is to remember rather than to
reenact an event.[40] The uniqueness of the event can be recited but not
repeated. However, what can be reenacted is the *meaning* of the event.[41]
Indeed, for the tradition to continue, for the story to have perpetual and
perpetuated meaning, it must be internalized.

By the internalization of memory through ritual, we become our
ancestors' contemporaries. Present and past converge at the moment
of celebration and commemoration. Memory is the stimulus, and ritual
and liturgy are the vehicles that bind past and present, ancestor and
descendant, ancient experience and contemporary faith. Performing a
ritual identifies who, where, and when a person is who performs it.

The expectation that commemoration of the Exodus would bring
about a personal as well as a communal experience of liberation is
expressed by the Hasidic master Menahem Nahum of Chernobyl. He
suggests that two types of liberation are necessary for Passover observance to be considered complete. One type celebrates the liberation
of Israel from Egypt. The second type is the liberation of each person from that particular thing that enslaves then. Unless individuals
liberate themselves from their own particular "Egypt," the celebration
of Passover is not complete. Before the people can experience liberation, all individuals must first be liberated from the fetters that restrain
them. Only redemption that commences with the individual can conclude with the community.[42]

The Hebrew word for memory is *zahkar*. But memory does not
merely signify mental recall, but includes a call to action. Liturgy and
ritual serve as vehicles to prevent memory from deteriorating into an
abstract reminiscence. Remembrance through observance of the festivals stifles the proclivity toward abstract theological speculation,
toward intellectual voyeurism devoid of commitment. As Heschel put
it, "An esthetic experience leaves behind the memory of a perception

and enjoyment; a prophetic experience leaves behind the memory of a commitment."[43] Participation in the life of the faith community is a prerequisite for commemorating events in the history of that faith community. For example, the Passover liturgy tells of four sons. Of these, the wicked son asks, "'What does this ritual mean to you?' (Exod. 12:26), that is, to you and not him. Since he excludes himself from the community and denies God's role in the Exodus, you shall confront him and say: 'This is done because of what God did for me when I went out of Egypt' (Exod. 13:8). For me and not for him. Had he been there, he would not have been redeemed." The continuity of the faith community depends upon its ability to perpetuate its memories.

Unless Jews recapture and preserve their memories, they will do to themselves what massacres, pogroms, and Holocaust were unable to accomplish—to obliterate Judaism, to make of it a forgotten memory. They will perpetrate upon themselves what Heschel called a "second Holocaust," not a genocide of Jewish people but a genocide of Judaism as a religious faith, and as the raison d'être for Jewish existence.[44] Again, to quote Heschel: "The tasks begun by the patriarchs and prophets and continued by their descendants, are now entrusted to us. We are either the last Jews or those who will hand over the entire past to generations to come. We either forfeit or enrich the legacy of the ages....We of this generation are still holding the key [to the sanctuary hidden in the realm of the spirit]. Unless we remember, unless we unlock it, the holiness of the ages will remain a secret of God."[45]

Rendezvous with God

Among the primary goals of living in the covenant are the consummation of a romance with God, the creation of one's life as a work of art, encountering a source of meaning that transcends us, and deepening the consciousness of our self-understanding. Four often converging paths are envisaged as propelling us toward these goals. They are the word, the world, the deed, and the self.

The spiritual pilgrimage commences with an inward gaze, with the individual's encounter with one's own self. It is told, for example, that once Rabbi Yitzhak of Vorki spent the Sabbath with a simple Jewish farmer. The farmer asked the rabbi to teach him some Torah, but the rabbi was curious as to what he could learn from the farmer. That particular week, the scriptural reading began with the verse "See I [God] have set before you this day blessing and curse" (Deut. 11:26). The farmer reflected upon the possible meaning of the first two words of the verse, and he said in Polish: *Pac Sobie,* meaning "See the I; look at yourself." The rabbi of Vorki was so impressed with this insight that he would quote it to his disciples each year when that verse was read in the synagogue.[1]

In order to encounter the self, one must know who and where one is. Descriptive Jewish theology responds to these questions by identifying and locating the individual within the context of the covenant and by explicating the theological, ethical, and halakhic implications of living in the covenant. Depth-theology, however, focuses on the individual's encounter with these basic questions before imposing a theological rubric, before setting forth an inventory of expected deeds.

According to the Bible, the first question ever posed to a human being was: "Where are you?" (Gen. 3:9). It is a fundamental question that drives the spiritual quest. "Where am I in my life?" is a question that each person must pose to himself.

> Once there was a schoolboy who like many of us, would wake up in the morning and forget where he put his things the night before. So, one night, before going to sleep, he devised a solution to his problem. Before he got into bed, he took a piece of paper and a pencil and he wrote himself a note: "My eyeglasses are on the table next to the bed. My pants are on the chair next to the table. My shirt is draped over my pants. My shoes are on the floor under the bed. My socks are in my shoes. And, I am in the bed." He placed the list on his bed-stand and he went to sleep. The next morning when he awoke, he took his list from his bed-stand and to his astonishment, he found everything on the list. But, when he came to the last item—"And, I am in the bed," he looked at the empty bed and asked himself, "So, if I am not in the bed, then where am I?"[2]

This first recorded question of "Where are you?" is posed by God to Adam. God does not ask it because he requires information about Adam's whereabouts. According to a Hasidic view, God poses the question to "Adam" (being not only the name of the first human being, but also denoting every human person) to stimulate human beings to reflect upon their existential situation, to acquire awareness of who and where "Adam" is.[3] In this view, an encounter with God, a rendezvous with God, requires a prior encounter with one's own self. The spiritual quest begins with individuals and their existential situation, not with theological constructs.

For scripture, a rendezvous with God begins with God's calling to an individual by name, and either awaiting or provoking a response. As Heschel reminds us, religion begins with God's question and our response, with God's quest for a rendezvous with each of us, with our making God's questions our questions. Where are you? is such a question. The question, Where are you? includes the question, Who are you? These two questions coalesce in the quest for self, in the search for meaning. As Heschel writes, "Religion consists of God's question and man's answer. The way to faith is the way of faith. . . . Unless God asks the question, all our inquiries are in vain."[4] Finding oneself leads to a connection with the transcendent.

Like so many "Adams" after him, the first Adam, the first human being, seeks to avoid God's question and resists appropriating it as his own question. But, is God's query really a question? A question asks for information and often can easily be resolved by the conveyance of a fact. Questions such as, What time is it?, What is your address?, Where are you right now?, are easily answered, but a problem is something altogether different. A question is a product of the intellect alone, but a problem involves the whole person. A question is an exercise for the mind; a problem is homework for the soul. Unlike a question, a problem is the outcome of perplexity and often of anxiety; it is not easily answered. God's query to Adam poses a problem rather than a question. God is not asking Adam, Where are you situated? What are your geographic coordinates? Rather, God is asking, What is your existential situation? Where are you in your life, and where are you going? According to scripture, after the liberation from Egypt, the Israelites wandered in the wilderness for forty years until they came to the promised land. The process of finding the promised land is a paradigm for finding the promised self.

Were God simply asking a question, Adam could have offered a simple answer, as did Abraham: "I am here." But precisely because Adam recognizes that his situation has changed because he had eaten of the forbidden fruit, and because he was both perplexed and anxious about his altered situation, he knows not how to respond. Rather, he hides from God and tries to avoid both God's query and the implications of his new situation. Adam is anxious about his situation. As some of the biblical commentators suggest, Adam was hiding not only from God but also from himself. God's inquiry is a challenge: You can run, but you cannot hide. You sometime must emerge from your hideout. You must eventually ask yourself, Where am I in my life?

When commanding Adam and Eve not to eat of the forbidden tree, God identifies death as the punishment for disobeying that commandment (Gen. 2:17). After posing queries and after listening to Adam's and Eve's responses, God announces the "verdict" of human mortality: "Dust you are, and to dust you shall return" (Gen. 3:19). As a result of their sin, Adam and Eve are exiled from the Garden of Eden into a world of challenges, labor, and pain. Death now becomes the inevitable fate of each human person. No longer naive children basking and playing naked in the Garden of Eden, Adam and Eve are condemned to death. Ironically, because of their sin, Adam and Eve acquire the vital characteristics of human nature. By sinning, by making the *wrong* choice, they demonstrate that they are capable of moral volition, of making *a* choice. By sinning, they become not only more completely human, but also godlike.

Paradoxically, by disobeying God, Adam and Eve acquire creative freedom; they activate the "image of God" implanted by God within themselves. Now, God realizes, human beings have become "like God," having choice and "knowing good and evil" (Gen. 3:22). While in the Garden of Eden, Adam and Eve are devoid of self-awareness, moral choice, and creative ability. However, after they sin they become like God: free, creative beings. Yet, they also become unlike God—mortal.

Ironically, confronting the reality of human mortality serves as a catalyst for dealing with the challenges of life, the problems that propel the spiritual quest.

When Adam and Eve are informed of their mortality, they have no frame of reference to understand what it means. No one yet had died. They had not yet witnessed death. However, unlike Adam and Eve, we have witnessed death. We recognize the reality of human mortality. We are aware of own mortality. Though Adam and Eve could not yet fathom the grim fact that each life is terminal, that each of us lives under an inevitable death sentence, we can and we must confront this distressing fact of life. Because Adam was initially unaware of the nature of death, it is not surprising that he avoided a confrontation with his own mortality; we, however, do not have that luxury. We do not share the naïveté of Adam and Eve. Nonetheless, precisely because the awareness of the certainty of death evokes such horror and despair, throughout history human cultures have attempted to deny or to obscure death's inevitability and reality. For example, one of the most ancient myths, the Babylonian *Epic of Gilgamesh*, tells how after the death of his heroic friend and companion, Enkidu, Gilgamesh sets out on a quest to find a way of escaping death. Having failed and in despair, Gilgamesh returns to his native land, where he dies.[5]

Franz Rosenzweig, who died an early death from amyotrophic lateral sclerosis (ALS), characterizes the history of Western philosophy as an ongoing attempt to transform the confrontation with death into the denial of death. Rosenzweig reads Western philosophy as an elegant mind game aimed at escaping the inevitability of human mortality, a kind of intellectual version of Gilgamesh's quest. In Rosenzweig's words, "All cognition of the All originates in death, in the fear of death. Philosophy takes upon itself to throw off the fear of things earthly, to rob death of its poisonous sting, and Hades of its pestilential breath.... It bears over the grave which yawns at our feet with every step.... [Philosophy attempts] to distract us from its [death's] perennial dominion." However, concludes Rosenzweig, "A person's terror, trembling before the inevitable sting of death condemns the compassionate lie of philosophy's cruel lying."[6]

Our naïveté about human mortality has been ripped away by our experience. Death confronts us at every turn, on every newscast, on the front page of the daily newspaper. The mass media make confrontation with death unavoidable. Life has become a blind date with death from which no one is immune, no one is safe. We are reluctantly reaching a gnawing and knowing acceptance of Ecclesiastes' simple statement of stark reality: "There is a time to die" (Eccles. 3:2). Like Adam, who is told, "Dust you are and to dust you shall return" (Gen. 3:19), each human being must inevitably realize that he or she lives under a sentence of death from which there is no escape, that confronting the reality of one's own mortality is not a task we can leave for another day. There are too many constant reminders that death can overtake us either by warning or by surprise, either in old age or in youth, at any time, that everyone lives on borrowed time. In a museum in Russia, there is an exhibit of a human skull. On the skull, it is written: "Once I was like you, but one day, you will be like me."

As life confronts us while death awaits us, each of us is caused to pause to consider how to infuse the blink of eternity that is each human life with purpose and meaning. Conscious of our infinitesimal finitude when set against the vast expanse of creation, the quest for a life of purpose, a life that matters, a life worth living, erupts as an urgent priority. Though there is no remedy for death, confronting death can serve as a powerful stimulant for coming to grips with questions such as, Where am I?? Who am I ? What is the meaning of my life?

Few have posed these existential issues with a sharper poignancy than the seventeenth-century philosopher Blaise Pascal, who wrote:

> When I consider the short duration of my life, swallowed up in the eternity before and after, the little space which I fill, and even can see, engulfed in the infinite immensity of spaces of which I am frightened and I am astonished at being here rather than there, why now rather than then? Who has put me here? By whose order and direction have this place and time been allotted to me? The eternal silence of those infinite spaces frightens me.[7]

Contemplation of death, an encounter with death, a confrontation with the self, can help teach us how to infuse our lives with meaning, how to live a life that matters. Over the door of a laboratory where autopsies are performed is a sign that reads: "Here is where death teaches life."

The quest for self and for meaning relates to the quest for truth, for authenticity. But where is truth to be found? What is the nature of the truth we seek? According to the Jewish mystics, the search for truth begins with the awareness that in our world truth is veiled, incomplete. Each grain of truth is surrounded by shells of falsehood. A goal of life is to encounter the truth behind the veils of illusion. Consequently, the greatest obstacles in the search for truth, in the search for self, are self-delusion and self-deception, that is, living a lie and taking it to be the truth. Truth means sincerity, honesty, integrity. It means doing what we say, living our stated commitments, becoming our convictions. One must try to navigate between truth and illusion, appearance and reality, self-realization and self-delusion.[8] Just as a person is forbidden to deceive his or her neighbor, a person is also forbidden to deceive his or her own self.

Once Rabbi Bunem of Peshisha was asked, "Who is pious?" He answered, "A person who does more than the law requires." He was then asked, "What does the law require?" His answer: "Scripture commands us: 'You shall not deceive your neighbor'" (Lev. 25:17). He was then asked, "What is required of the pious person?" His answer: "Not to deceive one's own self."[9] To find truth, to attain integrity, to escape self-deception, a person has to uncover the divine inner nature secreted in each and every human being, but particularly within one's own self.

The "Musar" movement that developed in nineteenth-century Lithuania taught that the most challenging book for a person to understand is the book of his own life. Harder than comprehending the most difficult text is truly understanding the text and the context of a person's own existence. The task of self-understanding is a never-ending, arduous process of lifelong learning, a curriculum that few really master. Rabbi Simha Zisel Ziv Braude, one of the leaders of the Musar movement, put it this way: "A person lives with their own body and soul for a lifetime. A person eats, drinks, and sleeps with themselves. No one can take a single step without themselves. Each individual knows all of their deeds, all their own most private thoughts, joys and sorrows.... And despite all of this, a person does not really know themselves on as much as a single point, unless such an individual is very wise, and has toiled and labored at it."[10]

Because no two people are the same, each individual needs not only constant introspection but also sincere and even brutal self-analysis. In this process, pride is a formidable stumbling block that must be overcome. Pride is inimical to spiritual development, and to a rendezvous with God, for three major reasons. First, pride is self-deceptive, and spiritual development is always sabotaged by self-deception. Pride tricks us into thinking we are more important than we really are. It fools us into believing that we have no faults, no shortcomings. Arrogance stifles the process of self-improvement by convincing us that we have no need to improve. It does not allow us to see ourselves as we really are. "Pride is literally a form of blindness," writes Moses Hayyim Luzzatto, "which prevents even a person who is otherwise wise from seeing their own shortcomings."[11]

Second, pride is dangerous because it stifles relationships. The ego stands as a barrier, restricting our ability to transcend ourselves in order to be able to forge a relationship with someone else, especially with God.

In this regard, the verse, "I stood between God and you" (Deut.5:5), is taken by a Hasidic master to mean that the "I," the ego, often stands as a barrier between God and us, obstructing the divine-human relationship.[12] Indeed, according to the mystics, we find ourselves when we lose ourselves in God. A rendezvous with God, among other things, can provide an antidote to narcissism, pride, and egocentricity. In other words, pride is dangerous because it is self-destructive and destructive of relationships: "Pride precedes destruction and a haughty spirit goes before a fall" (Prov. 16:18).

Third, pride is dangerous because it is a form of the greatest sin— idolatry. Idolatry means treating something other than God as if it were God. Pride is treating one's own ego as if it were God.[13] Arrogant persons worship only their own needs, their own selves. In contrast, humility entails recognizing one's abilities, but not making too much of them, not using them as a means of lording over others, or as a barrier between others and oneself. Rather than meaning a loss of identity and self-esteem, humility can offer a proper perspective for understanding the nature of reality and the dependence of the human person upon the transcendent. As Menahem Nahum of Chernobyl points out, rather than restricting us, humility liberates us from egocentricity, thereby allowing us to expand consciousness and to embrace limitless possibilities made inaccessible by the restraints of the human ego.[14]

The Ba'al Shem Tov considered sadness and depression to be the reverse side of pride. Pride is ego obsession where we inflate ourselves beyond all realistic proportions; depression is another form of ego obsession where we deflate ourselves beyond all realistic proportions.[15] Manifested as either pride or depression, ego obsession is self-deceiving and self-defeating, blocking creativity and interfering with the formation of meaningful relationships.

Humility is the opposite of pride. Authentic humility is meant to be a strength, not a weakness. When a person claims humility as an excuse for inaction, it becomes inauthentic, a weakness rather than a strength. Humility can serve as a conduit to articulating human meaning, to living in the covenant, but it can never become an excuse for evading challenges. Humility is the enemy not of self-esteem but of pride. Humility is a necessary ingredient in the creation of an artful life, a life of meaning, goodness, and significance. In his authoritative study of creativity, Silvano Arieti writes, "An attitude of humility, of willingness to make even the smallest contributions and to accept a life of commitment and dedication, must be part of the potentially creative person's way of life."[16]

Introspection not only is a vehicle to self-understanding but also provides an entrée to a rendezvous with God. For medieval Jewish philosophers such as Isaac Albalag, "knowing one's own soul inevitably leads to knowledge of God."[17] Or, as Joseph Albo writes, "If you know yourself, you will know your Creator."[18] In this view, the divine is accessible within the self, the path to God involves a journey inward to the center of the soul. As Judah Loew wrote, "Within the human being dwells the soul which is a spark of God." Scripture describes God as a fire (Deut. 4:24). In Loew's view, the human soul is a spark of this fire, that is, part of the divine.[19]

Though Loew uses figurative language to describe the human soul as part of God, other sources are more explicit. For example, the seventeenth-century Jewish mystic Elijah Di Vidas commented on the verse in Deuteronomy (32:9), "For the portion [Hebrew: *helek*, literally, 'part'] of the Lord is God's people." Di Vidas writes, "The soul of each member of the people of Israel is an actual part [*helek*] of God."[20] Probably influenced both by Loew and by Di Vidas, Shabbtai Sheftel Horowitz of Prague comments on the same verse in Deuteronomy and writes, "It is known that the souls of the people of Israel are a part of God above." The phrase "a part of God above" derives from Job 31:2. Horowitz uses the phrase "a part of God above" to describe the soul as embodying a divine element.[21] This idea that the human soul is a part of God, that the human soul is divine, means that the divine may be encountered not only by going out into the world but also by going inward into the self. In this view, self-understanding, knowing oneself, one's own soul, inevitably entails a rendezvous, a communion with God.

Not only the soul but also the body can serve as a place for a rendezvous with God. For example, Judah Loew interpreted the phrase in Job (19:26), "From my flesh, I shall see God," to mean "When one contemplates the form of the human body, one is able to arrive at a knowledge of God."[22] Furthermore, as the *Zohar* states, "The soul cannot operate without the body."[23] Without the body, the divine image implanted within the human being could not become manifest. The divine image requires a vehicle to express itself so that it may realize its essence, actualize its potential, and accomplish its divinely ordained mission. The body is this vehicle, for without the body, the divine image embedded within the human soul would remain unrealized, dormant, comatose.[24]

The claim that individual spiritual development can and should be cultivated through the body as well as the soul found strong resonance in Hasidism. That the most mundane physical actions could serve as conduits to spiritual self-development is articulated in the Hasidic concept of "divine worship through human materiality." The Ba'al Shem Tov taught that individuals are able to further their spiritual development and to bring about the unification of the divine forces in this world and in the supernal realm by the performance of everyday actions, such as eating, drinking, sexual relations, business activities, and social interactions with one's friends. In a similar vein, the Talmudic rabbi Bar Kappara asked, "What short text is there upon which all the essential principles of the Torah depend?" His answer: "In *all* your ways, know God" (Prov. 3:6).[25] In this view, all human experience, no matter how mundane, has the potential of enabling an individual to liberate and to elevate sacred sparks that relate to one's own self, one's own soul.

Commenting on the biblical phrase "From my flesh, I shall see God" (Job 19:26), the Ba'al Shem Tov observed, "From the physical, we perceive the spiritual."[26] His comment reiterates a Talmudic theme that teaches that even the most elemental functions of the human body can become invitations to the most exalted spiritual activities: worship of God and study of the Torah. Consider this Talmudic text:

> Rabbi Akiva said: Once I went in after Rabbi Joshua to a privy. [From watching him there] I learned three things.... Ben Azzai said to him [i.e., to Akiva]: Did you dare to take such liberties with your master? He [i.e., Akiva] replied: It is a matter of Torah and I am required to learn....Rav Kahana once hid under Rav's bed. He heard him chatting [with his wife] and joking and doing what he required [i.e., engaging in intercourse]. He said to him: One would think his mouth had never touched the dish before! He [i.e., Rav] said: Kahana, what

are you doing here?; it is rude. He [i.e., Kahana] replied: It is a matter of Torah and I need to learn.[27]

Not only the physical body but the physical world can serve as a path to spiritual fulfillment and as a passageway to the divine. Encountering the natural world is a second path on the spiritual journey. For example, commenting on the verse in Psalms 8:4, "I look at the heaven the work of God's fingers," Nahman of Bratzlav told this parable:

> Once a prince lived far away from his father the king. Each day he longed for the presence of his father. One day he received a letter from his father, and he was overjoyed and treasured the letter. Yet, the joy the letter gave him only increased his longing even more. He would sit and cry: "Oh, if I could only see my father and touch his hand. Merciful father, how I would love to touch and kiss even your little finger." And, while he was crying, feeling the longing for a touch of his father, a thought came to his mind, "Do I not have my father's letter, written in his own hand? And, is not the handwriting of the king comparable to his hand?" And, suddenly, a great joy burst forth in the heart of the prince.[28]

The world is a disguise worn by God. Our task is to unmask God, to encounter the divine beneath its disguise. As Maimonides and others observed, contemplation of nature and study of the natural sciences are not ends in themselves but means to a higher end, that is, greater appreciation for and awareness of the wisdom and majesty of God. Maimonides writes: "And what is the way that will lead to the love and awe of God? When a person contemplates God's great and wondrous works and creatures and from them obtains a glimpse of God's wisdom, which is incomparable and infinite, one will straightaway love, praise and glorify God, and long with an exceeding longing to know God's great Name."[29]

As has been discussed, according to a Musar tradition, one's own self is a book requiring study and reflection. Others, however, likened the natural world to a book. By means of encounter with this book, one comes into contact with its Author.[30] For Maimonides and others, scientific explorations of the cosmos, the natural world, and the human body can lead to an awareness of God, and to an appreciation of God's creative power and wisdom. However, as Heschel points out, scientific investigation can also deprive us of the awe and wonder that "the works of creation" (*ma'aseh bereshit*) can provide. For Heschel, it is precisely this awe, wonder, and "radical amazement" that can stir the individual, as Abraham was stirred, to look beyond creation toward the Creator, when one can exclaim with the psalmist: "This is the Lord's doing; it is marvelous in our eyes" (Ps. 118:23). For Heschel, it is precisely such awe that can engender faith. As Heschel writes, "Awe precedes faith; it is at the root of faith. We must grow in awe in order to reach faith."[31]

Beginning with the Bible, awareness of the wonders of creation was described as evoking an attitude of gratitude toward the Creator, both for the creation of the world and for the creation of one's own self. In the words of the psalmist, "I will give thanks to you for I am awesomely and marvelously made. Wondrous are your works; my soul exceedingly knows this" (Ps. 139:14).

Unlike the attitude of entitlement that focuses upon the self and its expectation of being owed something more, the attitude of gratitude focuses upon appreciation for the gift and acknowledgment of the Giver. Thanksgiving is a recognition of divine grace, a testimony to God's providential care, an act of reciprocity for blessings bestowed. The "sovereign self" is often drawn to ask: "What more am I entitled to?" The person of faith will inquire: "How can I repay the Lord all God's bountiful dealings with me?" (Ps. 116:12).

Gratitude is a major feature of the religious personality. The motto of the person of faith is: I thank; therefore, I am. Faith without gratitude to God is a premise without a conclusion. Before seeking the meaning of life, or eliciting meaning from life, one must first gratefully acknowledge the gift that is one's own life. Such gratitude expresses the awareness that we are not self-made, that our existence is a gift of God. The life of meaning entails reciprocation for the gift of life by laboring to transform life as mere existence into life as an art form.

Life is a gift of God's love, a manifestation of the divine largesse. As ibn Gabirol wrote: "Before I came to be, your enduring love came to me. You, who created something from nothing; you created me.... Who has taught me wisdom and showed me wonders?...Truly, it was you who made me, not I."[32]

The surprise of being alive evokes wonder. One discovers that that which is readily taken for granted is actually the miraculous in disguise.

Nahmanides observed that "a person has no share in the Torah" unless the miraculous nature of daily occurrences is acknowledged.[33] As the daily liturgy says, "We thank you for your miracles which are with us daily, for your continued marvels."[34]

Grateful awareness of gestures of divine largesse is a response not primarily to miracles of biblical proportions but to daily mundane occurrences, such as waking in the morning, eating a piece of bread, donning new clothing. Even the most mundane action of all, going to the bathroom, is an occasion for offering a blessing of gratitude to God and for acknowledging God's wisdom as our creator. This blessing says:

> Blessed are you, Lord our God, King of the universe, who with wisdom fashioned the human body, creating openings, arteries, glands and organs, marvelous in structure, intricate in design. Should but one of them, by being blocked or opened, fail to function, it would be impossible to exist. Praised are you, Lord, healer of all flesh who sustains our body in wondrous ways.[35]

In receiving a gift, we reciprocate with a prayer. The Jewish liturgy contains a plethora of prayers that acknowledge divine gifts we tend to take for granted, for example, the gifts of life, breath, bread, children, clothing, health, and—as has been noted—even regular excretory function. These acknowledgments, these prayers, often come in the form of blessings that begin "Blessed are you, Lord." Once God has been addressed in the second person, "you," God's presence in our daily lives is acknowledged. Reciting the blessing acts as a stimulus to evoke awareness of the presence of God, to serve as a vehicle to a rendezvous with God, even in the most mundane forms of the daily routine. As Heschel has observed, "This is one of the goals of the Jewish way of living: to experience commonplace deeds as spiritual adventures, to feel the hidden love and wisdom [of God] in all things."[36]

The self is one path on the spiritual journey; the natural world is a second. A third path is the encounter with the sacred word. Prayer and study are actions in which the self meets the word. The sacred word is a rendezvous point for the meeting of the human soul and the divine.

God is not an inaccessible monarch, hidden in an impregnable fortress, but a constant companion, easily accessible, always available, sometimes hidden but never remote. Of the Hasidic master Israel of Koznitz, it is told that when he prayed to God in the solitude of his room, he would address God over and over in the Polish language with the words *moi kochanku* (my darling); and of one of the Hasidic masters who perished during the Nazi occupation, it is told that he would cry in his sleep, "God, please do not ever let me become far from you."[37] When a disciple of the Rabbi of Kotzk informed his master that the Rabbi of Lubavitch taught that "Gott is in himel arein" (God is in heaven), the Rabbi of Kotzk replied, "Nein, Gott is in pipuk arein" (No, God is in our guts).[38]

Prayer is an experience of intimacy with God, of making love with God. The words of prayer are the vehicles to achieving this intimacy. It should not be surprising, therefore, that the Hasidic masters described prayer and study of sacred texts as "copulation with God" (Hebrew: *zivug im ha-Shekhinah*). In the words of the Ba'al Shem Tov, "Prayer is copulation with God [Hebrew: *Shekhinah*]. Just as there is swaying when copulation begins, so, too, one must sway at first and then remain immobile and attached to the divine with great attachment."[39] Through prayer, the human breath, the human soul, achieves intimacy and union with its divine source. As a Hasidic text puts it:

> When your prayers are pure and untainted, then surely the holy breath that rises from your lips will be joined to the breath of heaven that constantly flows into you from Above. Regarding the verse, "Every breath shall praise God" (Ps. 150:6), our masters have taught it to mean that with each breath that you breathe God is praised. And, as each breath leaves you, it ascends to God and then returns to you from Above. In this way, that part of God that is within you becomes reunited with its Source.[40]

There could be no spiritual achievement without intensive study of the tradition. Spiritual development and Jewish cultural illiteracy are mutually exclusive. Both Jewish continuity and Jewish spirituality are inconceivable without an ongoing intensive study of sacred texts. There can be no authentic Jewish existence detached from lifelong study of the sacred literary canon of Jewish religious tradition. For the Jewish mystics, the primary goal of life is cohesion to God (Hebrew: *devekut*).[41] Study is one of a number of paths to achieving it. Therefore, study is a means to an end rather than an end in itself. Study that does not enhance self-knowledge, learning that does not bring about spiritual self-transformation, is a non sequitur. In this regard, Mendel of Kotzk is reputed to have said the following to a scholar who was erudite but nothing more: "What good is understanding a text if one does not thereby attain a better understanding of oneself?" Furthermore, it is also told that an eminent scholar once approached Mendel of Kotzk and boasted that he had gone through the entire Talmud. Unimpressed, the rabbi retorted, "So, you have gone through the Talmud, but how much of the Talmud has gone through you?"[42] No passive voyeur, no casual tourist surveying the landscape of learning, the student of the Torah is one committed to *live* what he learns. As Kierkegaard said, "Truth exists for the particular individual only as he himself produces it in action."[43]

Study of the Torah is not merely an academic exercise, but an experience in which all aspects of the person should be engaged. Not distinct from experience, study *is* experience. Learning can be life's greatest adventure. Through study a person can become what he knows; a person can build life as a work of art from the raw materials bequeathed by tradition; an individual can translate classical sacred texts into a contemporary lifestyle. In pursuing the gift of knowledge, one can acquire the blessing of wisdom.

According to the Gospel of John (1:1), "In the beginning there was the word, and the word was with God, and the word was God." According to the Jewish mystics, however, it was the opposite. In the beginning there was God, and God became the word. God infused the divine Name, the divine presence, into the letters and words of the text of the Torah. Consequently, by entering the sacred word, we encounter God. God, truth, and self-knowledge can be found in the sacred text, in the word of God.

In Hebrew, a word for a "letter" of the alphabet is *teivah*. But *teivah* is also the word for "ark." The Ba'al Shem Tov interpreted God's command to Noah to enter the ark as a command to each person to enter the sacred word.[44] Through study of the Torah and in prayer, a person enters the word. The sacred word is an invitation for a rendezvous with God. Entering the holy word is the sacred "work of the heart" (*avodah she-ba-lev*).

The sacred text was considered a point of convergence between the human and the divine. As far back as thirteenth-century Spanish Jewish mysticism, we find the name of God equated with the Torah. In the *Zohar*, the Torah, which embodies the name of God, is correlated with the body of the "community of Israel," which in turn is identified with both *Shekhinah* and the people of Israel.[45] This subsequently led to an equation between God, the Torah, and Israel.[46] This equation is often found in Hasidic literature. One popular expression of the relationship of the community of Israel to the Torah is the claim that the soul of each Jew is identified with each of the letters that constitute the Torah and that the totality of the letters of the Torah constitutes the name of God. For example, Nathan Shapiro of Krakow reiterates other kabbalistic texts when he writes, "Each member of the people of Israel has a soul that is one of the many letters of the Torah."[47] In the sacred text, the soul, the word, and the divine converge. Through the sacred word, the individual encounters God, his or her own soul, self-knowledge, and the wisdom of the past that may then be applied to the perplexities of the present.

The Talmudic rabbis deferred the rebuilding of the Temple and the restoration of the sacrificial cult to the messianic era that would commence at the twilight of history. Until then, the Torah serves as the people of Israel's sanctuary, as their homeland while in exile. Until the messianic advent, study and prayer replace sacrifice. Study and prayer fulfill the primary function of sacrifice—bringing a person closer to God. In the Talmud there already is the claim that study of the Torah not only equals but surpasses the offering of sacrifices. Reflecting on the etymological relationship between the Hebrew world for "sacrifice" (*korban*) and the Hebrew word for "near" (*karov*), it has been observed that though the sacrifices served to bring those far from God near to God, those who study the sacred word are *already* close to God by virtue of their preoccupation with God's Torah.[48] The text of the Torah is a door to intimacy with its Author. Study of the Torah is an entrée to love of God and to communion with God.

According to Saadya Gaon, the Torah is the only viable foundation for Jewish identity. As Saadya put it, Israel is a people *only* by virtue of the Torah.[49] By offering the Torah, God initiates the covenantal relationship. By receiving the Torah, the people of Israel ratifies its commitment to living in the covenant. Judaism is how the individual Jewish person articulates that commitment.

It is significant that classical Jewish literature uses the word "Torah" to denote Judaism. The term "Judaism" was introduced by Greek-speaking Jews in ancient times to denote the "ism" of the Judeans. The origins of the English word "Judaism" derive from the Greek *Judaismes*, that first appears in 2 Maccabees (2:21) and in Galatians (1:13–14). However, Talmudic literature uses the word "Torah," to denote the religion of the Jews, as in the famous story of the gentile who comes to learn the entire Torah (i.e., Judaism) while standing on one foot.[50]

As "Judaism," the Torah is the only authentic and viable foundation of individual and communal Jewish life. Study of the Torah is the only historically demonstrated foundation for Jewish continuity. Jewish life that does not derive its essential sustenance from Jewish learning is a fallacy, a fraud. Consequently, a Jewishly illiterate communal leadership poses a dire threat to Jewish survival and continuity.

Not only study of the Torah but observance of its laws and commandments is a sine qua non for authentic Jewish life. Jewish law prescribes in the most minute detail how every action could be the expression of faith in the form of a deed. Jewish religious law serves as the skeleton of Jewish faith, giving it stability and structure. Without observance, faith would be ephemeral. Without a continuity of sacred deeds, the tradition would dissipate.

Sacred deeds, *mitzvot*, are the details of the covenant. Performing sacred deeds is living in the covenant. Their performance is a symphony of deeds, singing a song of love to God. The word *mitzvah*, often translated as "commandment," more correctly means a "covenantal commitment" that flows from the love that binds the Jewish individual in covenant to God. Observance of the commandments is the Jew's primary way of manifesting love of God. As Levi Yitzhak of Berditchev put it, "The word '*mitzvah*' means 'to bind' which is to say, those who properly perform a *mitzvah* bind themselves in love to God."[51]

Sacred deeds provide an opportunity each moment of each day for a rendezvous with God. Though God's Name is ineffable, unspoken, it can be articulated through performance of the sacred deed. God's ineffable name contains four Hebrew letters: *yod, he, vov. he. Mitzvah* also contains four Hebrew letters: *mem, tzade, vov, he.* In *atbash*, a system of Hebrew letter interchange where the first letter of the alphabet equals the last letter, and so forth, *mem* becomes *yod, tzade* becomes *vov; mitzvah* then becomes *yod, he, vov, he,* the ineffable name of God. Through proper performance of the *mitzvah*, we speak God's name in our deeds. We meet God in the sacred deed.

According to Leo Baeck, the *mitzvah* is also a vehicle by means of which individuals can articulate their having been created in the image of God. Through performance of the *mitzvot*, sacred deeds, human beings can become holy as God is holy (Lev. 19:2). Performing the *mitzvot* expresses the human capacity for creativity, for becoming God's partner in the ongoing unfolding of creation.[52]

Halakhah, Jewish law, elucidates the details of the *mitzvot.* For example, scripture tells us to observe the Sabbath, but it provides few details about how to do so. Halakhah fleshes out the particulars of how to do so, of the specific deeds that constitute the details of living in the covenant. Yet, halakhah, which means the "going," sets down a path to a destination rather than being itself a destination. It would therefore be a mistake to confuse the path with the destination, transversing the path with arrival at the destination.

From this perspective, observance with ulterior motives, observance that does not lead to communion with God, may be compared to a body without a soul. Treating the observance of Jewish law as the ultimate goal of the religious life of the Jew is potentially a form of idolatry. For example, Rabbi Mordecai Leiner of Izbica commented on the verse in the Ten Commandments "You shall not make unto yourself a graven image" (Exod. 20:4). He said, "This means you must not endow the commandments of the Torah with any real existence in their own right, for they are only instruments of God"; that is, the commandments are ways of bringing the person toward God, but they should not be considered as ends in themselves.[53]

The medieval preoccupation with the "reasons for the commandments" (*ta'amei ha-mitzvot*) reminds us that laws and commandments are means to an end rather than ends in themselves. This approach of the medievals altered earlier views in biblical and early rabbinic literature that considered the commandments as ends in themselves. To a substantial degree, for the medieval Jewish philosophers, the goal of observance was anthropocentric, while for the medieval Jewish mystics it was primarily theocentric. The philosophers considered the laws and commandments as tools in the process of human development— morally, physically, spiritually and intellectually. In this view, observance offered a blueprint for the creation of life as a work of art, for the realization of human potential. For the mystics, however, the primary motivation for observance is to fulfill a divine need, to "empower" God's presence in the world, to help engender unity and balance among the fragmented aspects of the divine that are manifest in our world (see chapter 8).

Already in rabbinic literature, in which many blessings speak of God as "King of the Universe," observance of the commandments and laws was linked to bearing witness to the "Kingdom of Heaven" (*malkhut shamayim*), to divine sovereignty over creation.[54] And, in this regard, the Talmudic rabbis reminded us that a king is only a king de jure but not de facto, unless his people acknowledge him as king by observing the laws of his kingdom, by bearing witness to his presence and sovereignty.[55] The medieval mystics, however, went further, not only by considering human observance to be a need of God but by considering observance as a means to actualize the divine presence, divine grace, and God's power in the world. A radical expression of this motif appears in kabbalistic literature. Commenting on the phrase (Lev. 22:31), "You shall do (or make) them" (i.e., the commandments), the *Zohar* says, "Whosoever does the Torah's commandments and follows its paths...The Blessed Holy One says, [it is] as if he made Me...because he followed the ways of the Torah and did the commandments and directed the Kingdom properly, so to speak, he made a divine name above."[56]

For the medieval Jewish philosophers, observance of the commandments helps to improve the state of the self, society, and God's world. For the mystics, observance helps "strengthen" God, to provide "balance" in the Godhead, and through doing so, it induces the flow of divine grace and power to our world. On the other hand, sin, transgression, and moral vice stifle the creation of life as a work of art, mar the divine image, and—for the mystics—enhance the power of evil, of "the other side" (*sitra ahara*) over the self, the sacred word, the world, and even the Godhead.[57] As the *Zohar* puts it, "Whosoever transgresses the laws of the Torah causes damage above [i.e., to the Godhead], damage below [i.e., to the world], damage to themselves, and damage to all the other worlds."[58]

Yet, there is an antidote for sin—repentance or "return." Sin disrupts the covenantal relationship; repentance restores it. Sin brings about alienation; repentance restores at-one-ment. Paradoxically, sin makes repentance both possible and necessary. Repentance points to the purpose of creation. According to a midrash, "The purpose and aim of all creation is atonement."[59]

Repentance is compared to rebirth. Unlike birth that happens to us, such rebirth happens because of us. "Born without the intervention of his will," writes Leo Baeck, the individual "is reborn precisely because of the intervention of his will. His existence was created but he himself creates it anew. Therein the creative power of man is realized."[60] Through repentance, human creatures can re-create themselves in the image of their creator.

For some, repentance is motivated by fear of God's punishment. According to Isaiah Horowitz, for example, such motivation is flawed because it is egocentric. Rather, in his view, one should repent out of love.[61] From this perspective, true love must be not only love but also true. According to the Talmud, "If love depends on a [transient] thing, when that thing ceases, love ceases. When love does not depend on a [transient] thing, it never ceases."[62] This Talmudic statement teaches that authentic love must be unconditional, that it cannot be self-love masquerading as love of another; it cannot be self-interest pretending to be altruism. Nor can it be a passing fancy disguising itself as a lifelong commitment.

For the person who loves, the alienation caused by a misdeed against a beloved causes a fissure in a cherished relationship that inevitably becomes unbearable. Reconciliation becomes not only desirable but crucial. Repentance out of love flows from a desire for "return," for healing the rupture of relationship, rather than from fear of punishment or retaliation, or from the expectation of reward. The more intense the love, the more significant the relationship, the greater the yearning for reconciliation. In this regard, Elijah Di Vidas commented: "Sin causes the alienation of the love between an individual and God, as it is written, 'Your sins have separated you from your God' (Isa. 59:2). Therefore, since a lover does not wish their beloved to become estranged, the one who is obliged to the other should confess the faults to the beloved saying 'Truly, I have sinned against you. Do not leave me because of my offense.' "[63]

To effect complete reconciliation, the return must be mutual, reciprocal:

> Consider the parable of a prince who was far away from his father, the king. His friends said to him: Return to your father. He replied: I cannot; I have not the strength. Thereupon, his father sent word to him saying: Come back as far as you are able, and I will go the rest of the way to meet you. So says God: "Return to me, and I shall return to you" (Mal. 3:7).[64]

Religious existence consists of an ebb and a flow. In sin and repentance the person moves from God to God. In ibn Gabirol's words, "I flee from you, to you."[65]

Not only sin but also evil and absurdity stifle the human quest for meaning, holiness, and goodness. The persistence of evil and absurdity in our world and in our lives, historically and theologically, represents the most challenging obstacle to faith and meaning. How Jewish religious faith can respond to this challenge is the subject of the chapter that follows.

Meaning Despite Evil and Absurdity

For many Jewish thinkers who affirmed God as the ultimate reality, demonstrating the existence of God is as unnecessary as a lover having to prove the existence of his or her beloved. Or, as Søren Kierkegaard observed: What can be more impertinent than to interrupt an audience with an enthroned king in order to debate the king's existence?

Beginning with the Hebrew Bible, the dominant form of Jewish faith in God has been rooted in a personal commitment rather than in the affirmation of abstract intellectual propositions, in bearing witness to God's presence in the world and in our lives rather than adducing "proofs" for God's existence or definitions of God's nature. As Leo Baeck wrote:

> For Judaism, religion does not consist simply in the recognition of God's existence. We possess religion only when we feel that our life is bound up with something eternal, when we feel that we are linked with God and that he is our God. And he is our God, as the phrase has it, if we love him, if we find through him our trust and humility, our courage and our peace, if we lay ourselves open in our innermost being to his revelation and commandment.... To know of this one God in whom all things find meaning, to bear witness to him...is what Israel taught mankind....And thereby man experiences in himself the meaning of the entire world.[1]

Nonetheless, in their attempt to rationally demonstrate what they already believed, philosophical theologians throughout the centuries formulated various "proofs for the existence of God."[2] Among them is the "argument from design" or "teleological proof," which seeks to infer the existence of God, of a designer of creation, from the order and intricate design of the natural world. That purpose and meaning inhere in the design of the creator, and hence in human life, flows from this claim.

Critics of the teleological argument have focused upon three of its points of vulnerability. The first is that the existence of order and design in the universe does not necessarily point to the existence of a divine designer, or to a meaning or purpose for the world's or for human existence. The universe is "just there," eternal, uncreated. Indeed, as the Nobel Prize–winning physicist Steven Weinberg has allegedly said—perhaps in response to Einstein's famous quip that God does not play dice with the universe—the more we understand the universe, the more we see it is pointless. A second demurral emerged in response to the formulation of the teleological argument by the eighteenth-century Deists. A favorite analogy the Deists offered was to compare the universe to a watch found by someone. In this view, the existence and the intricacies of a handcrafted watch demonstrate the existence and design of the creator of the watch. For the Deists, the intricate design in nature demonstrates the existence of God who designed the universe. Yet, for the Deists, God's continuous involvement with and providence over creation cannot also be assumed. God creates the universe and then "lets it be." Such a view does little to promote the claim to human meaning or the claim that God manifests any ongoing concern about either creation or creatures, including human beings.[3]

The third and most poignant challenge to the "argument from design" is the coexistence of disorder with order, evil with good, destructive as well as creative forces in the natural world.[4] In this view, even were one to accept the claim that nature manifests intricate order and design, and even were one to affirm that such order and design indicate the existence of a divine designer, the presence of disorder, disruption, and "natural evils" remains unexplained and poses a critical challenge to the claim that a benevolent divine designer (i.e., God) has created the universe and continues to manifest providential care regarding it.

A medieval or even an early modern understanding of nature could readily support the "argument from design." Medieval Aristotelian physics presented an orderly portrait of the natural realm, while early modern physics compared the operation of the universe to a meticulously designed and efficiently running clock. However, some more recent investigations into nature offer an altogether different picture that poses a poignant challenge to the teleological argument, and consequently to the belief that God created an ordered and benevolent world with meaning and purpose.

Though the medievals were keenly aware of "red tooth and claw," that is, the violence and terror that pervade the animal kingdom, they seemed oblivious to catastrophic events in the cosmic realm. Often, they explained earthly catastrophes such as earthquakes and plagues either as punishment for sin, or as the workings of the demonic, or both. Nonetheless, they perceived the universe as a benign and orderly realm, largely beyond the ken of their understanding. In contrast, contemporary scientists speak about the "law of entropy," which posits a growing element of disorder in the cosmos. Scientists warn of the possibility of the random impact of asteroids and comets upon our world that could obliterate life on our planet as we know it. They describe "magnetic impulses" in our universe that could readily obliterate the earth. They describe and predict cosmic catastrophes such as the collision of galaxies, including our own. They depict the enormous obliterating destructive power of "antimatter," "black holes," and "dark energy." On earth, they warn of "pandemics" as natural occurrences—unrelated to human sin or demonic forces—that could decimate earth's human population, of the eventual onset of an ice age, and of the devastating effects of alterations in climatic conditions with their negative impact on coastal regions, water and food supply, human health, and economic conditions. These and similar observations portray our universe and our world as a "dangerous neighborhood," as a cold and dark place, indifferent to human existence, meaning, and well-being, replete with threats and disorder, violence and catastrophe—all of which is a radical departure from earlier views of the natural world. Thus, despite the intrinsic design we observe in the universe, evidence of disorder and cataclysm offers a profound challenge to the benign and even benevolent views of nature that underlie various formulations of the "argument from design."

The medievals were already wont to identify two varieties of evil: natural and moral, the former characteristic of the workings of nature, the latter the result of aberrant human behavior (i.e., sin).[5] Consistent with the theological "doctrine of divine retribution," with its deep roots in the biblical narrative, they often related one to the other and perceived natural catastrophes such as floods, earthquakes, and illness as divine punishment for either individual or communal transgression of God's will.[6] Furthermore, besides natural and moral evil, nineteenth- and twentieth-century thinkers—Jewish and non-Jewish, theists and atheists—identified absurdity as a powerful challenge to human meaning . In a world and in a society where absurdity mightily prevailed, they asked, how could individual meaning and purpose be claimed and sustained? As Albert Camus observed, the pervasive presence of absurdity in daily life leads a person to pose the most fundamental philosophical question, Why not commit suicide?[7]

Throughout its long history, Judaism has never been oblivious to the perennial omnipresence of evil and absurdity in our world. The words of Job (9:24) echo throughout Jewish history and experience: "The earth is given into the hands of the wicked." It is a premise of Jewish theology, confirmed by the harsh experience of the Jewish people in history, that ours is an unredeemed world where "the Evil Inclination, Satan, the Angel of Death hold sway."[8] Shortly after the Holocaust, Martin Buber wrote, "We [Jews] demonstrate with the bloody body of our people the unredeemedness of the world."[9] The pervasive presence in human experience of absurdity and evil poses the most powerful challenge to faith and to meaning.

Some of the medieval philosophical theologians tried to define "evil" out of existence by subtle rhetorical maneuvers. In contrast, the medieval Jewish mystics recognized the power and the presence of evil and sought to confront it head-on, understanding the challenge it poses to the quest for faith and meaning. The medieval Jewish mystics also recognized the realm of the good and the holy. Yet, for them, there is an additional realm that pervades our world, our lives, that offers a challenge of its own and that may be more pervasive than either extreme: the realm of the intermingling of good and evil, of evil within good. Though the task of contending with evil is formidable, the task of separating the evil from the good without destroying the good is even more difficult. More frustrating than the fact that evil is real and powerful is the fact that evil thrives so well disguised as the good. Redemption is therefore contingent upon the separation of good and evil, and not only upon the defeat of evil and the absurd.[10]

Even our best social, religious, educational, and political insti- tutions, even our most righteous people, represent a commingling of good and evil. For example, Mendel of Kotzk explained the verse in Leviticus (7:1), "This is the law of the guilt offering; it is most holy," to mean: "Where is guilt to be found? In the most holy."[11] In this regard, the Ba'al Shem Tov observed that a Hebrew word for "sin" (*heit*) is spelled *het, tet, alef.* The *alef,* the last letter, is silent. Why, then, is it needed? In Hasidic Hebrew, *alef* is often an abbreviation for *alufo shel olam,* "The leader of the world," that is, God. According to the Ba'al Shem Tov, the *alef* in *heit* relates to the nature of sin. In his view, like all things, even sin requires God's presence to exist. Sin, therefore, is placing God in a place where God does not belong, intermingling the divine and the demonic, God with evil.[12] The problem, then, is not only how to contend with evil, how to do good, but also how to root out the evil from the good—in our deeds, our society, our institutions, and our own selves—without destroying the good that has given evil and sin a home.

Both Hebrew scripture and the Talmudic rabbis saw human expe- rience as a failed experiment of God. Human history demonstrates that God initially had been too utopian, optimistic, hopeful, and perhaps naive about the future of humankind. Though containing many sto- ries, much of the Hebrew scriptures may be read as the story of God's hopes and expectations for humankind, and humanity's frustration and betrayal of those expectations.

Does Scripture ever tell us that God saw that human righteousness was great on the earth and that God was glad to have created human beings? Rather, Scripture tells us, "The Lord saw how great was human wickedness on earth and how every plan devised by man's mind was nothing but evil all the time. And the Lord regretted having created human beings, and God's heart was saddened" (Gen. 6:5–6; cf. 8:21). As the old limerick puts it:

> God's plan had a hopeful beginning
> Then man spoiled his chances by sinning.
> We know that the story
> Will end with God's glory
> But right now, the other side's winning.[13]

That God's initial hopes must be modified, that the divine plan for creation must be revised in light of how the world God created turned out to be, is found in many classical Jewish sources. For example, according to rabbinic tradition, the revelation at Sinai was supposed to initiate the redemption of the world, the messianic era, but it does not. As Moses receives the Torah, the people build the Golden Calf. God's plan is once more frustrated. God's hopes are once more betrayed. Redemption does not come. The Talmudic rabbis compare the people's worshiping of the Golden Calf at the time and place of the making of the covenant at Sinai to a bride betraying her groom in the honeymoon bed (see also chapter 8).[14] Humankind turned out differently than God had expected. God's novel failed to follow the original plot.

Already in thirteenth-century Spain, Nahmanides observed that the problem of evil is "the most difficult matter which is at the root both of faith and apostasy, with which scholars of all ages, peoples and tongues have struggled."[15] Further, in *The Ethics of the Fathers*, the Talmudic rabbis concluded that "it is not in our power to understand either the suffering of the righteous or the prosperity of the wicked."[16] In other words, insofar as the challenge of evil and absurdity to faith and meaning is concerned, there is no "final solution," especially not a theological one. In the final analysis, there are responses but no solutions.

As has been noted earlier (chapter 4), a midrash tells of a person who was traveling from place to place when he saw a palace *doleket*. "Is it possible that there is no master who cares for this palace?" the person wondered. Then the master of the palace appeared and said, "I am the master of this palace."[17]

According to this parable, the palace is the world, the person is every person, and the master of the palace is God. The Hebrew term *doleket* is ambiguous. According to some of the commentators, it means a "shining" or "luminous" palace (*birah*), representing a world of beauty, marvels, and order. This reading of the text interprets it to mean that a gaze at the grandeur and wonder of creation leads to the inevitable conclusion that the palace, that is, the world, has a lord, a creator, a caretaker. This is a rabbinic version of the "argument from design." Other readings, however, translate the word *doleket* as a "burning" palace, a palace in flames, a conflagration. Such a reading of the text interprets it to mean that the world is aflame with evil, that absurdity overwhelms our world, and that even God is in some way trapped in our world of evil and absurdity.[18]

The palace is aflame; nonetheless, it does have a master. God is the master of the palace, of the world. God is the ultimate creator, the ultimate artist. But, like every artist, God learns to accept that there always is a gap between what an artist expects a work to be and what it actually turns out to be. As Isaac Bashevis Singer wrote, "every artist, every creator, painfully experiences the chasm between his inner vision and its ultimate expression." God, claims Singer, is no different. Singer continues:

> God was for me an eternal *belle lettrist*. His main attribute was creativity. . . . I quoted to myself that passage from the midrash that says God created and destroyed many worlds before He created this one. Like my brother and myself, God threw his unsuccessful works into the wastepaper basket. The flood, the destruction of Sodom, the wanderings of the Jews in the desert, the wars of Joshua, these were all episodes in a divine novel, full of surprise and adventure.[19]

Singer draws here upon a midrashic tradition that describes God as continuing to create and to destroy worlds until he manages to create one with which he is sufficiently satisfied: "The Holy One went on creating and destroying worlds until God created this one and declared— This one pleases me; those did not please me."[20]

God, the creator, the artist, God entrapped in the palace, is not the God of the philosophical theologians. This is not the static omnipotent God of the Jewish Aristotelians. Rather, here is a God of pathos and of passion, a being capable of artistic proclivities, a God who makes mistakes and tries to rectify them, a God who creates and who redeems but who also requires human assistance and human partnership in the process of creation and redemption.

In contrast, medieval philosophical theologians press hard to convince us that God must be perceived as a rational, statically perfect being devoid of emotion or pathos.[21] To ascribe emotion or error to God is, in their view, a mistaken apprehension of the divine that borders on heresy. To be sure, this approach offers a rationalistic view of God, of the world God created, and of ourselves. In this view, the human being, created in God's image, is a rational being; the human being, following this Aristotelian perspective, is the "rational animal." The world is a rational place, following rational laws of cause and effect. In such a world, divine retribution functions with the reliability, the consistency, and the rationality of any of the laws of nature.[22] Evil is punished and virtue is rewarded with the same predictable regularity as the sun's rising and the seasons' changing in their ordained sequence. Evil is the product of human deeds; to imply that God has any relationship to evil is, in this view, to impugn divine perfection.

Such a portrait of reality is very comforting. To live in a rational world, governed by a rational God with fellow humans who think and act rationally, means that everything is "in order" and "under control." Everything is predictable, reasonable. But where do evil, absurdity, trauma, and tragedy fit in to this portrait of reality? How can the existence of meaningless tragedy, of irrational catastrophe, be explained? The answer is: it cannot.

As David Hume reminds us, "Epicurus' old questions are yet unanswered. Is he [God] willing to prevent evil, but not able?, then he is impotent. Is he able but not willing?, then he is malevolent. Is he both able and willing?, whence then is evil?"[23] In other words, the problem of theodicy, that is, "the justification of God" in the face of evil and absurdity, rests upon three assumptions: *God is benevolent. God is omnipotent. Evil is real.* Not willing to compromise God's perfection by questioning divine benevolence or omnipotence, medieval philosophical theologians have tended to confront the problem by defining "evil" out of existence, an example of conversion by redefinition. "Evil," they claim, is the "privation of the good," a non-entity, and therefore there is no problem of evil.[24] Yet this argument is not convincing anymore than it is to say that a dead relative is not really dead but is only experiencing a privation of life, or that a sick child is not ill but is only experiencing a privation of health. The relative is still dead and to be mourned. The child is still sick and the parents worry. Bad things are bad things, not "privations" of good things.

In order to maintain the rationalistic, mechanistic view, evil is either defined into oblivion, or human beings are identified as its exclusive cause, or both. As the product of human sin, evil is explainable, rational. It is the effect of an identifiable cause. Evil that appears to have no identifiable cause appears to be irrational, and therefore it must be explained away, defined away. Either there is a cause (perhaps known only to God) but we remain unaware of it, or evil is relegated to being an apparency rather than a reality.

The linguistic and intellectual acrobatics of these philosophical theologians seem to be a means for defending the notion of divine perfection and divine rationality, a way of getting God "off the hook" for meaningless suffering and for absurd tragedy. It seems that, to these thinkers, protecting the perfection of God and reaffirming the rational quality of existence is more crucial than forthrightly confronting the problematic existence of inexplicable evil and pervasive human tragedy. The dysteleological surd—the factor within existence that has no purpose or meaning—cannot be integrated into their neatly systematic apprehension of reality and therefore must be swept under the theological rug in order to maintain the notion of a statically perfect and rigidly rational God.[25] Despite the elegant semantic arguments of the philosophers, evil and absurdity continue to run rampant in the world and in everyday human experience.

The dominant Jewish theology of divine retribution that describes God as a celestial accountant tabulating our debits and our credits in order to determine whether it is "cost-effective" to maintain us, pervades biblical, rabbinic, and liturgical texts. Though based upon a rationalistic assumption, though positing a cause-and-effect relationship between sin and punishment in an almost scientific manner, this theology must be severely questioned when it is so facilely applied to enormous human catastrophes such as the European Holocaust.[26] In the final analysis, as has been noted, there is no solution to evil and absurdity, only responses rooted in an alternative theological approach, an approach that understands the nature of God differently than the philosophical theologians. As Dostoyevsky reminds us, all the wisdom of all the philosophers cannot explain the death of a child to the child's mother.[27] As was already noted, such an alternative approach that understands God to be an artist who makes mistakes, would not be foreign to Jewish theological discourse. It is found in rabbinic literature and is amplified by Jewish mystical literature, and it offers an alternative to the views of the philosophical theologians and to the doctrine of divine retribution.

It is no more anthropomorphic to portray God as a disappointed artist than it is to portray God as a totally rational being. All concepts of God, deriving as they do from the human mind and heart, are necessarily anthropomorphic. However, one might suggest that some so-called anthropomorphisms may in fact be theomorphisms.[28] Both our rational nature and our artistic nature may be reflections of God's nature within us rather than projections of our nature onto God.

Nahman of Bratslav translated the verse "Let us make humans in our image and likeness" (*kidmuteinu*) (Gen. 1:26) as "Let us make humans endowed with an imagination."[29] In medieval Hebrew, *ha-koah ha-medameh* is the term used to denote the imaginative faculty of the human soul, the human imagination. In Nahman's view, the essential human trait is imagination, creativity, fantasy, which reflects an attribute of the divine nature. All that we know of God to this point (i.e., Gen. 1:26) in the biblical narrative—that God is a creator—would support the portrayal of the essence of human nature as a reflection of the divine attribute of imagination and of creativity. Like God, humans can be rational beings, but like God, they can simultaneously be creators, artists, and imaginative beings.

Being of a creative and an artistic temperament, humans, like God, share the frustrations endemic to artistic creativity. Like God, human beings are susceptible to the foibles and mistakes endemic to the artistic process. Like God, humans become aware of the fact that destruction is part and parcel of the process of creation.

As an omnipotent, rational, "divine dictator," as a "celestial accountant," God cannot afford to make mistakes, to err; otherwise, God's perfect nature would be irredeemably compromised. As an artist, however, God must make mistakes. God must destroy as part of the process of creating. Even God cannot make an omelet without breaking the eggs. As an artistic creator, it is consistent with God's nature to make mistakes.

Some rabbinic sources contend not only that is God a fallible creator but that God the creator is also God the destroyer. Furthermore, these sources maintain that God's act of destruction is sinful, that sometimes in destroying what God created, God sins! Finally, these texts take the radical theological position that human beings can take actions that atone for God's sin. God needs us to redeem his sins. In the Talmud, for example, we read:

> Rabbi Simeon ben Pazzi pointed out a contradiction [between the verses]. One verse says, "And God made the two great lights" (Gen. 1:16), and immediately the verse continues, "The greater light [i.e., the sun]...and the lesser light [i.e., the moon]." The moon said unto the Holy One, "Sovereign of the Universe! Is it possible for two kings to wear one crown?" God answered: "Go then and make yourself smaller." "Sovereign of the Universe!," cried the moon, "Because I have suggested that which is proper must I then make myself smaller?" On seeing that it [i.e., the moon] would not be consoled, the Holy One said: "Bring an atonement *for me* for making the moon smaller." That is what is meant by Rabbi Simeon bar Lakish when he declared, "Why is it that the he-goat offering offered on the new moon is distinguished in that there is written concerning it '*for* the Lord' (Num. 28:15)? Because the Holy One said, 'Let this he-goat be an atonement *for me* for making the moon smaller.'"[30]

The Lurianic kabbalah describes destruction, evil, and imperfection as endemic aspects of the process of creation. Because it is the nature of the creative process to include destruction, and because a creation by its very nature must be imperfect, even God cannot create without destroying. Even God cannot create a perfect world. The Lurianic doctrine of *zimzum* (divine contraction) has God withdraw within, going into "exile" into God, into the Godhead, thereby corrupting God's initial, absolute perfection, as the first step in the process of creation. Furthermore, the Lurianic concept of the "breaking of the vessels" teaches that there is an initial flaw in creation, and that this cosmic flaw reaches back to the divine creative process itself.[31]

According to the Jewish mystics, God has two "faces." On the one hand, God is the *Deus Absconditus*, the hidden God, whose essence is existence, and of whom nothing can be known by human beings. Beyond human apprehension or comprehension, called *Ein Sof* (Infinite) by the mystics, this is God as God actually is. *Ein Sof* also transcends all relationships. On the other hand, God is also the *Deus Revelatis*, the revealed God, the manifested God, God as God is revealed to us, God who creates the world and who enters into a relationship with creation and its creatures, God who is present in the world, in history, and in our lives. Though *Ein Sof* remains beyond all dichotomies, the revealed God, according to the Jewish mystics, is manifest in complementary polar opposites, such as those represented by the divine attributes of justice and mercy. From this perspective, the manifested "face" of God is perfect not in the Aristotelian sense of being static and unchanging but "perfect" in a different way. The Hebrew word for "perfection" is *shleimut*, which denotes completeness, wholeness. Such wholeness is manifested by the balance and polarity of divine attributes such as justice and mercy, transcendence and immanence, intellect and passion, rationality and imagination. Our world reflects these polarities. These divine attributes are reflected in God's creation, and especially in human beings.[32]

A major trend in classical Jewish thought perceives reality as being characterized by polarity. In the words of Judah Loew of Prague, "Everything that exists in the world is either of a certain essence or its opposite."[33] According to a medieval text, "God made each thing and its opposite....All things cleave to one another, the pure and the impure. There is no purity except through impurity."[34] The *Sefer Yetzirah*, for example, states: "God has set each thing to correspond with another, the good against the evil, and the evil against the good."[35] For there to be up there must be down, for black there must be white, for good to be perceived there must also be evil, for repentance to be required sin must be present, for there to be mercy there must be justice. The major concepts of Jewish theology are not expressed in definitions that together constitute a systematic theology but as descriptions of complementary polar opposites.

Philosophy offers definitions. Classical Jewish thought offers descriptions. These descriptions are offered not *de fine*—to define, to limit—but to present an entity or an idea in its fullness, in its totality. These descriptions are offered as pairs of complementary polar opposites, such as, God is both transcendent and immanent, human nature simultaneously embraces the "image of God" (Gen. 1:26) and "dust and ashes" (Gen. 18:27, Job 42:6). The world embraces the polarities of light and darkness, good and evil. Creation entails destruction, good entails evil, meaning entails absurdity. One cannot exist without the other. Without evil, good would be unrecognizable and unattainable. Free moral choice between good and evil would be unrealizable. Without the challenge of absurdity, meaning would be meaningless. Without destruction, creation could not occur. From this perspective, the existence of evil and absurdity flow from the nature of creation and from the nature of the creative process. Because it is an essential feature of the creative process to include destruction, and because creation by its very nature must be imperfect, creation must embody dichotomies such as good and evil, meaning and absurdity. That creation embodies evil as well as good also derives from the empirical observation that evil is a component of created existence. Indeed, for some of the Jewish mystics, the polarity of good and evil extends even to the Godhead. According to the mystical treatise *Sefer ha-Bahir*, though God is good, there is nonetheless a divine attribute that is called "evil."[36]

In this view, evil and absurdity are ontologically necessary components of existence. Rather than concluding that the necessary existence of evil inescapably leads to nihilism and despair, and rather than perceiving the human condition as one of random victimization, rather than seeking ways of justifying God (i.e., "theodicy"—the justification of God), this position asserts to the contrary that the human person can respond to evil and absurdity by becoming an active protagonist in the ongoing battle to contain the evil element within the self and within the world. This approach aims at reducing the power of evil in the self, and in the world by means of the performance of sacred and redemptive deeds. Evil and absurdity are understood to be facts of life, features of existence to be reckoned with, rather than problems to be solved. In this view, human deeds can either fuel or stifle the growth of evil and absurdity in our world; they can either accelerate or retard redemption. For example, the Lurianic idea of the *parzufim* (divine faces) relates to the re-creation that must follow the catastrophic "breaking of the vessels" that is an integral part of the creative process. Lurianic kabbalah provides human beings with a role in rectifying God's mistakes, of atoning for the destruction that God implants within the process of creation. Human deeds can organize the *parzufim* as part of *tikkun*, the process of the repair of the flaws that form part of the initial fabric of creation, and even the repair of imbalances and flaws within the divine realm.

Though most of the medieval Jewish philosophers stressed divine omnipotence as a crucial feature of a self-sufficient, static God, the notion of divine omnipotence seems either unknown or irrelevant to biblical and rabbinic theology. Certainly, biblical and rabbinic sources discussed the "power" of God, but omnipotence, as it was understood by many of the Jewish philosophers, does not seem to have been characteristic of Jewish thought until the Middle Ages, probably through Islamic philosophical influence.[37]

The understanding of the divine nature, reflected throughout scripture, particularly in the classical prophetic writings, and amplified in rabbinic literature, particularly in texts where God is denoted by *Shekhinah*, emphasizes divine pathos with the human condition and not divine omnipotence.[38] In this view, God is a participant in human suffering and a victim of moral evil. God shares in the vicissitudes of human experience.[39]

From the assumption that God is not omnipotent, that God is affected by human deeds, flows the claim that God's power in the world, as well as the power of evil and absurdity, is contingent upon the nature and quality of human actions. Thus, "anthropodicy" replaces theodicy as the issue at hand. Rather than trying to justify God's deeds and evil human deeds that God might prevent, the problem becomes the justification of human deeds vis-à-vis other human beings and vis-à-vis God.

Many rabbinic and kabbalistic texts are oblivious to the problem of how to reconcile divine omnipotence with the existence of evil. They rather assume that the presence of God in our world is not omnipotent, and that God must rely on human effort to increase the divine power in our world. Human deeds can serve either to enhance or to reduce that divine power. Evil in the world becomes a reality for human beings to ameliorate by means of sacred deeds rather than a concept to be made consistent with the theological doctrine of divine omnipotence. Those midrashic and kabbalistic sources that describe the divine reliance upon human beings took seriously and literally the statement in Psalms (68:35): "Give strength to God." For example, a midrash reads: "Hence Moses' plea: 'And now, I pray you, let the strength of the Lord be enhanced' (Num. 14:17)....When human beings do not do God's will, then if one dare say such a thing, 'The Rock that begot you [i.e., God], you weakened' (Deut. 32:18)....Whenever Israel does the Holy One's will, they enhance the power of the Almighty."[40] In the words of the *Zohar*, "The Holy One, as it were, said: When Israel is worthy below, my power prevails in the universe, but when Israel is found to be unworthy, she weakens my power above."[41]

For many of the medieval Jewish philosophical theologians, especially those influenced by Aristotle, God is statically perfect, self-sufficient, thought contemplating its own perfection, and omnipotent. In this view, were God to change, to express emotion, to enter into relationships with imperfect beings such as human beings, God's perfection would be compromised. This, however, is not how God is understood by the biblical prophets, the Talmudic rabbis, the medieval Jewish mystics, or the Hasidic masters. Theirs is a God of reason and emotion, intellect and passion, concerned about and involved with an imperfect world and its creatures, and in need of human beings to act as God's partners in the continuous work of creation. God, in this view, has power but not necessarily omnipotence. Such a God is not, like that of the philosophers, "a powerless prisoner of his own perfection."[42] Such a God is not content just "to be," but needs creative self-expression, relationship, and human assistance to complete the creative process God initiated.

In medieval philosophical theology influenced by Aristotle, God is portrayed as being self-sufficient. Beginning with the Enlightenment, philosophers claimed that human beings are self-sufficient. This claim of the medieval philosophers threatened to undermine the nature of religion, for if God were completely self-sufficient and statically perfect, then he could neither desire nor require a relationship with imperfect human beings, as this would compromise God's perfection and self-sufficiency. However, such a view would also undermine the fundamental theological presupposition of Judaism that God has entered into a covenantal relationship with the people of Israel and with humankind. The modern claim regarding human self-sufficiency aimed at undermining, among other theological claims, the belief in revelation. A corollary of this view is that without God's revelation of the Torah that provides a blueprint for enacting human meaning by following its teachings, God would be irrelevant to the human enterprise, and Judaism would be merely a matter of peoplehood and culture. Because creation is an expression of divine revelation, the dismissal of revelation would also discredit the claim that God created the world with meaning and purpose.

To address revelation is to address the nature of God. Like the phenomenon of creation, the phenomenon of revelation presumes that God does not want to be alone, statically perfect, and self-sufficient, that God seeks relationship with creation, with human beings. In this view, God is in need of human beings to continue the work of creation that God had initiated. God reveals to humankind in the Torah a blueprint for how human beings can elicit meaning in life by living in the covenant with God, how human beings can articulate meaning by utilizing the revealed teachings of the Torah to create their lives as works of art. In this view, neither is God self-sufficient as the medieval philosophers claimed, nor are human beings self-sufficient as the Enlightenment and other modern thinkers claimed. Rather, God has reached out to humankind through revelation in an act of grace and love in order to enter into a covenantal relationship with human beings. This relationship is one of mutual need, of interdependence, rather than of individual self-sufficiency.

For some of the Jewish mystics, even *Ein Sof* is not completely self-sufficient. Rather, *Ein Sof* needs to manifest itself, to express itself, through creativity. Through the mysterious unfolding of the divine "personality," the need for creative self-expression leads to the manifestation of the features of the divine in what the mystics called the *sefirot*. The last of the ten *sefirot* is called *Malkhut* or *Shekhinah*. For the Jewish mystics this is the aspect of God closest to us, the aspect of God that "births" our

world. As such, *Shekhinah* is usually described as having "female" features. She is the "mother of the world," the mother of humankind, the
manifestation of the divine presence in our world. From this perspective,
the aspect of God closest to us is a "she." This unfolding of the "divine
personality" eventually leads to the creation of the universe, including
our world and ourselves. Hence, God requires relationship with an other
to truly become "perfect" in the sense of "completeness" (*sheleimut*). The
world and the human creature in the world represent the "divine need"
for an other.

Each of us is God's "other." As Arthur Green puts it, "In order to
be God's 'other,' we have to be all that the eternal One is not: transi-
tory, corporeal, mortal. God, as it were, seeks out an opposite—and
a partner—in us."[43] The very existence of this "other" is the purpose
for the unfolding of the divine personality, the culminating purpose of
divine creativity, the fulfillment, as it were, of a "need of God."[44] Again,
here is a polarity: our need for God, and God's need for us. In this view,
human beings are not created only "in the image of God" but also "*for*
the image of God."

For the Jewish mystics, by entering into a relationship with our
world, and by entering into a covenant with human beings, God freely
chooses self-restriction, *zimzum* ("self-contraction," as the Lurianic mystics put it), and self-limitation in terms of the presence and existence of
the divine power and presence in our world. By choosing to enter into a
covenantal relationship, a partnership, God, in effect, becomes dependent upon us. By sharing the divine attribute of freedom with us, God
thereby restrains divine power and freedom.

Human free will is a precarious gift God gives human beings to
allow them to be truly human, that is, free moral agents. In this view,
God chooses to limit divine power so that humans may exercise their
freedom. Because freedom of choice entails the option of making the
wrong choices, evil then becomes the price that humans must pay and
that God must tolerate.[45] Ironically, through making the wrong choice,
through sin, the first human beings activate their divine image, their
free will, the attribute that they share with God.[46]

The Jewish mystics taught that everything in our world is in a state
of exile, of alienation, challenged by the evil and absurd dimensions of

human existence. This includes not only the human condition but also the *Shekhinah*, the divine presence in our world. The spiritual quest begins with the awareness that existence means existence in exile. To think otherwise must be viewed as an act of nonawareness—even worse, as an act of self-deception. As Mendel of Kotzk said, it is bad enough to be in exile, in a state of alienation, but it is even worse to be in exile and not to be aware of it.

According to the Jewish mystics, the necessary catalyst for stimulating the flow of transcendent divine grace is the human performance of sacred deeds. In this regard, commenting on the verse in Psalms (121:5): "The Lord is your shadow," Levi Yitzhak of Berditchev said, "Just as a person's shadow does whatever a person does, so does God, as it were, do whatever a person does. Consequently, a person should perform sacred deeds such as showing compassion to those in need, so that God will likewise bestow divine goodness upon the world's creatures."[47]

This idea, central to Jewish mysticism, is that human deeds not only influence God but also influence God's relationship to us. There is a flow upward of our activities and their effects upon God. However, there is also a perpetual downward flow of divine blessing and grace from God toward us that is affected by our activities. When the flow upward is characterized by human acts of goodness, virtue, and unification, it affects the downward flow in a good and positive way. But when the flow upward of human deeds is characterized by sinful and undesirable acts, it affects the downward flow in a negative way. In this view, the nature and quality of divine grace is, in a very direct way, related to the nature and quality of human deeds.[48]

Though unredeemed, the world is yet redeemable. There is a partnership between God and human beings with foundations in an interdependent divine-human covenant. Both divine grace and human deeds are necessary in order to achieve the goal God and we both desire—the redemption of the world. Human beings are not passive bystanders in the drama of existence but active protagonists. As our fate lies in God's hands, so the destiny of God's world, God's creatures, and the divine presence in our world lays in each of our hands. We need God and God needs us to accomplish the task of redemption. A rabbinic midrash comments on the verse in Psalms: "My heart shall rejoice in your [i.e., God's] salvation" (Ps. 13:6). "Rabbi Abbahu taught: This us is one of those difficult verses that declare that the salvation of God depends upon the salvation of God's people. Note that it is not written, 'My heart shall rejoice in my salvation,' but in *your* salvation, by which the verse means: Your salvation, i.e., God's salvation, depends upon our salvation."[49]

According to this paradox, God has chosen us out of love to help realize the divine purpose for the world. Our relationship to God is not one of passive compliance but of active assistance. God's presence in our world, God's power in our world, paradoxically becomes linked to our attitudes and deeds. The theological boldness of this idea is already expressed by the Talmudic rabbis. For example, commenting on the verse in Isaiah (43:12) "You are my witnesses says God," a second-century rabbi said, "When you are my witnesses, I am God. But, when you are not my witnesses, it is as if I am not God."[50] Following this tradition of the Talmudic rabbis, the medieval Jewish mystics, and the Hasidic masters, Jews perceived God as a neighbor in distress, as a relative in need of our help, our love. In Yiddish, they called God *Gottenu*— our little God; *Tattenu*—our little father.

From this perspective, human purpose and meaning derive from our being a need of God, from our role as God's partners in covenant, and God's "partners in the work of creation."[51] Human meaning derives from the human mission to serve as God's partners in helping to fulfill and complete the initial creation of the world and of each human person created by God, and the place to begin is with one's own self. Each commandment we observe can meet a need of God. As Isaiah Horowitz writes, "All the commandments fulfill needs of the *Shekhinah*."[52] In this view, each person has a choice: either to amplify or to reduce the presence and power of evil and absurdity in our world. Though evil, absurdity, and alienation (*galut*) are features of our world, their disposition in our world depends on our deeds, on how we exercise the gift of human freedom and how we articulate human meaning. Not only are we affected by our deeds, but so is the *Shekhinah*, God's presence in our world.

We are beckoned to collaborate with God to accelerate the time of redemption when evil and absurdity will be overcome. As a midrash puts it in the form of a parable: "Once a prince was betrothed to a princess. A certain day was appointed for festivities before the wedding. The prince was looking forward to his wedding day, and the princess was looking forward to her wedding joy. . . . So does the Holy One look forward for redemption for Israel and Israel awaits redemption for the Holy One."[53] This approach takes literally the verse in Zechariah that is included in the daily Jewish liturgy: "On *that* day, God will be one and God's name will be one" (Zech. 14:9). In other words, presently God is not really one. Only in the messianic future when evil and absurdity are subdued will God truly be one. The human task is to work toward the goal of making God one through redemptive deeds, through deeds of loving-kindness, through living in the covenant.[54]

Hope Despite Experience

Evil and absurdity are endemic features of life in a premessianic world. Christianity teaches that we live in a world where the Messiah already has come. Judaism teaches that we live in a "messy" world, where messianic redemption is yet to come. As a midrash puts it, "In this world of strife and tribulations, the Evil Inclination, Satan and the Angel of Death hold sway."[1] According to the Talmudic rabbis, in the messianic world, in eschatological rather than historical times, the forces of evil will be defeated. Then, for example, God will slay the Evil Inclination.[2]

Jewish teachings caution against confusing the eschatological with the historical, the utopian with the contemporary, messianic with premessianic times. Throughout Jewish religious literature, there are admonitions against "hastening the end," against confusing pretenders with the Messiah, against understanding sociopolitical events in messianic terms.[3]

According to a variety of rabbinic traditions, various junctures in human history were ripe for the advent of the messianic redemption—a time of peace and spiritual fulfillment, a time when evil will be subdued. However, human actions thwarted the redemptive plan of God. As was noted in the previous chapter, according to one such tradition, such a juncture was the time of the revelation of the Torah at Sinai. However, here as elsewhere, God's plan for humankind was frustrated by human deeds, by human sins, and redemption had to be deferred to an indeterminate future. Rather than initiating the redemptive era, the people thwarted God's plan by building and worshiping the Golden Calf.

As was discussed earlier (in chapter 5), the rabbis compared the revelation at Sinai to a wedding between God and the people of Israel. However, they also compared the people's worship of the Golden Calf at the time and place of the making of the covenant at Sinai to a bride betraying her groom in the honeymoon bed.[4]

Moses descends from the mountain carrying the two tablets described by scripture as written with "the finger of God" (Exod. 31:18). According to a rabbinic tradition, the entire Torah was written on those tablets. Moses sees the people worshiping the idol, the Golden Calf, and he smashes the tablets.[5] Later on, we read: "Moses carved two stone tablets, like the first" (Exod. 34:4). As a midrash comments on this verse, "God said to Moses: It was I who wrote the first tablets, as it says— 'written with the finger of God.' But now, *you* write the second tablets and I will assist you."[6]

Rabbinic commentators and Jewish mystics reflected upon this story. They asked: Why was the first set of tablets written by God while the second set was written by Moses? Are the two sets different? Why did Moses break the first set? The following is one line of interpretation offered to answer these questions.

The first set of tablets, written by God, was completely spiritual. It represented a perfect Torah for a perfect and redeemed world. It represented the "essential" Torah—the Torah as it really is; the Torah whose abode is in heaven, the spiritual realm. In this view, Moses did not break the tablets out of anger; he broke them from his realization, after seeing the people worshiping the Golden Calf, that redemption could not yet come, that the world remained sinful, corrupt, and unredeemed. Moses realized that the perfect Torah, the spiritual Torah, the Torah written by the hand of God, had no place in such a world. It could not operate in the world as it is. Moses therefore broke the first set of tablets.

Later on, Moses wrote a second set. The first set was written by God, the second by a human being. The first Torah was completely spiritual for a redeemed world. The second is a remolded Torah, shaped for an unredeemed world. In this view, God compromises the divine plan for the world, the Torah, to allow it to speak to a world replete with evil, strife, and absurdity, to an imperfect world. The completely spiritual Torah is meant for a world of peace, devoid of violence, injustice, and corruption. The actual Torah that we have deals with violence, war, murder, crime, deception, and sin, which are features of human existence in our world. The text of the Torah that we have does not address a perfect world, a utopian world. It addresses both the hopeful and the ugly side of human nature and experience. It does not demand perfection. It carries God's word, God's will, God's commandments for a messy world, not for a messianic world. As the Talmud reminds us, the Torah is given to human beings and not to angels.[7] In our world of falsehood, deception, and sin, of evil and absurdity, the Torah of absolute truth, perfection, and spirituality could not endure, nor could it be endured by the world. As the *Zohar* says, "The world could not endure the Torah if she had not garbed herself in the garments of this world."[8] Gershom Scholem summarized this teaching as follows:

> The first tablets contained a revelation in keeping with the original state of man [before Adam sinned]....This was the truly spiritual Torah, bestowed upon a world in which Revelation and Redemption coincided, in which everything was holy and there was no need to hold the powers...[of evil] in check....But the utopian moment soon vanished. When the first tablets were broken "the letters engraved on them flew away," that is, the purely spiritual element receded....On the second tablets the Torah appears in a historical garment....A hard shell is placed around the spiritual Torah, indispensable in a world governed by the powers of evil.[9]

The Jewish mystics taught that the Torah is in exile in our world and is alienated from its completely spiritual nature.[10] Indeed, everything in our world is in a state of exile, alienation. This includes not only the Torah and the human condition but also the *Shekhinah*, God's presence in the world. For the Jewish mystics, the path toward redemption begins with the awareness of the unredeemed state of the world, with the realization that human history is out of sync with God's dreams, that human history is a divine disappointment, that God's hopes for a redeemed world have been sabotaged by undesirable human deeds. The spiritual quest begins with the awareness that existence in history means existence in exile, in alienation, in a world where evil, strife, and absurdity run rampant.

As was discussed in the preceding chapter, the Talmudic rabbis and the medieval Jewish mystics considered our world to be like a palace aflame, and the human condition as a source of frustration of God's hopes and plans. They depicted endemic "flaws" in both the process and the product of God's creation. They perceived evil, strife, and absurdity as ontological features of the human condition, exacerbated by sinful human deeds. Such views led the Talmudic rabbis to question the propriety of God's creating the world, and the human species in particular. For example, one Talmudic text describes how God took counsel with the angels about God's plan to create human beings. The angels discourage God from proceeding with the plan, yet God creates human beings anyway. After witnessing the sins of the generation of the Flood and of the Tower of Babel, the angels subsequently affirm the wisdom of their counsel. God responds by quoting a verse from Isaiah (46:4), which is taken to mean that God will nonetheless bear with the undesirable features of human existence under all circumstances.[11]

A second Talmudic text reports one of only six occasions in the Talmud where the view of the school of Shammai prevailed over the view of the school of Hillel. At dispute was whether or not it was better that God had created human beings. The school of Hillel claimed that it was better that human beings had been created. The school of Shammai claimed that it would have been better had humans not been created. After two and a half years of debate, a decision was reached: It would have been better had human beings *not* been created, but now that they have been created, people should examine their deeds, and if they find fault with them, they should make amends.[12]

Whether a divine mistake or an expression of God's irrational exuberance and hope, human beings are condemned to freedom, and to contend with evil and absurdity in a premessianic world. For the Talmudic rabbis, though existing in an alienated condition in our world, the Torah nonetheless provides a foundation for hope and meaning. God is the Giver of the covenant; the people of Israel are its recipient; but the Torah represents its content. According to the Talmud, the Torah is the raison d'être of the universe and of human existence.[13]

The Torah provides meaning and purpose to God's creation and to the human creature.[14] Serving as a touchstone of meaning, purpose, insight, wisdom, and spiritual direction, the Torah is also depicted as a powerful antidote to the forces of evil and absurdity.[15]

According to a midrash, discussed in the preceding chapter: "Abraham may be compared to a man who is traveling from place to place when suddenly he saw a palace aflame. 'Is it possible that there is no master who cares for this palace?,' the man wondered. Then, the master of the palace appeared and said, 'I am the master of this palace.'"[16] According to this midrash, although Abraham recognizes the presence of evil and absurdity in the world, he continues to affirm his newly discovered faith. Indeed, according to another legend, the evil king Nimrod cast Abraham into a fiery furnace to test his faith.[17] Here, at the very beginning of Judaism, the first Jew is already cast by an evil dictator into a crematorium. Yet, both Abraham and his faith survive. As his descendants will later learn, Abraham learns about living in a world aflame with evil and absurdity. Abraham learns that it is sometimes necessary to have faith in God in spite of God, despite how God's world is run.

As the person of faith is required to bear witness to God, so may the person of faith doubt God and even bear witness against God. Faith includes wrestling with God. Only after Jacob struggles with the divine is he called "Israel," which means "to wrestle with God" (Gen. 32:29). Out of the crucible of faith emerges an anguished cry, a protest against evil and absurdity: "Lord, how long shall I cry to you and you will not hear, even cry out to you of violence and you will not save.... The wicked encompass the righteous, wrong judgment proceeds....Wherefore do you hold your tongue when the wicked devours the person more righteous than he?" (Hab. 1:1–3). Similarly, the Talmudic rabbis comment on the verse in Exodus (15:11), "Who is like unto you among the mighty [*elim*] O Lord?," saying "Read not *elim* [mighty] but *elmim* [silent]. Who is like you among the silent, O Lord, seeing the suffering of his children and remaining silent."[18] Believing in God in spite of God, embracing faith over experience, the prophets and rabbis cajoled God to emerge from silence and to act.

This tradition of Jewish "protestantism" was begun by Abraham (see Gen. 18:25) and was perpetuated by his descendants. The covenant requires God to act with justice and benevolence. When God does otherwise, he may be called to account.

Rabbinic sources depict God as obeying the laws of the covenant. In other words, God is considered a "person" in Jewish law, heeding its precepts, bound to its obligations. This rather startling notion—that God is a "person" under the law—is established in the Talmud: "Rabbi Lazar said: A human king issues a decree and he may choose to obey it or he may choose to have only others obey it. Not so the Holy One. When God issues a decree, God is the first to obey it, as it is stated, 'And they shall observe my commandments, I am the Lord,' i.e., I am the one who is first to observe the commandments of the Torah."[19] As a person under the law—albeit God's own law—God may be called to account for the apparent failure to honor the legal obligations to which he became committed. As Israel is liable to God for its violations of the covenant, so is God liable to Israel for his violations of the pact made with the people.

The story of Abraham and of the faith he founded is a story of hope despite experience. It is a story of the audacity of hope in the face of evil and absurdity. In Jewish theology, hope coalesced into an expectation for messianic redemption. No other people in the ancient world developed such an idea.[20]

The day in the Jewish liturgical calendar that is dedicated to recognizing the presence of tragedy, evil, and absurdity is Tisha B'Av —the Ninth of Av. Jewish tradition recounts a litany of Jewish catastrophes that occurred on this day throughout history. Yet, in keeping with the tradition of finding hope, even within abject despair, a tradition developed that also identified this day of tragedy with the onset of hope: "On the Ninth of Av, the Messiah will be born."[21]

Messianic redemption is often viewed as a collaborative effort of God and human beings. God can initiate messianic redemption as an expression of divine grace, but first the world must be made ready for redemption by human effort. As Heschel puts it: "At the end of days, evil will be conquered by the One; in historic times, evils must be conquered one by one."[22] The teachings of the Torah provide the road map for preparing the world for messianic redemption through the performance of sacred and redemptive deeds. Along these lines, a story in the Talmud reports a dialogue between Rabbi Joshua ben Levi and the Messiah. The rabbi inquires, "When will you come?" The Messiah responds, "Today." When the Messiah fails to come, the rabbi inquires of Elijah the prophet. Elijah explains that the Messiah was citing a verse in Psalms (95:7): "Today—if you hearken to God's voice."[23] Similarly, the Hasidic master Mendel of Kosov was once asked why the Messiah had not come. Commenting on the verse in Samuel (2 Sam. 20:27): "Why has the son of Jesse [i.e., the Messiah], not come either today or yesterday?" he said, "The reason is provided by the question itself. Why has he not come? Because we are today just as we were yesterday."[24] In this view, human beings are not innocent bystanders in the cosmic drama. The challenge is to labor to redeem oneself, the world, and the divine presence in the world. The human task is to work in partnership with God to subdue evil and absurdity, and eventually to initiate messianic redemption. As Abraham Heschel has written:

Who is man? A being in travail with God's dreams and designs, with God's dream of a world redeemed, of reconciliation of heaven and earth, of a mankind which is truly in His image, reflecting His wisdom, justice, and compassion. God's dream is not to be alone, to have mankind as a partner in the drama of continuous creation. By whatever we do, by every act we carry out, we either advance or obstruct the drama of redemption; we either reduce or enhance the power of evil.[25]

The dominant view in Jewish theology is that messianic redemption is an eschatological event to occur in the distant future, an event that will one day take place in historical and geographic coordinates, centered in the Holy Land, with clear sociopolitical features.

According to many Jewish traditions, the Messiah already exists but cannot come until a certain juncture in history. Whether or not that juncture has arrived is purposefully left vague. However, when that juncture will be reached, the obvious question becomes: What prevents the messianic advent? One response is that the people of Israel prevent the messianic advent because they have not adequately observed the laws and commandments, cultivated the moral virtues, or discerned the secret meanings of the Torah. In this view, each individual can accelerate or retard messianic redemption. Each individual can play a significant role in the messianic drama. Each individual can serve as a "miniature messiah" with a mission, a purpose, a goal. From this perspective, God alone can send the Messiah. The role of the people as a whole or of any individual is not to bring the Messiah but rather to create conditions conducive to the advent of the Messiah, to remove impediments to the Messiah's advent. In this view, the Messiah does not bring redemption. Rather, the messianic advent is a sign that the time of redemption has arrived and that the world has been made ready for redemption. God seeks human assistance and collaboration in the transition from historical to eschatological times.[26]

The idea in Lurianic Kabbalah of liberating the "sparks" articulates a messianic motif. In this view, the human role is to liberate all the sparks of divinity trapped in the shells of impurity so that they can reunite with the Source from which they originally derived. When the "great *Tikkun*," that is, when the liberation of all the sparks has occurred, things will revert to their originally perfected state. With the ultimate reparation, the messianic age would commence. It therefore becomes the human task to liberate these sparks, especially the particular sparks that reside in one's own soul. In Hasidic teaching, the individual is obliged to redeem not only the sparks in their own souls but also the sparks scattered in various places that relate to the spark of their own soul. When all the sparks of the soul of the pre-Fall Adam are redeemed, they will join together to reconstitute the soul of Adam before the Fall. That soul is also the soul of the Messiah. The soul of the first Adam before the Fall is the soul of the second Adam, that is, the Messiah. If a single human being fails in his mission to redeem the part of Adam's soul that is his own, messianic redemption cannot occur. Here, again, we see the Jewish mystics' emphasis on the crucial role that every action of each individual plays in the drama of existence and redemption.

In various Jewish mystical traditions, the messianic drama is consigned to the individual human soul. If repairing the divine realm is too great and long a process, if reconstituting the entire soul of the original Adam proves too daunting a task, if the redemption of the people of Israel in the sociopolitical realm is unattainable because of historical conditions, then an alternative form of messianic redemption becomes available for the here and now, that is, the redemption of the individual soul. From this perspective, messianic redemption is not only the climax of a historical process but the acme of individual spiritual development. Because sending the Messiah is a task best left to God, the mystics encouraged individuals to focus on personal redemption, the redemption of their own souls.

Besides their obvious references to concrete geographic places, terms like "Zion," "Jerusalem," the "Land," and the "Land of Israel" took on another dimension of meaning in various Jewish mystical texts. Rather than being identified solely with geographic locations relating to the place where messianic redemption would commence, they came to be identified with various spiritual states of being. Just as "Jerusalem" referred to the place where messianic redemption would commence, it also was used to refer to an elevated spiritual state representing the attainment of individual spiritual redemption.[27] Thus, for example, the well-known statement in the Passover Haggadah—"Next year in Jerusalem"—became a double entendre. On one level, it means geographic residence in Jerusalem at the commencement of the messianic era at the end of history, in eschatological times. On another level, it meant that the individual should aspire to the spiritual state of "Jerusalem," that is, a state of individual redemption.

Just as the Land of Israel became identified with an individual spiritual state of redemption, exile (*galut*) came to refer not only to a physical location outside the Holy Land but to a condition of individual spiritual exile or alienation. Messianic redemption therefore came to be understood as a process whereby the human soul progresses from a state of alienation to a state of fulfillment, that is, to a messianic state of being. Each individual achieving this state of being can thereby attain what some Hasidic texts call "individual redemption" (*geulah peratit*) as distinguished from the "collective redemption" (*geulah kelalit*) of the entire people of Israel, or of the cosmos, or of the world of the divine.

The means whereby individual redemption can be achieved, the techniques by means of which an individual can become his own messiah, come as no surprise. They include observance of the commandments, cultivation of the moral virtues, and winning the war against the

"Evil Inclination" within the self. According to the teachings of the Ba'al Shem Tov, individual redemption entails the fulfillment of the biblical verse "Draw near to my soul and redeem it" (Ps. 69:19). For the Ba'al Shem Tov, "'the exile of the soul' is called the 'Evil Inclination.'"[28] In this view, the exile and the redemption of the soul are spiritual states. Having attained a state of spiritual redemption, one is spiritually in the "Land of Israel," though geographically one may continue to dwell in the Diaspora, the "exile."

According to prophetic Kabbalah, as articulated by Abraham Abulafia, each individual is potentially a messiah.[29] By actualizing one's spiritual nature, each person can become his own messiah. The Abulafian process of self-development that can lead to prophecy can also lead to individual messianic redemption. Messianic redemption, in this view, is indicative of an inner spiritual development rather than a change in sociopolitical realities. The initial object of messianic redemption is the individual soul rather than the entire people of Israel, the cosmos, or the supernal realm. An indication that a state of individual redemption has been achieved is *devekut*, the state of intimate communion with God. The soul is redeemed when it merges with God in mystical intimacy, when one has reached the state of "[God] is me and I am God."[30] Yet the individual who has achieved individual redemption must still pursue the mission of redeeming others. The primary task is to redeem one's own soul. The ultimate task, however, is the redemption of the whole. According to certain Hasidic teachings, individual redemption consists of affecting the reunion of the human soul with God in mystical intimacy. The individual's spark is redeemed as a prelude to the eventual liberation of all the sparks.

In this view, messianic redemption need not be a future expectation assigned to a certain place at an indeterminate time. Rather, it can be attained in the here and now. As one Hasidic master put it:

> The quintessence of our worship [of God] is to restore and complete the part of the Messiah that corresponds to each and every one of us . . . and when the enterprise of restoration (*Tikkun*) of the complete stature [of the Primordial Adam] is accomplished, he [the Messiah] will be the righteous one, the foundation of the world, in a perfect manner, a great and unencumbered pipe, prepared [to receive] the

influx and vitality [from the supernal realm]...hence every individual of Israel should become in the category of the righteous in order to sustain the world in a perfect manner....because all [the people] are in the category of the "righteous" and are a pipe for this world, i.e., serving as a vehicle for the existence of the world, they will inherit the land [i.e., they will be redeemed].[31]

Besides belief in messianic redemption, hope crystallized around another eschatological belief—the afterlife.

Survey data from opinion polls consistently report that most American Jews do not believe in an afterlife. Yet a survey of the sacred and significant texts of Judaism reveals that every important Jewish religious thinker, from Talmudic to modern times, has depicted belief in an afterlife as a fundamental feature of Jewish faith.[32] Judaism affirms belief in an afterlife; like many of the *conversos*, most American Jews do not.

An analysis of survey data shows that about 80 percent of American Christians believe in an afterlife, as do about 65 percent of Americans who affirm no specific religious faith (including atheists and agnostics). Of all groups surveyed, belief in an afterlife has been consistently the lowest among American Jews: 46 percent in polls done in the late 1990s. However, of all groups surveyed, belief in an afterlife has increased the most among American Jews: from 19 percent in the 1970s to 46 percent in the 1990s, an increase of 142 percent.[33]

From time immemorial, human beings have asked: What's next? Is this life all that there is? What can I hope for when my life ends? Is death the end, the annihilation of all that I am? Or, as Tolstoy poignantly put it: Is there any meaning in my life that will not be destroyed by the inevitable death that awaits me?[34] Historically and theologically, Judaism has affirmed that though death is inevitable, something of ourselves can survive our physical death, that some form of individual self-perpetuation is available beyond the grave.

Unlike other religions and philosophies, Judaism never has avoided the inevitability or the reality of death. Already in Genesis, the first human being is told: "Dust you are and to dust you will return" (Gen. 3:19). Ecclesiastes (3:2) states, "A season is set for everything: a time to be born and a time to die." In contrast, much of Western culture historically has sought to deny the reality of human mortality. We readily use euphemisms to disguise death. Yet in an age such as our own, where acts of terrorism, war, and genocide continue to punctuate daily life, where life is a blind date with an uncertain future, death cannot be avoided.

Jewish children preparing for bar or bat mitzvah are taught the traditional blessing to be recited after the reading of the Torah that says, "Eternal life (*hayei olam*) you [God] have implanted within us." It does not say that God has assured us eternal life, but that like a seed implanted within the soul, God has implanted within us the *potential* for life after death, for self-perpetuation. The task in life, then, is to nurture and to develop this seed. Hence, belief in the afterlife is not a way of escaping the responsibilities of life in this world as some claim, but is rather a challenge to imbue life with a meaning that will outlast it. As Abraham J. Heschel wrote: "Survival beyond death carries, according to Judaism, demands and obligations during life here and now. Conditions are attached to the hope of survival. . . . Eternity is not an automatic consequence of sheer being. . . . It must be achieved, earned."[35] How a person lives their life determines what of themselves can be perpetuated beyond death.

For Bahya ibn Pakudah, the belief that there is no afterlife, no ultimate accountability for the way we have lived, no possibility of self-perpetuation beyond our years on earth, readily leads to nihilism, hedonism, escape from moral responsibility, and obsession with trivialities. Bahya presents this view in his ethical treatise, *Duties of the Heart*.[36] This work, and Moses Hayyim Luzzatto's *Paths of the Upright*, have been the two most influential works of Jewish ethical literature (*sifrut ha-musar*). Stating the dominant, representative view of Jewish religious literature about the afterlife, Luzzatto writes, "The purpose for which human beings were created is realized not in this world but in the World to Come. Human existence in this world is but a preparation for existence in the World to Come which is the goal."[37] For ibn Pakudah, Luzzatto, and others, life in this world should focus on developing our spiritual, moral, and creative potentialities during life to prepare for the next step, to help ensure some form of self-perpetuation in the World to Come.

While alive, we reside in the dimensions of time and space. But the afterlife may well be a different dimension of existence that transcends time and space. To conceive of such a dimension of existence is beyond our abilities, since everything we know and experience exists within time and space. This is precisely why an afterlife can be neither proved nor disproved by science. Science examines the realm of space-time, not what is beyond it. If the afterlife is beyond time and space, it would not be a *place* like heaven or hell. Rather, it would be a *state* of being beyond the dimensions of this world. For human beings to try to grasp the nature of the afterlife would be like a person blind from birth trying to describe color. About the nature of the afterlife, we have speculation but no experience.

One view of the afterlife is that the body dies, but the soul survives. Consider an analogy of the soul and the body to an astronaut. In space, astronauts are totally dependent upon their space suit for existence in space, but it is not so of astronauts in the totally different atmosphere of the earth. Similarly, the body may be merely a capsule designed for life in this world. In the totally different atmosphere of the next world, it might not be required. Or, to use another analogy—can the caterpillar conceive of what life is like as a butterfly? For the caterpillar, a cocoon means death, but for a butterfly it means a new life, a new beginning, a radically different type of existence. According to Joseph Albo, people weep at the thought of death for the same reason a newborn weeps when it emerges from the womb. There it was secure and unafraid, but now a new dimension of existence is opening up for it, and it is predictably frightened of the unknown.[38]

Passing down a name, genes, and family traditions is a way of continuing and perpetuating our lives and those of our forebears. Children and grandchildren can perpetuate more than DNA. Children can perpetuate values, wisdom, memories, deeds, dreams, and love. They can serve as a link between past and future. They can provide us with a biological as well as a spiritual form of self-perpetuation and continuity. A medieval commentary compares one's children to one's deeds. Like children, our deeds are generated by us.[39] Like children, the effects of our deeds allow part of us to survive us, and provide meaning for a life well lived.

The doctrine of the resurrection of the body made its debut in ancient Jewish history. It became a central belief of the Talmudic and medieval rabbis. To those who doubted it, the Talmud rhetorically asks: If those who never lived can live, why cannot those who once lived, live again?[40] Initially, the doctrine of resurrection was a response to the problem of evil. The earliest textual reference seems to be the well-known story in 2 Maccabees (7:9) of Hannah and her seven sons. After her sons are tortured to death, Hannah addresses their oppressor: "You wretch. You release us from this life but the King of the World will raise us up because we have died for God's laws, to an everlasting renewal of life." Resurrection of the body developed in response to the Jewish passion for justice. Justice unavailable in this world is guaranteed by God in the World to Come. Like other forms of life after death, the rabbis taught that resurrection either has to be earned by performance of good deeds during life or that it serves as the redress for a life abruptly and unjustly ended by violence or disease. In this view, belief in life after death of some variety relieves one of the expectation that everything will be finally decided in the here and now.

Resurrection is also an affirmation of the spiritual significance of the human body, for it is the body that is resurrected. Jewish spirituality is not only about the soul but about the body as well. According to the *Zohar*, the body is the instrument through which the soul carries out the commandments. Without the body, the soul would be a mute vagabond spirit; spiritual life would be unattainable, meaning unrealizable.[41]

The emphasis in Jewish communal life on the community and its needs can readily deflate the significance of the individual. Resurrection, however, teaches that each individual is inestimably precious to God in their individuality, that without individual self-perpetuation, there can be no communal continuity.

There is a blessing, recorded in the Talmud and recited first thing each morning as part of the daily liturgy: "My God, the soul that you have placed within me is pure. You it was who fashioned it. You it was who blew it into me. You it is who preserves it in me. And, you it will be who will take it from me, only to return it to me in the time yet-to-be.... Praised are you, God, who restores souls to lifeless bodies."[42]

According to this prayer, resurrection occurs not only at the end of history in the messianic era but each morning when the sleeping person awakens. In this view, a person need not wait until death to experience resurrection. It can happen every day. In this regard, it is told that a skeptic once came to the Rabbi of Kotzk to mock him. "They say you can perform miracles, like resurrecting the dead," the skeptic sarcastically said. "Yes," said the Rabbi of Kotzk, "but I prefer to resurrect the living."[43]

The idea of the immortality of the human soul is an idea that apparently came into Judaism under the influence of Greek philosophy in late antiquity and that gained popularity in medieval times. In this view, the soul is the essence of the human person. The soul represents a spiritual quality that we share with God.[44] According to some of the Jewish mystics, the soul may be divine, a spark of the great spiritual flame that is God. The divine mandate is for each person during life to nurture and develop the soul, the part of us that is most like God—our creative, moral, spiritual and intellectual capacities. As Keats put it, "The world is a vale of soul-making."[45]

The desire to perpetuate our essence, our soul, is an innate human trait, and such self-perpetuation is a form of life after death. People can perpetuate themselves through acts of meaning, for example, creating works of art, literature, music, thoughts, or deeds that can survive their death. In this view, the afterlife entails committing oneself to perpetuating the lasting, the essential, within us. It is an expression of the biblical claim that humans have been created in the image and likeness of God, that the purpose of life is a life of purpose.

Though found in earlier Jewish sources, by the seventeenth century, belief in the transmigration of souls and reincarnation had become pervasive in the Jewish community, with some considering it an essential belief of Judaism. This teaching insists that a person deserves more than one crack at life in order to "get it right." Here, too, the penchant for justice plays a role. Because some people are born deprived while others are born advantaged, to expect the same achievement from both would be unjust. Therefore, each soul gets more than a single opportunity to fulfill its potential. In successive lives, the soul inhabits different bodies. What kind of body a person is assigned in a future life reflects the moral and spiritual quality of his former life. When the soul is adequately developed spiritually, it breaks out of the wheel of trans-migration and finds eternal repose within God. Reincarnation is also taught by the Jewish mystics. As a punishment for heinous sins a person can be reincarnated in a variety of animals or even in plants and stones; the worse the sin, the lower the life-form.[46]

The notion of transmigration of souls reminds us that we *are* who we *were*, that each person has a past that shapes his identity, his future, that no person creates himself from scratch. When Mark Twain first heard Henry Clay's phrase "a self-made man," Twain commented that a self-made man is about as likely as a self-laid egg. Transmigration points to an important religious insight: each person is more than she thinks she is; each life is richer and deeper than we imagine. As Browning so aptly put it: "Reach should exceed grasp, else what's a heaven for?"[47]

The Ethics of the Fathers compares this life to a vestibule, a wait-ing room, and the World to Come to a living room.[48] This life is but a prelude to the next, a prolegomenon to eternity. From this perspective, the quest for meaning relates to what survives us, to what we perpet-uate of ourselves. The path to meaning entails focusing our attention during life not on the ephemeral, the fashionable, the transient but on the lasting, the enduring, on that which both transcends us and can survive us. What we do in this life effects our disposition in the World to Come.

Confrontation with the reality of our own mortality is not meant to stimulate morbidity but rather to stimulate us to fashion our lives around that which we want to speak for us and of us when we are no longer here. This life offers each of us an opportunity to create enduring words, to perform enduring works, and to help perpetuate institutions whose work we value. Contemplation of life after death can lead us to perform actions aimed at making life in the here and now more mean-ingful, beautiful, and saturated with significance. In the final analysis, as Heschel reminds us, Judaism affirms an afterlife as a matter of faith, but exactly what it might be, we cannot now know.[49]

To conclude this chapter and this volume I offer the following words of philosopher Hans Jonas, which summarize many of the themes in this and preceding chapters. In an essay based upon his delivery of the prestigious Ingersoll Lecture in 1961, entitled "Immortality and the Modern Temper," Jonas wrote:

> Every new dimension of world-response opened up in its course means another modality for God's trying out his hidden essence and discovering himself through the surprises of the world adventure.... The advent of man means the advent of knowledge and freedom, and with this supremely double-edged gift the innocence of the mere subject of self-fulfilling life has given way to the charge of responsibility under the disjunction of good and evil. To the promise and risk of this agency the divine cause, revealed at last, henceforth finds itself committed; and its issue trembles in the balance. The image of God, haltingly begun by the universe, for so long worked upon—and left undecided—in the wide and then narrowing spirals of pre-human life, passes with this last twist, and with a dramatic quickening of the movement, into man's precarious trust, to be completed, saved, or spoiled by what he will do to himself and the world. And in this awesome impact of his deeds on God's destiny, on the very complexion of eternal being, lies the immorality of man.... We can build and we can destroy, we can heal and we can hurt, we can nourish and we can starve divinity, we can perfect and we can disfigure its image: and the scars of one are as enduring as the luster of the other. [This is] the immortality of our deeds.[50]

Notes

Chapter 1

1. On the Jews in Amsterdam during this period, see, e.g., Salo W. Baron, *A Social and Religious History of the Jews* (New York: Columbia University Press, 1973), vol. 15, 3–73.

2. On the period of the Inquisition and the *converso* dispersion, see, e.g., Salo W. Baron, *A Social and Religious History of the Jews* (New York: Columbia University Press, 1969), vol. 13, 3–158.

3. See Jose Faur, *In the Shadows of History* (Albany: State University of New York Press, 1992), 48.

4. On the theological issue of whether apostasy, i.e., in this case, the conversion of Jews to Christianity, is a "cardinal sin" without the possibility of reconciliation or repentance, see, e.g., Alexander Altmann, "TheEternality of Punishment: A Theological Controversy within the Amsterdam Rabbinate in the Thirties of the Seventeenth Century," *Proceedings of the American Academy for Jewish Research* 40 (1973): 1–88; Noah Rosenbloom, "Menasseh Ben Israel and the Eternality of Punishment Issue," *American Academy for Jewish Research* 60 (1994): 241–62. Legal issues often involved the marital status in a family where one party (often the husband) apostatized and another party (often the wife) did not, as well as relationships between parents and children, and other family members.

5. Cited in Faur, *Shadows of History*, 127.

6. See, e.g., ibid., 51. For this reason, leading *conversos* and their offspring like Isaac Cardoso and Menashe ben Israel wrote treatises defending belief in the afterlife.

7. See, e.g., Cecil Roth, *A Life of Menasseh ben Israel* (Philadelphia: Jewish Publication Society, 1934).

8. See, e.g., Jakob J. Petuchowski, *The Theology of Haham David Nieto* (New York: Ktav, 1970), 32–48, 69–106. It was not uncommon for *conversos'* views regarding rabbinic authority to be compared to the ancient Sadducees or the medieval Karaites, who also denied rabbinic interpretative authority. Many of Nieto's polemics were directed against a *converso* community in eighteenth-century England.

9. Shlomo Pines, "The Jewish Religion after the Destruction of Temple and State: The Views of Bodin and Spinoza," in *Studies in Jewish Religious and Intellectual History*, ed. Siegfried Stein and Raphael Loewe (University: University of Alabama Press, 1979), 223–28.

10. For a succinct summary of these views of Spinoza, see Steven Katz, ed., *Jewish Philosophers* (New York: Bloch, 1975), 137–46.

11. Cited in Yosef Hayim Yerushalmi, *From Spanish Court to Italian Ghetto* (Seattle: University of Washington Press, 1971), 319.

12. Gershom Scholem, *Shabbatai Sevi*, trans. R. J. Zwi Werblowsky (Princeton, N.J.: Princeton University Press, 1973), 818.

13. See ibid., 615.

14. Michael Meyer, *Response to Modernity* (New York: Oxford University Press, 1988), 11; Jacob Katz, "The Possible Connection of Sabbateanism, Haskalah and Reform Judaism," Hebrew section, in Stein and Loewe, *Studies in Jewish Religious and Intellectual History*, 83–100.

15. On Sanchez, see, e.g., Faur, *Shadows of History*, 87–109.

16. See Yerushalmi, *From Spanish Court*, 43.

17. See ibid., 114–16; Faur, *Shadows of History*, 111–12.

18. Cited in Yerushalmi, *From Spanish Court*, 46.

19. See Moses Mendelssohn, *Jerusalem*, trans. Allan Arkush (Hanover, NH: Brandeis University Press, 1983), 22–23, 97–98.

20. See, e.g., Meyer, *Response to Modernity*, 410 n. 11; Sidney Ayinn, "Kant and Judaism," *Jewish Quarterly Review* 59 (1988): 9–23.

21. See, e.g., Immanuel Kant, *Foundations of the Metaphysics of Morals*, trans. Lewis Beck (Indianapolis: Library of Liberal Arts, 1959).

22. Immanuel Kant, "What Is Enlightenment?" trans. Lewis Beck (Indianapolis: Library of Liberal Arts, 1959), 85. See also Nathan Rotenstreich, "Enlightenment: Between Mendelssohn and Kant," in Stein and Loewe, *Studies in Jewish Religious and Intellectual History*, 263–79.

23. See, e.g., Moritz Lazarus, *The Ethics of Judaism*, trans. Henrietta Szold (Philadelphia: Jewish Publication Society, 1900), vol. 1 pp. 123–38. See also Meyer, *Response to Modernity*, 54–56.

24. See, e.g., Faur, *Shadows of History*, 65. See also Meyer, *Response to Modernity*, 387.

25. See Julius Wellhausen, *Prolegomena to the History of Ancient Israel* (New York: Meridian, 1957).

26. See, e.g., Meyer, *Response to Modernity*, 64–66; Jerold S. Auerbach, *Rabbis and Lawyers* (Bloomington: Indiana University Press, 1990), 52–68.

27. See, e.g., Arthur A. Cohen, *The Myth of a Judeo-Christian Tradition* (New York: Schocken, 1971).

28. See Meyer, *Response to Modernity*, 286–89; Auerbach, *Rabbis and Lawyers*, 15, 17.

29. Steven Cohen, *American Modernity and Jewish Identity* (New York: Tavistock, 1983), 35; see also Elliot Abrams, *Faith or Fear* (New York: Free Press, 1997), 146–52.

30. Leonard Fein, *Where Are We?* (New York: Harper and Row, 1988), 225.

31. See, e.g., Bernard Susser and Charles Liebman, *Choosing Survival* (New York: Oxford University Press, 1999), 68–89; Steven Cohen and Arnold Eisen, *The Jew Within* (Bloomington: Indiana University Press, 2000), 13–42. The privatization of religion in America has been extensively examined by American sociologist Wade Clark Roof in his *Generation of Seekers* (San Francisco: HarperSanFrancisco, 1993).

32. Sylvia Barack-Fishman, *Negotiating Both Sides of the Hyphen: Coalescence, Compartmentalization and American Jewish Values* (Cincinnati: Publications of the Judaic Studies Department at the University of Cincinnati, 1995), 10–11.

33. See, e.g., Susser and Liebman, *Choosing Survival*, 86–89; Cohen and Eisen, *The Jew Within*, 12.

34. Judg. 17:6, 21:25.

35. Cohen and Eisen, *The Jew Within*, 7.

36. Ibid., 12.

37. The expression "condemned to freedom" was coined by Jean-Paul Sartre, and the "insecurity of freedom" was coined by Abraham Heschel, to describe the existential condition of modern people. The characterization of the contemporary person as being beset by anxiety, self-doubt, and boredom is found in the writings of many theologians, philosophers, and psychologists. See, e.g., Joseph B. Soloveichik, *Worship of the Heart* (New York: Ktav, 2003), 33–44.

38. Charles Taylor, *The Ethics of Authenticity* (Cambridge, Mass.: Harvard University Press, 1991), 37.

39. Abraham J. Heschel, *God in Search of Man* (Philadelphia: Jewish Publication Society, 1955), 411.

40. Charles Liebman, *The Ambivalent American Jew* (Philadelphia: Jewish Publication Society, 1973), 197.

41. Ibid., 150.

42. Susser and Liebman, *Choosing Survival*, 69.

43. See, e.g., Auerbach, *Rabbis and Lawyers*, xvi–xviii, 93–94.

44. See, e.g., Yehezkel Kaufmann, *Toledot ha-Emunah ha-Yisraelit* (Tel Aviv: Dvir, 1964), vol. 1, p. 23; Joseph Blenkinsopp, *A History of Prophecy in Israel* (Philadelphia: Westminster Press, 1983), 23–30.

45. See Schechter's letter to Rabbi Morris Joseph, quoted in Norman Bentwich, *Solomon Schechter: A Biography* (Philadelphia: Jewish Publication Society, 1938), 303.

46. Cited in Auerbach, *Rabbis and Lawyers*, 79.

47. Solomon Schechter, *Seminary Addresses and Other Papers* (New York: Burning Bush Press, 1959), 98.

48. See Auerbach, *Rabbis and Lawyers*, 18–19.

49. See ibid., 116.

50. See ibid., 47.

51. See ibid., 126. On Brandeis's Sabbatean roots, see Gershom Scholem, *The Messianic Idea in Judaism* (New York: Schocken, 1971), 167–75.

52. Auerbach, *Rabbis and Lawyers*, 18.

53. Eugene Borowitz, *Masks Jews Wear* (Port Washington, N.Y.: Sh'ma, 1980), 10, 208.

54. Franz Rosenzweig, *On Jewish Learning* (New York: Schocken, 1955), 54; Nahum N. Glatzer, ed., *Franz Rosenzweig: His Life and Thought* (New York: Schocken, 1970), 20, citing Rosenzweig's letter to his parents of December 5, 1909.

55. See Jonathan Woocher, *Sacred Survival: The Civil Religion of American Jews* (Bloomington: Indiana University Press, 1986), 92.

56. See, e.g., Egon Mayer and Barry Kosmin, *2001 American Jewish Identity Survey* (New York: City University of New York, 2002).

57. See Solomon Schechter, *Studies in Judaism: First Series* (Philadelphia: Jewish Publication Society, 1911), 180; Abraham J. Heschel, *The Insecurity of Freedom* (New York: Farrar, Straus and Giroux, 1966), 217.

Chapter 2

1. From an oral tradition conveyed to me by my mentor, Abraham Joshua Heschel.

2. Borowitz, *Masks Jews Wear*, 10, 208.

3. Woocher, *Sacred Survival*, 92.

4. See, e.g., Mayer and Kosmin, *2001 American Jewish Identity Survey*; see also Sidney Goldstein, "Profile of American Jewry: Insights from the 1990 Jewish Population Survey," *American Jewish Yearbook 1992* (Philadelphia: Jewish Publication Society, 1992), 77–173.

5. Steven Cohen, *Content or Continuity?* (New York: American Jewish Committee, 1991), 26.

6. Louis Jacobs, *A Jewish Theology* (New York: Behrman House, 1973), 281–83.

7. Abraham J. Heschel, *Moral Grandeur and Spiritual Audacity* (New York: Farrar, Straus and Giroux, 1996), 3.

8. See Gilbert Ryle, *The Concept of Mind* (New York: Barnes and Noble, 1949).

9. Schechter, *Studies in Judaism: First Series*, 180; Heschel, *Insecurity of Freedom*, 217.

10. Heschel, *God in Search of Man*, 322–25.

11. Eric Yoffie as cited in Dana Kaplan, ed., *The Cambridge Companion to American Judaism* (New York: Cambridge University Press, 2005), 15.

12. See Woocher, *Sacred Survival*, 72–80.

13. Cited in Arthur Hertzberg, ed., *The Zionist Idea* (New York: Atheneum, 1973), 319.

14. See, e.g., Byron L. Sherwin, "*Mai Hanukkah?* What Is Hanukkah?" *Central Conference of American Rabbis Journal* 50 (Fall 2003): 19–28.

15. See citations in Jerold Auerbach, *Are We One?* (London: Rutgers University Press, 2001), 41, 59.

16. See, e.g., Bialik's speech at the opening of Hebrew University in Jerusalem in 1925, cited in Hertzberg, *The Zionist Idea*, 284.

17. See Moshe Idel, "Pardes: The Quest for Spiritual Paradise in Judaism—Stroum Lecture, 1999," www.kheper.Net/topics/kabbalah/Idel/Pardes.htm (accessed November 16, 2006).

18. Leon Simon, ed. and trans., *Selected Essays of Ahad Ha-Am* (New York: Meridian, 1962), 147.

19. Jacob Neusner, ed., *To Grow in Wisdom: An Anthology of Abraham Joshua Heschel* (Lanham, Md.: Madison Books, 1990), 100.

20. Heschel, *Moral Grandeur*, 30.

21. Jacobs, *Jewish Theology*, 281.

22. Heschel, *Insecurity of Freedom*, 191.

23. Fein, *Where Are We?* 134, 142–43.

24. See, e.g., Eugene Borowitz, *Renewing the Covenant: A Theology for Post-modern Jews* (Philadelphia: Jewish Publication Society, 1991).

25. Barack-Fishman, *Negotiating Both Sides of the Hyphen*, 14; see also Abrams, *Faith or Fear*, 148.

26. For example, a discussion of *Tikkun Olam* is conspicuously absent in seminal studies of rabbinic thought such as, among others, Ephraim Urbach, *The Sages*, trans. Israel Abrahams (Cambridge, Mass.: Harvard University Press, 1987); Max Kadushin, *The Rabbinic Mind* (New York: Jewish Theological Seminary, 1952).

27. See, e.g., the study of the earliest uses of the term in rabbinic literature in the 2004 Hebrew University Ph.D. dissertation of Sagit Mor. See her Hebrew study, "*Tikkun Olam*: Its Early Meaning and Influence on Divorce Law during the Mishnaic Period," *Moed* 15 (2005): 24–51.

28. See Eugene Lipman, *"Mipne Tikkun ha-Olam* in the Talmud," in *The Life of Covenant*, ed. Joseph Edelheit (Chicago: Spertus College Press, 1986), 108.

29. See, e.g., Gilbert Rosenthal, *"Tikkun ha-Olam*: The Metamorphosis of a Concept," *Journal of Religion* 85 (April 2005): 214–40; Lawrence Fine, *"Tikkun*: A Lurianic Motif in Contemporary Jewish Thought," in *Ancient Israel to Modern Judaism*, ed. Jacob Neusner et al. (Atlanta: Scholars Press, 1989), 35–53. See also Arnold J. Wolf, "Repairing *Tikkun Olam," Judaism* 50 (Fall 2001): 479–82; Steven Plaut, "The Rise of *Tikkun Olam* Paganism," http/// www.israelnationnews.com/article.php3?id=1760 (accessed August 25, 2006).

30. See, e.g., Ismar Elbogen, *Jewish Liturgy*, trans. Raymond Schiendlin (Philadelphia: Jewish Publication Society, 1993), 71–72.

31. See, e.g., Byron L. Sherwin, *Kabbalah: An Introduction to Jewish Mysticism* (Lanham, Md.: Rowman and Littlefield, 2006), 105–7. See Isaiah Horowitz, *Shnei Luhot ha-Brit*(Jerusalem: Edison, 1960) vol. 3, p. 152b, sec. "Rosh Hashanah": "All the commandments are for the purpose of repair of the *Shekhinah (Tikkunei Shekhinah).*"

32. See, e.g., Hayyim Vital, *Sefer Sha'arei Kedushah* (Jerusalem: Eshkol, n.d.).

33. Rosenzweig, *On Jewish Learning*, 99.

34. Ibid., 98–99.

35. Ibid., 43.

36. Schechter, *Seminary Addresses and Other Papers*, 97.

37. Max Margolis, "The Theological Aspect of Reformed Judaism," *Yearbook of the Central Conference of American Rabbis* 13 (1903): 185–338.

38. Arthur Green, "New Directions in Jewish Theology in America," in *Contemporary Jewish Theology*, ed. Elliot N. Dorff and Louis E. Newman (New York: Oxford University Press, 1999), 487.

39. Zalman Schachter, *Jewish with Feeling* (New York: Riverhead, 2005), 187.

40. Jakob Petuchowski, "The Question of Jewish Theology," *Judaism* 7 (Winter 1958): 55.

Chapter 3

1. Heschel, *Insecurity of Freedom*, 217.

2. Jacobs, *Jewish Theology*, 1.

3. Woocher, *Sacred Survival*, 92.

4. Norman Frimer, "The A-theological Judaism of the American Community," *Judaism* 11 (1962): 144–54.

5. See, e.g., Robert G. Goldy, *The Emergence of Jewish Theology in America* (Bloomington: Indiana University Press, 1990); Byron L. Sherwin, "Thinking Judaism Through: Jewish Theology in America," in Kaplan, *Cambridge Companion to American Judaism*, 117–132.

6. See Lou Silberman, "Theology and Philosophy," in *Hebrew Union College–Jewish Institute of Religion at One Hundred Years*, ed. Samuel E. Karff (New York: Hebrew Union College Press, 1976), 389.

7. See, e.g., Kaufmann Kohler, *Jewish Theology: Systematically and Historically Considered*, 2nd ed. (New York: Ktav, 1968); see Solomon Schechter's essays, "The Dogmas of Judaism" and "The Doctrine of Divine Retribution in Rabbinic Literature," in his *Studies in Judaism: A Selection* (New York: Meridian, 1958).

8. Moses Maimonides, *Commentary to the Mishnah* [in Hebrew], ed. Joseph Kapah (Jerusalem: Mosad ha-Rav Kook, 1968), *Sanhedrin* 10:1.

9. See, e.g., Menahem Kellner, *Dogma in Medieval Jewish Thought* (New York: Oxford University Press, 1986).

10. Solomon Schechter, "The Dogmas of Judaism," in his *Studies in Judaism: First Series*, 180.

11. See Mendelssohn, *Jerusalem*, trans. Alfred Jospe, 72.

12. Schechter, "The Dogmas of Judaism," *Studies in Judaism: A Selection*, 180.

13. Petuchowski, "Question of Jewish Theology," 49.

14. Julius Guttmann, "The Principles of Judaism," *Conservative Judaism* 14, no. 1 (Fall 1959): 1.

15. Ibid., 6.

16. See Seymour Siegel, "The Unity of the Jewish People," *Conservative Judaism* 42, no. 3 (Spring 1990): 23.

17. *Talmud, Hagigah* 3b, in *Talmud* [with commentaries] (Vilna: Romm, 1895; reprint, New York: Otzar ha-Sefarim, 1958), 20 vols.; English translation: Isadore Epstein, *The Talmud*, 18 vols. (London: Soncino Press, 1935–61).

18. *Talmud, Sanhedrin* 34a.

19. On the Torah as a multifaceted mirror, see *Pesikta Rabbati*, ed. Meir Friedmann (Vienna: Herausgebers, 1880), 100b. On the seventy "faces" of the Torah, see *Numbers Rabbah* 13:15 in *Midrash Rabbah* [with commentaries], 2 vols. (Vilna: Romm, 1921). See also the discussion of Moshe Idel, "Infinities of Torah in Kabbalah," in *Midrash and Literature*, ed. Geoffrey Hartman and Sanford Budick (London: Yale University Press, 1986), 141–57. Idel maintains that beginning with late thirteenth-century Jewish mysticism the notion that the Torah has infinite meanings was introduced. Previously, the view that there are many but a limited reservoir of meanings prevailed. On infinite meanings, see also Gershom Scholem, "The Meaning of the Torah in Jewish Mysticism," in his *On the Kabbalah and Its Symbolism* (New York: Schocken, 1965), 50–86.

20. *Mishnah, Abot*, 3:15, in *Mishnah* [with commentaries] (Jerusalem: Horeb, 1952).

21. See, e.g., Jose Faur, *Golden Doves with Silver Dots* (Bloomington: Indiana University Press, 1986), xv–xvi, 123–24; Louis Jacobs, "Jews and Law," *Judaism* 37 (Spring 1988): 246–47; compare David Weiss Halivni, *Midrash,*

Mishnah, Gemara (Cambridge, Mass.: Harvard University Press, 1986), 102–15.

22. Louis Jacobs, *Faith* (New York: Basic Books, 1968), 175.

23. The approach outlined here obviates the need for the type of "experiential" theology advocated by Daniel Breslauer, for the "open Jewish theology" advocated by William Kaufman, or for the personalist "open traditionalism" advocated by Eugene Borowitz. Each of these authors tends to see Jewish theology in its earlier sense as being too systematic, "closed," and monolithic. Kaufman, for example, calls for a "theology of clarification rather than a dogmatic [systematic] theology." But, as is discussed later, Jewish theology need not be either systematic or dogmatic. Borowitz sets up a tension between traditionalism and existentialism, between Jewish tradition and individual choice. However, once the individual can act as the ultimate arbiter of what Jewish theology may be, then the authority of tradition is undermined and a claim to authenticity becomes problematic. The present view is that the broad boundaries offered by Jewish religious literature and the absence of a central theological authority like the Catholic curia provide the means for variety and multiplicity for the formulation of an authentic though "open" Jewish theology. Moving blatantly outside its broad parameters would deny authenticity to a theological foundation of Judaism. Just as American constitutional law cannot admit the propriety of certain concepts and options and still remain valid and authentic, a Jewish theology cannot exceed its broad boundaries and continue to remain valid and authentic. In other words, Jews cannot formulate any theology they wish and consider it a valid Jewish theology. This would invite anarchy, if not heresy. See Daniel Breslauer, "Alternatives in Jewish Theology," *Judaism* 30 (Spring 1981): 233–45; William Kaufman, *Contemporary Jewish Philosophies* (New York: Reconstructionist Press, 1976), 7; Eugene Borowitz, *A New Jewish Theology in the Making* (Philadelphia: Westminster Press, 1968), 108–9.

24. For want of a better English term, I am obliged to use the term "theology" despite its inappropriateness when dealing with the nature and implications of Jewish faith. Etymologically, the term means "the study of God," or "divine discourse." However, Jewish teachings emphasize that the nature of God is beyond the ken of human understanding or analysis. We can only speak about the ideas, perceptions, and experiences of God that we might have and that the classical sources discuss. The real subject of theology is not God per se but the human relationship with the divine, and the nature and implications of religious faith. Compare Saint Thomas Aquinas, *Summa Theologica* I,1, where theology is considered a way of knowing God as God knows God—a goal that Judaism would view as impudent if not intellectually impossible. See, e.g., Anton Pegis, ed., *Introduction to St. Thomas Aquinas* (New York: Modern Library, 1948), 3–15.

The medieval Jewish philosophers simply translated the Greek term that considered theology "divine knowledge" or "divine science" into Hebrew, e.g., *limud elohi, hokhmah elohit, torah ha-elohut, mada ha-elohi.* In modern Hebrew, the term "theology" (*teiologica*) is used. A viable alternative might be use of the term suggested by Abraham Isaac Kook in his *Orot ha-Kodesh: hokhmat ha-kodesh*, "sacred knowledge" or "knowledge of the sacred." See Samuel S. Cohon, *Jewish Theology* (Assen Netherlands: Royal Vangorcum, 1971), 9. I believe it incorrect to maintain that theology is new to Judaism as Breslauer and others claim; see Breslauer, "Alternatives in Jewish Theology," 234; Cohon, *Jewish Theology*, 5.

On the issue of authenticity and tradition in Jewish theology, compare Gershom Scholem, "Reflections on Jewish Theology," in his *On Jews and Judaism in Crisis* (New York: Schocken, 1976), 261–98.

Though these criteria for a valid Jewish theology are similar to those proposed by Jacob Neusner, my description and understanding of them differ significantly from his. Furthermore, my proposed methodologies for composing a theology of Judaism differ substantially from his. See Jacob Neusner, "The Tasks of Theology in Judaism," *Journal of Religion* 59 (1979): 71–86.

25. *Mekhilta de-Rabbi Yishmael*, ed. Hayyim Horovitz and Israel Rabin (Jerusalem: Wahrmann, 1960), sec. "Be-shalah," chap. 6, p. 175.

26. On the use in Jewish literature of the expression "a dwarf on the shoulders of a giant," see, e.g., Dov Zlotnick, "Al Makor ha-Mashal ha-Nanas ve-ha-Anak ve-Gilgulav," *Sinai* 77 (1975): 184–89; Hillel Levine, "Dwarfs on the Shoulders of Giants: A Case Study in the Impact of Modernization on the Social Epistemology of Judaism," *Jewish Social Studies* 40 (Winter 1978): 68–72; Byron L. Sherwin, *In Partnership with God* (Syracuse, N.Y.: Syracuse University Press, 1990), 1–5.

27. Cited and translated in Dov Zlotnick, "The Commentary of Rabbi Abraham Azulai to the Mishnah," *American Academy of Jewish Research Proceedings* 40 (1973): 163–64.

28. Schneur Zalman of Liady, *Likkutei Amarim (Tanya)* (Brooklyn: Otzar ha-Hasidim, 1965), chap. 5, pp. 18–19.

29. Mordecai of Chernobyl, *Likkutei Torah* (New York: Noble Printing, 1954), sec. "Le-Rosh ha-Shanah," p. 22b.

30. See, e.g., John Macquarrie, *Principles of Christian Theology* (New York: Scribner's, 1966), 5; D. S. Adam, "Theology," in *Encyclopedia of Religion and Ethics* (New York: Scribner's, 1908), vol. 12, p. 294; Cohon, *Jewish Theology*, 29; Jacobs, *Jewish Theology*, 1; Bernard Bamberger, *The Search for Jewish Theology* (New York: Behrman House, 1978), 5.

31. *Leviticus Rabbah* 35:7, in *Midrash Rabbah*.

32. *Exodus Rabbah* 30:13 in *Midrash Rabbah*.

33. See *Talmud, Berakhot* 57a; *Talmud, Pesahim* 49b; *Sifre on Deuteronomy*, ed. Meir Friedmann (Vienna, 1865), par. 345 on Deut. 33:4.

34. Samuel of Uceda, *Midrash Shmuel* (Jerusalem: Brody-Katz, n.d.), 61a–b.

35. *Zohar* (Vilna: Romm, 1882), vol. 2, p. 94b.

36. Moses Hayyim Ephraim of Sudlykow, *Degel Mahaneh Ephraim* (Jerusalem: Hadar, 1963), sec. "Aharei," p. 175.

37. See *Sifre on Deuteronomy,* par. 345 n. 8.

38. I obviously reject the long-standing view, rooted in Aristotle and developed in medieval and modern Christian theology, that considers theology as a science. See, e.g., Adam, "Theology," 293–95.

39. *Talmud, Pesahim* 6b.

40. See Samuel of Uceda, *Midrash Shmuel,* 61a–b. See also Faur, *Golden Doves,* 14.

41. In his *Dialoghi d'Amore,* Leone Ebreo distinguishes between lust, which can be satisfied, and love, which cannot. Lust can be quenched whereas love continues to regenerate itself. See Leone Ebreo, *The Philosophy of Love,* trans. F. Friedberg-Seeley and Jean H. Barnes (London: Soncino Press, 1937), 56.

42. See Samuel of Uceda, *Midrash Shmuel,* 60b.

43. Judah Loew, *Netivot Olam* (New York: Judaica Press, 1969), 1:32. This blessing derives from *Talmud, Berakhot* 11a.

44. See Moshe Idel, *Kabbalah: New Perspectives* (New Haven, Conn.: Yale University Press, 1988), 239, 399 n. 184.

45. *Mishnah, Abot* 3:19.

46. Samuel of Uceda, *Midrash Shmuel,* 61a–b.

47. Loew, *Netivot Olam,* 32.

48. On "expansive" and "restrictive" notions of "Torah," see Abraham J. Heschel, *Torah min ha-Shamayim* (London: Soncino Press, 1965), vol. 2, pp. 220–64, 360–417.

49. See *Leviticus Rabbah* 22:1 in *Midrash Rabbah,* and discussion of this text in Heschel, *Torah min ha-Shamayim,* vol. 2, pp. 236–37.

50. *Sifre on Deuteronomy,* par. 333. For parallels, see *Sifre,* ed. Louis Finkelstein (Berlin: Judischer Kulterband in Deutschland Abteilung Verlag, 1939), 265–66 n. 13.

51. See Solomon Schechter, *Aspects of Rabbinic Theology* (New York: Macmillan, 1909), 13–14: "The rabbis show a carelessness and a sluggishness in the application of principles which must be most astonishing to certain minds, which seem to mistake merciless logic for God-given truths.... It will, therefore, suggest itself that any attempt at an orderly and complete system of Rabbinic theology is an impossible task." On coherence without systematic thinking as a feature of rabbinic theology, see, e.g., Max Kadushin, *Organic Thinking* (New York: Bloch, 1938), 1–3; and Kadushin, *Rabbinic Mind,* 11–26. According to Heschel, though rabbinic thought is not systematic, it nevertheless represents a cohesive worldview that must be elicited from the corpus of rabbinic literature. See Abraham J. Heschel, *Torah min ha-Shamayim* (London: Soncino Press, 1962), 1:viii. It is significant that Heschel translated

the title of this work as *"Theology* of Ancient Judaism." Compare Steven Schwarzschild's unsubstantiated contention that a systematic rabbinic theology is not only desirable but possible. See Menachem Kellner, ed., *The Pursuit of the Ideal: Jewish Writings of Steven Schwarzschild* (Albany: State University of New York Press, 1990), 293 n. 64.

52. See Cohon, *Jewish Theology*, 43.

53. For example, despite his legion attempts to distinguish Jewish theology from Christian theology, Kaufmann Kohler's pioneering work, *Jewish Theology*, is heavily influenced by contemporary Protestant thought. Despite his insistence that Jewish theology be systematic, he fails in the attempt to present it as such.

54. From a letter from Schechter to Max Heller, quoted in Sefton Tempkin, "Solomon Schechter and Max Heller," *Conservative Judaism* 16:1 (Winter 1962): 55.

55. Heschel, *Moral Grandeur*, 4.

56. On the historical function and present problematics of natural theology and on the role of reason in Christian theology, see Macquarrie, *Principles of Christian Theology*, 39–48.

57. Heschel, *God in Search of Man*, 23 n. 8.

58. Ibid., 8–10.

59. Emil Fackenheim, *Quest for Past and Future* (Boston: Beacon Press, 1968), 99.

60. Levi ben Gershon (Gersonides), *Milhamot ha-Shem* (Leipzig, 1866), 150. See Norbert Samuelson, "Philosophical and Religious Authority in the Thought of Maimonides and Gersonides," *Central Conference of American Rabbis Journal* 16, no. 4 (October 1969): 31–43. Philosophy was considered superfluous at best and an entrée to heresy at worst by many Jewish thinkers. I hope elsewhere to demonstrate that if most of medieval Jewish philosophical literature had been discarded, it would have had little substantial impact on the subsequent development of Jewish religious thought. As a largely elitist endeavor, Jewish philosophical speculation had little lasting impact on Jewish life, unlike Jewish mysticism, which did. The criteria discussed later of acceptance by the faith community would historically disqualify much of medieval Jewish philosophical thought from claiming to be a valid expression of Jewish theology.

61. Bahya ibn Pakudah, *The Book of Direction to the Duties of the Heart*, trans. Menahem M. Mansoor (London: Routledge and Kegan Paul, 1973), 113.

62. "Rationality" has a wide variety of possible meanings. See, e.g., Bryan Wilson, *Rationality* (New York: Harper and Row, 1971). See Bamberger, *Search for Jewish Theology*, 4; Heschel, *God in Search of Man*, 20; Jacobs, *Faith*, 41–65, 201–9.

63. Fackenheim, *Quest for Past and Future*, 75.

64. Jacobs, *Jewish Theology*, 5.

65. *Talmud, Berakhot* 55a.

66. Compare the similar model for Christian theology advocated by Macquarrie, *Principles of Christian Theology*, 50. I believe that while for Christian theological discourse, descriptive theology is a departure (as Macquarrie suggests), for Jewish theology it would represent continuity with the past, particularly with regard to biblical, midrashic, kabbalistic, and late medieval and early modern east European traditional Jewish religious literature.

67. On "God, Torah, and Israel," see, e.g., Abraham J. Heschel, "God, Torah and Israel," in his *Moral Grandeur*, 191–208; Isaiah Tishbi, "Al Mekorei ha-Ma'amar Kudsha Berikh hu, Oraita ve-Yisrael—had hu," *Kiryet Sefer* 50 (1975): 480–92, 668–74.

68. *Pesikta de-Rav Kahana*, ed. Solomon Buber (Lyck: Mekitzei Nirdamim, 1868), 102a.

69. As an analogy, there are similarities and differences between the two things compared. In that theology demands commitment while aesthetics and art do not, the analogy cannot apply. See Bamberger, *Search for Jewish Theology*, 87. On Judaism as an art form, see, e.g., Alan Lazaroff, "Judaism as an Art," *Judaism* 30 (Summer 1981): 353–63; Sherwin, *In Partnership*, 9–15.

70. *Seder Eliyahu Rabbah ve-Seder Eliyahu Zuta*, ed. Meir Friedmann (Vienna: Ahiyasaf, 1904), sec. "Zuta," chap. 2, p. 172.

71. See, e.g., Idel, *Kabbalah*, 215.

72. On the expression, "a donkey carrying books," see Israel Davidson, *Otzar ha-Mashalim ve-ha-Pitgamim* (Jerusalem: Mosad ha-Rav Kook, 1969), no. 2851, p. 171 n. 39.

73. See, e.g., *Sefer ha-Bahir*, ed. Reuven Margaliot (Jerusalem: Mosad ha-Rav Kook, 1951), par. 115, p. 51. Note Judah Halevi, *Kuzari*, trans. Hartwig Hirschfield (New York: Schocken, 1964), 4:3, p. 202.

74. See, e.g., Joseph Karo, *Shulhan Arukh* (Reprint: Vilna: Romm, 1911), sec. "Yoreh De'ah," 274:7.

75. See David ibn Zimra, *Teshuvot ha-Radbaz* (Furth, 1781), vol. 3, no. 643, p. 43b. See discussion in Idel, *Kabbalah*, 214–15, and sources noted there.

76. *Talmud, Baba Metzia* 59a–b.

77. See, e.g., the interpretation of the Talmudic phrase "a partner in the work of creation" (*Talmud, Sabbath* 10a) in the beginning of Jacob ben Asher's *Arba'ah Turim* (New York: Grossman, n.d.), sec. "Hoshen Mishpat," where scholars of any generation who correctly interpret the Torah and declare a correct legal judgment are considered God's partners in the work of creation. On the human being as a coauthor of the Torah, see, e.g., Idel, *Kabbalah*, 215.

78. Meir ibn Gabbai, *Avodat ha-Kodesh* (Jerusalem: Levin-Epstein, 1954), pt. 3, chap. 23, pp. 85b–86a.

79. *Exodus Rabbah* 28:6, in *Midrash Rabbah*; see also *Midrash Tanhuma* [ha-Nidpas] (Jerusalem: Levin-Epstein, 1964), sec. "Yitro," no. 11, p. 96.

80. See Moses Hayyim Ephraim of Sudlykow, *Degel Mahaneh Ephraim*, sec. "Bereshit," p. 6.

81. Loew, *Netivot Olam*, 1:32.

82. Hayyim ben Betzalel, *Sefer ha-Hayyim* (Jerusalem: Weinfeld, 1968), sec. "Sefer Zechuyot," 1:1, p. 4.

83. Horowitz, *Shnei Luhot ha-Brit*, vol. 1, sec. "Beth David," pp. 39a–b (pp. 25b–26a in the Amsterdam edition).

84. See, e.g., Hayyim Vital, *Sha'ar ha-Gilgulim* (Jerusalem: Eshel, 1963), chap. 17, p. 48. Note Scholem, *On the Kabbalah and Its Symbolism*, 65, and sources noted there.

85. Jacobs, *Jewish Theology*, 6, 1. As Monford Harris notes, "An authentic Jewish theology always speaks in terms of specific historic situations." See Harris, "Interim Theology," *Judaism* 7 (Fall 1958): 305. For Harris, "The existence in the world of Jewish existence and how each Jew is to link his private existence to Jewish existence sets into motion a *Jewish* theological enterprise" (302).

86. Arthur A. Cohen, *The Natural and the Supernatural Jew* (New York: McGraw-Hill, 1964), 288. See also Cohen, "Theology," in , eds., *Contemporary Jewish Religious Thought*, ed. Arthur A. Cohen and Paul Mendes-Flohr (New York: Scribner's, 1987), 971–81.

Chapter 4

1. See, e.g., Fredrick Copelston, *A History of Philosophy: Medieval Philosophy* (Garden City, N.Y.: Image Books, 1962), 2:177–86.

2. On "depth-theology," see, e.g., Heschel, *Insecurity of Freedom*, 115–26.

3. This approach reflects the influence of phenomenological method, with its three levels of inquiry: the prereflective, the descriptive, and the reflective. It also reflects the influence of my mentor, Abraham Joshua Heschel, who utilized phenomenological method. For a similar approach using phenomenological method in Christian theology, see Macquarrie, *Principles of Christian Theology*, 30–36. In my view, this approach merely states in another way what many Jewish thinkers have been doing throughout the ages. However, while many Jewish thinkers not profoundly influenced by Jewish philosophy developed what is called here "descriptive theology," Jewish philosophers utilized philosophical theology. The utilization of both would seem well advised. Cohon's observation, in his *Jewish Theology*, 27, that "even when employing the methods of philosophy, the theologian utilizes them in a somewhat different way and with a different object in mind," is relevant.

4. See Louis Jacobs, *Hasidic Thought* (New York: Behrman House, 1976), 238.

5. See Abraham J. Twerski, *Let Us Make Man* (New York: CIS, 1987), 1.

6. Heschel, *God in Search of Man*, 3.

7. Cited in Paul Edwards, "Meaning and Value of Life," in *The Encyclopedia of Philosophy*, ed. Paul Edwards (New York: Macmillan, 1972), 3:468.

8. Joseph Campbell, *The Power of Myth* (New York: Doubleday, 1988), 229.

9. See Edwards, "Meaning and Value of Life," 468.

10. Carl G. Jung, *Modern Man in Search of a Soul*, trans. W. S. Dell and Cary E. Barnes (New York: Harcourt Brace, 1933), 61, 66.

11. Herman Hesse, *Reflections*, trans. Ralph Manheim (New York: Farrar, Straus and Giroux, 1974), 35.

12. Harold Kushner, *When All You've Ever Wanted Isn't Enough: The Search for a Life That Matters* (New York: Pocket Books, 1986), 20.

13. John Paul II, *Fides et Ratio: On the Relationship between Faith and Reason* (Boston: Pauline Books, 1998), 39, 40, 16.

14. Raymond Angelo Belliotti, *What Is the Meaning of Human Life?* (Atlanta: Rodopi, 2001), 7, 86.

15. Irving Singer, *Meaning in Life* (New York: Free Press, 1992), 24.

16. Ludwig Wittgenstein, *Notebooks 1914–1916*, trans. G. E. Anscome (New York: Harper and Brothers, 1961), 74.

17. See, e.g., Jacobs, *Faith*, 62–64.

18. Albert Camus, *The Myth of Sisyphus*, trans. Justin O'Brien (New York: Knopf, 1955), 3.

19. William Shakespeare, *Macbeth*, act 5, scene 5.

20. Ibn Pakudah, *The Book of Direction to the Duties of the Heart*, 109.

21. *Avot d'Rabbi Natan*, ed. Solomon Schechter (Vienna, 1887), version A, chap. 16.

22. Heschel, *God in Search of Man*, 169.

23. Solomon ibn Gabirol, *The Fountain of Life*, trans. Alfred B. Jacob (Stanwood, Wash.: Sabian, 1987), 3.

24. See, e.g., Elie Wiesel, *Souls on Fire* (New York: Random House, 1972), 158.

25. Cited in Isaac Heinemann, "The Purpose of Human Existence as Seen by Greco-Roman Antiquity and the Jewish Middle Ages," 129. This article was graciously sent to me by the library of the Jewish Theological Seminary of America as a separate pamphlet; its source is unclear.

26. Ibid., 141–51.

27. Ibid., 144.

28. See, e.g., Menahem Kellner, *Maimonides on Human Perfection* (Atlanta: Scholars Press, 1990).

29. Maimonides to *Mishnah, Abot* 1:14 in Maimonides' *Commentary on the Mishnah*. See Arthur David, trans., *Moses Maimonides: The Commentary to Mishnah Abot* (New York: Bloch, 1968), 14.

30. According to a midrashic text, Abraham, Judah, Job, and the Messiah come to the recognition of God through their own independent effort. See *Numbers Rabbah*, sec. "Naso," 14:2, in *Midrash Rabbah*.

31. See Eliezer Ashkenazi, *Sefer Ma'aseh ha-shem* (Venice, 1583), sec. "Ma'aseh Abot," chaps. 1, 2.

32. *Genesis Rabbah* 38:13 in *Midrash Rabbah*.

33. "Ma'aseh Avraham," in *Beit ha-Midrash*, ed. Adolph Jellenik (Jerusalem: Wahrmann, 1967), 2:118–19. See also Louis Ginzberg, *The Legends of the Jews* (Philadelphia: Jewish Publication Society, 1968), 1:195–203, and sources noted there.

34. *Genesis Rabbah* 39:1 in *Midrash Rabbah*.

35. Martin Buber, *I and Thou*, trans. Ronald Smith (New York: Scribner's, 1958), 110–11.

36. *Deuteronomy Rabbah* 4:4 in *Midrash Rabbah*.

37. *Mishnah, Abot* 3:14.

38. Leo Baeck, *The Essence of Judaism* (New York: Schocken, 1948), 119, 121.

39. Abraham J. Heschel, *Man Is Not Alone* (Philadelphia: Jewish Publication Society, 1951), 91, 241–42.

40. Judah Loew, *Be'er ha-Golah* (New York: Judaica Press, 1969), chap. 2, p. 38.

41. *Genesis Rabbah* 11:6 in *Midrash Rabbah*.

42. Judah Loew, *Tiferet Yisrael* (New York: Judaica Press, 1969), chap. 69, p. 216.

43. Ibid., chap. 69, p. 216.

44. *Zohar* vol. 1, p. 5a.

45. For the Hebrew original, see Yonah David, ed., *The Poems of Amittay* [in Hebrew] (Jerusalem: Achshav, 1975), 20–24.

46. *Talmud, Berakhot* 10a.

47. See the commentary of Samuel of Uceda on *Mishnah, Abot* 1:4 in his *Midrash Shmuel*, 16a.

48. See Jonah Gerondi, *Sha'arey Teshuvah* [*Gates of Repentance*], ed. and trans. Shraga Silverstein (New York: Feldheim, 1971), 2:26, p. 115.

49. *Talmud, Sanhedrin* 37–38.

50. Joseph B. Soloveichik, "Redemption, Prayer, Talmud Torah," *Tradition* 17 (1978): 64.

51. Joseph B. Soloveichik, *Halakhic Man*, trans. Lawrence Kaplan (Philadelphia: Jewish Publication Society, 1983), 101.

52. *Talmud, Sota* 14a.

53. See, e.g., *Talmud, Sabbath* 133b.

54. See David S. Shapiro, "The Doctrine of the Image of God and *Imitatio Dei*," *Judaism* 12 (Winter, 1963): 57–77.

55. This statement is attributed to Menahem Mendel Morgenstern, known as the "Rabbi of Kotzk"; see *Emet mei-Kotzk Titzmah* (Bnai Brak: Nezah, 1961), 51–52. A similar statement is attributed to Israel Friedman, the "Maggid of Ruzhyn"; see *Knesset Yisrael* (Warsaw: n.p., 1906), 16–17.

56. Moses Maimonides, *The Eight Chapters of Maimonides on Ethics*, ed. and trans. Joseph Gorfinkle (New York: Columbia University Press, 1912), 42 (Hebrew section), 84 (English section).

57. Soloveichik, *Halakhic Man*, 116.

58. Nahman of Bratzlav, *Likkutei Maharan* (1866; reprint, New York: Bratslaver, 1966), pt. 2, p. 10b. See Arthur Green, *Tormented Master* (University: University of Alabama Press, 1979), 341.

59. See Byron L. Sherwin, *Mystical Theology and Social Dissent* (London: Oxford University Press, 1982), 118–21.

60. Judah Loew, *Derekh Hayyim* (New York: Judaica Press, 1969), chap. 3, p. 148.

61. Moses Maimonides, *Mishneh Torah* [with commentaries], 6 vols. (reprint, New York: Friedman, 1963), sec. "Sefer Mada—Hilkhot Teshuvah," 5:3–4.

62. See Sherwin, *Mystical Theology and Social Dissent*, 119.

63. See Abraham J. Heschel, *Kotzk* [in Yiddish] Tel Aviv: Menorah, 1973, vol. 1, pp. 131–36.

64. See Abraham J. Heschel, *The Earth Is the Lord's* (New York: Henry Schuman, 1950), 9; see also Jakob Petuchowski, "The Beauty of God," in Edelheit, *Life of Covenant*, 125–31.

65. Loew, *Derekh Hayyim*, sec. 2, p. 24, and "Introduction," p. 9; also Loew's *Hiddushei Aggadot* (New York: Judaica Press, 1969), 3:40.

Chapter 5

1. See Ryle, *Concept of Mind*.

2. See, e.g., John Cottingham, *On the Meaning of Life* (London: Routledge, 2003), 72.

3. See Ben Zion Bokser, ed. and trans., *The Prayerbook* (New York: Hebrew Publishing, 1961), 7. A version of this text is also recited during the concluding service (*Ne'ilah*) for the Day of Atonement. See Philip Birnbaum, *High Holiday Prayerbook* (New York: Hebrew Publishing, 1951), 1006; Daniel Goldschmidt, *Mahazor Le-Yamim Nora'im—Yom Kippur* (New York: Leo Baeck Institute, 1970), 782.

4. *Talmud, Sabbath* 88a. See Emil Fackenheim, "Can There Be Judaism without Revelation?" in his *Quest for Past and Future*.

5. See, e.g., *Genesis Rabbah* 1:1, in *Midrash Rabbah*, on the Torah as a blueprint for creation.

6. *Exodus Rabbah* 32:2 in *Midrash Rabbah*.

7. See Nelson Gleuck, *Hesed in the Bible* (New York: Ktav, 1975).

8. Irving Singer, *The Pursuit of Love* (Baltimore: Johns Hopkins University Press, 1994), 2.

9. See, e.g., Elijah Di Vidas, *Reshit Hokhmah* (Jerusalem: Or ha-Musar, 1984), sec. "Shaar ha-Ahavah," vol. 1, chap. 2, p. 367, quoting *Zohar*, vol. 3, p. 267b.

10. Singer, *Pursuit of Love*, 13.

11. See, e.g., Sherwin, *Mystical Theology and Social Dissent*, 135, and sources noted there.

12. Loew, *Netivot Olam*, sec. "Ahavat ha-Shem," chap. 1, p. 38.

13. See, e.g., Henry Slonimsky, *Essays* (Chicago: Quadrangle Books, 1967), 15.

14. *Talmud, Sanhedrin* 37–38.

15. *Numbers Rabbah* 12:8 in *Midrash Rabbah*. See also *Talmud, Ta'anit* 26b; *Song of Songs Rabbah* 3:11 in *Midrash Rabbah*; *Exodus Rabbah* 52:5 in *Midrash Rabbah*; *Numbers Rabbah* 12:8 in *Midrash Rabbah*; *Midrash Tanhuma*, ed. Solomon Buber (Vilna: Romm, 1885); sec. "Pekuday," 8, vol. 2, p. 6a, and sec. "Numbers--Ba-midbar," 5, p. 3a; *Pesikta de- Rav Kahana*, ed. Bernard Mandelbaum (New York: Jewish Theological Seminary, 1962), 1:3, 22:5, vol. 1, pp. 7, 329; *Pirke de Rabbi Eliezer* (New York: Ohm, 1946), chap. 41, p. 97b. For scriptural roots of the portrayal of Israel as God's bride, see, e.g., Isa. 62:5; Jer. 2:1–3; Hosea 2:16–18; Ezek. 16, 23. Some scholars understand certain biblical festivals as having been observed originally as celebrations of a sacred marriage between God and Israel. See, e.g., Helmer Ringrenn, *Israelite Religion* (Philadelphia: Fortress Press, 1966), 190, 198–99. See p. 197 on the Song of Songs as being rooted in the idea of a sacred marriage. This was the interpretation of the Song of Songs ascribed by subsequent Jewish and Christian exegetes. On "sacred marriage" rituals practiced by the medieval mystics, see Scholem, *On the Kabbalah and Its Symbolism*, 138–46.

16. On the Torah as a song, see, e.g., *Midrash on Psalms* [in Hebrew], ed. Solomon Buber (Vilna: Romm, 1891), 119:41, p. 249b: "David said, 'Oh how I love your Torah' (Ps. 119:97).... It is always with me. I have not neglected it at all. And because I have not neglected it, it has been to me not a burden, but a song."

17. Moses Hayyim Ephraim of Sudlykow, *Degel Mahaneh Ephraim*, sec. "Yitro," p. 111.

18. On biblical sources for the renewal of the covenant, see, e.g., Josh. 24:22–27; 2 Kings 23:3–4; Neh. 9:32–37, 10:1. The term "before the Lord," when discussing the covenant, refers to the renewal of the covenant.

19. See, e.g., Ringrenn, *Israelite Religion*, 193.

20. This is an oral tradition I heard years ago.

21. Rashi to Exod. 19:1, in *Mikra'ot Gedolot* [Hebrew scripture with commentaries], 5 vols. (New York: Tanach, 1959), paraphrasing *Talmud, Berakhot* 63b: "The Torah is as beloved every day to those who study it as the day it was given from Mount Sinai." See also Rashi to Deut. 11:13 and 26:16 in *Mikra'ot Gedolot*. Note *Midrash Tanhuma*, sec. "Ki-Tavoh, para." 3, vol. 2, p. 23b.

22. See Martin Buber, *Tales of the Hasidim: Later Masters*, trans. Olga Marx (New York: Schocken, 1948), 116.

23. See, e.g., Bokser, *Prayerbook*, 95.

24. *Sifre*, pars. 32–33, pp. 54–55.

25. Abraham J. Heschel, *A Passion for Truth* (New York: Farrar, Straus and Giroux, 1973), 186.

26. Ibid., 192.

27. Heschel, *God in Search of Man*, 74.

28. See Sherwin, *Mystical Theology and Social Dissent*, 131–32.

29. See Heschel, *Man Is Not Alone*, 93.

30. See ibid., 87.

31. See ibid., 164.

32. *Talmud, Megillah* 6b.

33. See Blaise Pascal, *Pensees*, trans. A. J. Krailsheimer (New York: Penguin Books, 1966), 149–53.

34. See Martin Buber, *Tales of the Hasidim: Early Masters*, trans. Olga Marx (New York: Schocken, 1947), 97.

35. Heschel, *Man Is Not Alone*, 162–63.

36. According to Hasidic theology, each Jew is *aiver ha-Skekhinah*, "a limb of God," a "divine member." This is similar to the Catholic idea that in being part of the church, one is part of the Corpus Christi, the Body of God. Dismemberment means separation from the divine. For Judaism, remembrance is an entrée to re-memberment. See Byron L. Sherwin, "*Corpus Domini*: Traces of the New Testament in East European Hasidism?" *Heythrop Journal* 35 (1994): 267–80.

37. Halevi, *Kuzari*, 1:21–26, pp. 46–47.

38. Three Jewish thinkers who relate fundamental ideas of Jewish theology to the holydays are the fifteenth-century Spanish commentator Isaac Arama, the sixteenth-century mystic Judah Loew of Prague, and the early twentieth-century German philosopher Franz Rosenzweig. See Isaac Arama, *Akedat Yitzhak* (Pressburgh, 1849), sermon no. 67, p. 99b. Arama relates six theological concepts to the festivals listed in Leviticus 23, as follows: Sabbath—creation, Passover—God's power, *Shavuot*—revelation, Rosh Hashanah—providence, Yom Kippur—repentance, *Sukkot*—immortality. See the discussion of Arama by Menahem Kellner, *Dogma in Medieval Jewish Thought*, 159–61. On Judah

Loew, see Sherwin, *Mystical Theology and Social Dissent*, 39–40. Rosenzweig relates the Sabbath and the "pilgrimage festivals" to creation, revelation, and redemption. See Franz Rosenzweig, *The Star of Redemption*, trans. William H. Hallo (New York: Holt, Rinehart and Winston, 1970), 308–28.

39. This text in the Haggadah is based on *Mishnah, Pesahim* 10:5, 6. See the insightful analysis by Baruch M. Bokser, *The Origins of the Seder* (Berkeley: University of California Press, 1984), 86–87.

40. See, e.g., Monford Harris, "The Passover Seder: On Entering the Order of History," *Judaism* 25 (Spring 1976): 167–74.

41. Certain Jews, such as Yemenites and Russian Caucasians, do "reenact" the Exodus as part of their Passover observance. However, this is an ethnic curiosity rather than a normative practice.

42. Menahem Nahum of Chernobyl, *Ma'or Einayim* (Jerusalem: n.p., 1966), sec. "Tzav," pp. 130–31.

43. Heschel, *God in Search of Man*, 212.

44. See, e.g., Richard Rubenstein, *Power Struggle* (New York: Scribner's, 1974), 128.

45. Heschel, *The Earth Is the Lord's*, 107.

Chapter 6

1. Yoetz of Rakatz, *Siah Sarfei Kodesh* (Lodz, Poland: n.p., 1931), pt. 2, p. 116.

2. See, e.g., ibid., pt. 2, p. 29b; Heschel, *The Earth Is the Lord's*, 106–7.

3. See, e.g., Martin Buber, *Hasidism and Modern Man*, trans. Maurice Friedman (New York: Horizon Press, 1958), 130–36.

4. Heschel, *God in Search of Man*, 137.

5. *The Epic of Gilgamesh*, trans. N. K. Sanders (New York: Penguin Books, 1972).

6. Rosenzweig, *Star of Redemption*, 3–5.

7. Compare the translation in Pascal, *Pensees*, par. 68.

8. Heschel, *Passion for Truth*, 156–65.

9. Yoetz of Rakatz, *Siah Sarfei Kodesh*, pt. 3, p. 5.

10. Cited in Abraham Menes, "Patterns of Jewish Scholarship in Eastern Europe," in *The Jews*, ed. Louis Finkelstein (Philadelphia: Jewish Publication Society, 1928), 174.

11. Moses Hayyim Luzzatto, *Mesillat Yesharim—The Path of the Upright*, trans. Mordecai M. Kaplan (Philadelphia: Jewish Publication Society, 1936), 207–8, 212, 422.

12. See Buber, *Tales of the Hasidim: Early Masters*, 149.

13. On pride in Jewish ethics, see, e.g., Byron L. Sherwin and Seymour J. Cohen, *How to Be a Jew: Ethical Teachings of Judaism* (Northvale, N.J.: Jason Aronson, 1992), 81–90, and sources noted there. On the equation of pride

with idolatry, see, e.g., the Hasidic sources collected in *Leshon Hasidim* (Lwow, 1876), 36.

14. See, e.g., Menahem Nahum of Chernobyl, *Ma'or Einayim* (Jerusalem: n.p., 1966), 39, 353–54.

15. See, e.g., sources cited in Aryeh Kaplan, *The Light Beyond: Adventures in Hasidic Thought* (New York: Maznaim, 1981), 287–300. This insight was later discussed by psychoanalyst Heinz Kohut in his *Analysis of the Self* (New York: International Universities Press, 1971).

16. Silvano Arieti, *Creativity* (New York: Basic Books, 1976), 380.

17. See Alexander Altmann, *Studies in Religious Philosophy and Mysticism* (Ithaca, N.Y.: Cornell University Press, 1969), 4.

18. Joseph Albo, *Sefer ha-Ikkarim—The Book of Principles*, trans. Isaac Husik (Philadelphia: Jewish Publication Society, 1946), 3:6, vol. 3, p. 54.

19. Judah Loew, *Netzah Yisrael* (New York: Judaica Press, 1969), chap. 51, p. 195. See Sherwin, *Mystical Theology and Social Dissent*, 137.

20. Di Vidas, *Reshit Hokhmah*, sec. "Sha'ar Ha-Ahavah," chap. 3, sec. 7.

21. Shabbtai Sheftel Horowitz, *Shefa Tal* (Frankfurt, 1719), "Introduction." See the discussion of this motif and of this text in Louis Jacobs, "The Doctrine of the 'Divine Spark' in Man in Jewish Sources," in *Studies in Rationalism, Judaism and Universalism*, ed. Raphal Loewe (New York: Humanities Press, 1966), 87–196.

22. Loew, *Derekh Hayyim*, 3:4, p. 143.

23. *Zohar*, vol. 2, p. 244a.

24. See Sherwin, *Mystical Theology and Social Dissent*, 107–23; Byron L. Sherwin, *Toward a Jewish Theology* (Lewiston, N.Y.: Edwin Mellen Press, 1991), 132–58.

25. *Talmud, Berakhot* 63a.

26. Jacob Joseph of Polnoyye, *Toledot Yaakov Yoseif* (Jerusalem: Sifrei ha-Musar Va-Hasidut, 1960), vol. 1, p. 51.

27. *Talmud, Berakhot* 62a.

28. See Heschel, *God in Search of Man*, 99.

29. Maimonides, *Mishneh Torah*, sec. "Sefer ha-Mada--Hilkhot Yesodei ha-Torah," 2:2; note Bahya ibn Pakudah, *Duties of the Heart*, trans. Moses Hyamson (Jerusalem: Boys Town, 1965), 1, 133.

30. Levi ben Gershon (Gersonides), *Commentary on the Torah*, 113a–b.

31. Heschel, *God in Search of Man*, 77.

32. T. Carmi, ed., *The Penguin Book of Hebrew Verse* (New York: Penguin Books, 1981), 316.

33. See Heschel, *God in Search of Man*, 51; Nahmanides to Exod. 13:16 in *Mikra'ot Gedolot*.

34. Cited in Heschel, *God in Search of Man*, 48.

35. See *Talmud, Berakhot* 60b.

36. Heschel, *God in Search of Man*, 49.

37. Buber, *Tales of the Hasidim: Early Masters*, 289.

38. For another version of this story, see Israel Arten, *Emet ve-Emunah* (Jerusalem: n.p., 1969), 19.

39. See Simeon Mendel of Guvarchov, *Sefer Ba'al Shem Tov* (Lodz, Poland: n.p., 1938), vol. 1, p. 144, n. 45.

40. *Likkutim Yesharim* (Lwow, 1863), 15b.

41. See, e.g., Sherwin, *Mystical Theology and Social Dissent*, 124–43; Scholem, *Messianic Idea in Judaism*, 203–27.

42. Heschel, *The Earth Is the Lord's*, 83.

43. Søren Kierkegaard, *Training in Christianity*, trans. Walter Lowrie (Princeton, N.J.: Princeton University Press, 1944), 201.

44. See Simeon Mendel of Guvarchov, *Sefer Ba'al Shem Tov*, 122.

45. See Scholem, *On the Kabbalah and Its Symbolism*, 47.

46. On the development of the phrase "God, Torah and Israel are One," see Isaiah Tishbi, "Al Makorei ha-Ma'amar Kudsha Brikh hu, Torah ve-Yisrael had hu," *Kiryat Sefer* 50 (1975): 668–74; see also Heschel, *Moral Grandeur*, 191–205.

47. Nathan Nata Shapiro, *Megaleh Amukot—Ve-Ethanan* (Bnai Brak: n.p., 1992), no. 186, p. 155.

48. See, e.g., Herman A. Glatt, *He Spoke in Parables: The Life and Works of the Dubnow Maggid* (New York: Bithmar, 1957), 60.

49. Saadya Gaon, *The Book of Beliefs and Opinions*, trans. Samuel Rosenblatt (New Haven, Conn.: Yale University Press, 1948), bk. 3, sec. 7, p. 158.

50. *Talmud, Sabbath* 31a. The usual modern Hebrew word for "religion" is *dat*, a term already found in the biblical book of Esther. *Dat yehudi* is often used to denote "Judaism." But *dat* does not denote "religion." Rather, it refers to "customary practices." It sometimes is used with *din* (law), as when describing a practice as *ke-dat ve-din* (according to customary practice and law). In the Jewish wedding ceremony, one finds the phrase *ke-dat moshe ve-yisrael*, i.e., the marriage is established "according to the customary practices of Moses and Israel."

51. See Levi Yitzhak of Berditchev, *Kedushat Levi* (Jerusalem: Mosad l'Hotzaat Sifrei ha-Musar ve-ha-Hasidut, 1958), 33. Note Eugene Kullman, "Tikvah and Mitzvah," *Conservative Judaism* 10, no. 4 (Summer 1956): 34–5.

52. Baeck, *Essence of Judaism*, 155.

53. See Jacobs, *Hasidic Thought*, 205.

54. On the "Kingdom of Heaven," see, e.g., Schechter, *Aspects of Rabbinic Theology*, 65–115.

55. *Pirkei d'Rabbi Eliezer*, trans. Gerald Friedlander (London: n.p., 1916), chap. 11, p. 80.

56. *Zohar* vol. 3, pp. 113a–b.

57. See Sherwin, *Kabbalah*, 105–33.

58. *Zohar* vol. 3, p. 122a.

59. *Genesis Rabbah* 2:4 in *Midrash Rabbah*, as cited in Baeck, *Essence of Judaism*, 167.

60. Baeck, *Essence of Judaism*, 170.

61. Horowitz, *Shnei Luhot ha-Brit*, sec. "Sha'arei Teshuvah," vol. 3, p. 175b; see also Albo, *Sefer ha-Ikkarim* 4:25, pp. 225–26.

62. *Mishnah, Abot* 5:16.

63. Di Vidas, *Reshit Hokhmah* (Tel Aviv: Esther Press, n.d.), sec. "Sha'ar ha-Teshuvah," chap. 3, p. 113a.

64. *Pesikta Rabbati*, 44:9, pp. 184b–185a.

65. H. Shirman, ed., *Solomon ibn Gabirol: Selected Poems* [in Hebrew] (Jerusalem: Schocken, 1964), "Keter Malkhut," p. 1.

Chapter 7

1. Baeck, *The Essence of Judaism*, 97–98.

2. In general, see, e.g., John Hick, ed., *The Existence of God* (New York: Macmillan, 1964). On "proofs" for the existence of God in medieval Jewish philosophical theology, see, e.g., Harry A. Wolfson, "Notes of Proofs of the Existence of God," *Hebrew Union College Annual* 1 (1924): 575–96. For an example of the "argument from design," see, e.g., ibn Pakudah, *The Book of Direction to the Duties of the Heart*, 109.

3. See, e.g., William Paley, "The Watch and the Watchmaker," in Hick, *The Existence of God*, 99–104; on critiques of the "argument from design," see pp. 104–36, especially those of David Hume and John Stuart Mill, pp. 104–36.

4. On the "problem of evil" or "theodicy" in Jewish theology, see, e.g., Byron L. Sherwin, *Studies in Jewish Theology* (London: Vallentine Mitchell, 2007), 46–58.

5. See, e.g., Moses Maimonides, *Guide of the Perplexed*, trans. Shlomo Pines (Chicago: University of Chicago Press, 1963), bk. 3, chap. 12, pp. 441–45.

6. See, e.g., Robert Gordis, *The Book of God and Man* (Chicago: University of Chicago Press, 1965), 135–56.

7. Camus, *Myth of Sisyphus*, 3.

8. *Beit ha-Midrash*, "Midrash va-Yoshah," vol. 1, p. 55.

9. Cited in Ernst Simon, "Martin Buber: His Way between Thought and Deed," *Jewish Frontier,* 15:2 February 1948, 26.

10. See, e.g., Heschel, "Confusion of Good and Evil," in his *Insecurity of Freedom*, 127–50.

11. See Heschel, *Passion for Truth*, 40.

12. Moses Hayyim Ephraimof Sudlykow, *Degel Mahaneh Efraim*, sec. "Ekev," pp. 236–37.

13. I could not find a source for this limerick.

14. *Talmud, Sabbath* 88b.

15. Moses Nahmanides (Ramban), *Kitve Rabbenu Moshe ben Nahman*, ed. Charles Chavel (Jerusalem: Mosad ha-Rav Kook, 1963), vol. 1, p. 193.

16. *Mishnah, Abot* 4:5.

17. *Genesis Rabbah* 39:1, in *Midrash Rabbah*.

18. See Heschel, *Passion for Truth*, 272–75.

19. Isaac Bashevis Singer, *Gifts* (Philadelphia: Jewish Publication Society, 1985), 11.

20. *Genesis Rabbah* 3:7, 9:2, in *Midrash Rabbah; Midrash on Psalms*, 34:1, p. 123a.

21. See, e.g., Abraham J. Heschel, *The Prophets* (Philadelphia: Jewish Publication Society, 1962), 221–67.

22. For a comparison of the doctrine of divine retribution to the laws of nature, see Hans Kelsen, "Causality and Retribution," *Journal of the Philosophy of Science* 8 (1941): 533–56; also in his *Society and Nature* (Chicago: University of Chicago Press, 1943).

23. David Hume, *Dialogues Concerning Natural Religion* (New York: Hafner, 1966), 66.

24. See, e.g., Maimonides, *Guide of the Perplexed*, bk. 3, chap. 10, p. 439: "all evils are privations."

25. The term "dysteleological surd" was coined by Edgar S. Brightman, *A Philosophy of Religion* (New York: Prentice Hall, 1940).

26. See, e.g., Sherwin, *Studies in Jewish Theology*, 46–74.

27. I could not relocate the exact source of this quote, which I believe is found in Dostoyevsky's *Brothers Karamazov*.

28. See, e.g., Heschel, *The Prophets*, 270–78.

29. See Green, *Tormented Master*, 341–44.

30. *Talmud, Hullin* 60b.

31. See, e.g., Gershom Scholem, *Major Trends in Jewish Mysticism* (New York: Schocken, 1941), 260–78; Louis Jacobs, *Seeker of Unity* (New York: Basic Books, 1966), 49–63.

32. See, e.g., Sherwin, *Kabbalah*, 47–84.

33. See, e.g., Loew, *Hiddushei Aggadot*, vol. 2, p. 89; Sherwin, *Mystical Theology and Social Dissent*, 70–82; Heschel, *God in Search of Man*, 336–48, and sources noted on p. 347 n. 10. Compare the notions of polarity as a way of apprehending truth in Morris Raphael Cohen, *Reason and Nature* (New York: Harcourt Brace, 1931), and Alan Watts, *The Two Hands of God* (New York: Collier, 1969).

34. *Midrash Temurah* in *Beit ha-Midrash*, vol. 1, p. 106.

35. *Sefer Yetzirah* (Jerusalem: Levin-Epstein, 1965), chap. 4, par. 4, p. 20b.

36. *Sefer ha-Bahir,* par. 162, p. 71. For the roots of the idea of an evil or demonic element of God in the Bible, see the discussion of Exodus 4 in Ringrenn, *Israelite Religion,* 73.

37. See, e.g., Heschel, *Moral Grandeur,* 159.

38. See, e.g., Heschel, *The Prophets;* Heschel, *Moral Grandeur,* 182–84.

39. See, e.g., *Talmud, Megillah* 29a; *Talmud, Hagiga* 15a; *Mekhilta de Rabbi Yishmael,* chap. 14, sec. "Bo," p. 52; see also Heschel, *Torah min ha-Shamayim,* vol. 1, pp. 65–92.

40. *Pesikta de-Rav Kahana,* ed. Mandelbaum, vol. 2, 25:1, p. 380.

41. *Zohar,* vol. 2, p. 65b.

42. See Daniel Jeremy Silver, *Maimonidean Criticism and the Maimonides Controversy* (Leiden: Brill, 1965), 139.

43. Arthur Green, *Seek My Face, Speak My Name* (Northvale, N.J.: Jason Aronson, 1992), 66.

44. See Heschel, *Man Is Not Alone,* 215. See the discussion and earlier sources brought in the sixteenth-century work, Horowitz, *Shnei Luhot ha-Brit,* "The Great Gate," pp. 45b–57a.

45. See, e.g., Eliezer Berkovits, *God, Man and History* (New York: Jonathan David, 1959), 79.

46. See, e.g., Loew, *Derekh Hayyim,* on *Mishnah, Abot* 3:15, p. 148.

47. Levi Yitzhak of Berditchev, *Kedushat Levi* (Brooklyn: Derbarendiger, 1966), sec. "Naso," pp. 315–16; see also Horowitz, *Shnei Luhot ha-Brit,* 46a.

48. See, e.g., Sherwin, *Kabbalah,* 119–34.

49. *Midrash on Psalms,* chap. 26, p. 166b.

50. *Sifre,* par. 346, pp. 403–4.

51. *Talmud, Sabbath* 10a.

52. See Horowitz, *Shnei Luhot ha-Brit,* vol. 3, sec. "Rosh ha-Shanah," p. 152b.

53. *Midrash on Psalms* 14:6, pp. 57b–58a.

54. *Zohar* vol. 3, p. 77b; see Heschel, *Moral Grandeur,* 163–72.

Chapter 8

1. *Beit ha-Midrash,* vol. 1, p. 55.

2. *Talmud, Sukkah* 52a.

3. See, e.g., Moses Maimonides, *Epistle to Yemen* [in Hebrew] in Moses Maimonides, *Iggarot* (Jerusalem: Mosad ha-Rav Kook, 1944), 69–193. Note that in the nineteenth century, some liberal Jewish thinkers interpreted the sociopolitical "Emancipation" of the Jews in messianic terms.

4. *Talmud, Sabbath* 88b.

5. See the discussion and sources brought in Heschel, *Torah min ha-Shamayim,* vol. 2, pp. 348–50.

6. *Exodus Rabbah* 47:2 in *Midrash Rabbah.*

7. *Talmud, Sabbath* 89a.

8. *Zohar* vol. 3, p. 152a.

9. Scholem, "The Meaning of the Torah in Jewish Mysticism," in his *On the Kabbalah and Its Symbolism*, 69–70.

10. See Heschel, *God in Search of Man*, 270–71.

11. *Talmud, Sanhedrin* 38b.

12. *Talmud, Erubin* 13b.

13. *Talmud, Sabbath* 88a.

14. See, e.g., the parable of the fish in water, *Talmud, Avodah Zarah* 3b; *Talmud, Sanhedrin* 99b: "a person is created to labor in the Torah; happy are those who are worthy of being receptacles of the Torah."

15. See Schechter, *Aspects of Rabbinic Theology*, 272–75, and sources noted there.

16. *Genesis Rabbah* 39:1 in *Midrash Rabbah*.

17. *Genesis Rabbah* 38:13 in *Midrash Rabbah*.

18. *Mekhilta de-Rabbi Yishmael*, 142.

19. *Palestinian Talmud* (Krotoschin, 1886), sec. "Yebamot" 4:12.

20. Joseph Klausner, *The Messianic Idea in Israel*, trans. W. F. Stinespring (New York: Macmillan, 1955), 13.

21. See *Lamentations Rabbah*, 1, 16, par. 51, in *Midrash Rabbah*; *Emet mei-Kotzk Titzmah*, par. 456, p. 141.

22. Heschel, *God in Search of Man*, 377.

23. *Talmud, Sanhedrin* 98a.

24. Buber, *Tales of the Hasidim: Later Masters*, 96.

25. Abraham J. Heschel, *Who Is Man?* (Stanford, Calif.: Stanford University Press, 1965), 119.

26. See Moshe Idel, *Messianic Mystics* (New Haven, Conn.: Yale University Press, 1998), 150; see Sherwin, *Kabbalah*, 210–19.

27. On the "spiritualization" of the Land of Israel and Jerusalem, see, e.g., Marc Saperstein, "The Land of Israel in Pre-modern Jewish Thought," in *The Land of Israel*, ed. Lawrence Hoffman (Notre Dame, Ind.: Notre Dame University Press, 1986), 201–4; Bernard Weinryb, *The Jews of Poland* (Philadelphia: Jewish Publication Society, 1973), 326–28.

28. *Sefer Ba'al Shem Tov al Nah ve-Aggadot ha-Shas* (Jerusalem: Otzar Midrash, 1968), 31.

29. See, e.g., Idel, *Messianic Mystics*, 70.

30. See, e.g., ibid., 84.

31. Menahem Nahum of Chernobyl, *Ma'or Einayim*, 110.

32. See, e.g., Louis Jacobs, *Principles of the Jewish Faith* (New York: Basic Books, 1964), 398–454.

33. Andrew Greeley, "Pie in the Sky While You're Alive: Americans' Belief in Life after Death and Supply-Side Religion," www.agreeley.com/articles/piesky.html (accessed November 16, 2006).

34. Leo Tolstoy, "A Confession," in *The Portable Tostoy*, ed. John Bayley (New York: Penguin Books, 1978), 683.

35. Heschel, *Moral Grandeur*, 373.

36. Ibn Pakudah, *The Book of Direction to the Duties of the Heart*, 278, 311–12, 351.

37. Luzzatto, *Mesillat Yesharim*, 28–30.

38. Albo, *Sefer ha-Ikkarim* , 4:32, p. 322.

39. See Rashi's commentary to Gen. 6:9 in *Mikra'ot Gedolot*.

40. *Talmud, Sanhedrin* 91a.

41. See *Zohar*, vol. 2, p. 244a. Note *Zohar* vol. 1, p. 103b. See Isaiah Tishbi, *Mishnat ha-Zohar* (Jerusalem: Mosad Bialik, 1957), vol. 2, p. 115.

42. See Bokser, *Prayerbook*, 5.

43. From an oral tradition.

44. On the human soul as a "part of God," as a spark of the divine flame, see Jacobs, "The Doctrine of the 'Divine Spark' in Man in Jewish Sources," 87–196.

45. Keats's letter to George and Georgiana Keats in John Keats, *Selected Poetry and Letters* (New York: Holt, Rinehart and Winston, 1964), 329.

46. See, e.g., Gershom Scholem, *On the Mystical Shape of the Godhead*, trans. Joachim Neugroschel (New York: Schocken, 1991), 197–250.

47. See Robert Browning as cited in Louis Untermeyer, ed., *A Concise Treasury of Great Poems* (New York: Simon and Schuster, 1942), 326.

48. *Mishnah, Abot* 4:16.

49. See Heschel, *Moral Grandeur*, 411.

50. Hans Jonas, "Immortality and the Modern Temper," *Harvard Theological Review* 55 (January 1962): 15–17.

Bibliography

Abrams, Elliot. *Faith or Fear*. New York: Free Press, 1997.

Adam, D. S. "Theology." In *Encyclopedia of Religion and Ethics*. 12 vols. New York: Scribner's, 1908.

Albo, Joseph. *Sefer ha-Ikkarim—The Book of Principles*. 6 vols. Translated by Isaac Husik. Philadelphia: Jewish Publication Society, 1946.

Altmann, Alexander. "The Eternality of Punishment: A Theological Controversy within the Amsterdam Rabbinate in the Thirties of the Seventeenth Century." *Proceedings of the American Academy for Jewish Research* 40 (1973): 1–88.

———. *Studies in Religious Philosophy and Mysticism*. Ithaca, N.Y.: Cornell University Press, 1969.

American Jewish Yearbook 1992. Philadelphia: Jewish Publication Society, 1992.

Arama, Isaac. *Akedat Yitzhak*. Pressburgh, 1849.

Arieti, Silvano. *Creativity*. New York: Basic Books, 1976.

Arten, Israel. *Emet ve-Emunah*. Jerusalem: n.p., 1969.

Ashkenazi, Eliezer. *Sefer Ma'aseh ha-Shem*. Venice, 1583.

Auerbach, Jerold. *Are We One?* London: Rutgers University Press, 2001.

———. *Rabbis and Lawyers*. Bloomington: Indiana University Press, 1990.

Avot d'Rabbi Natan. Edited by Solomon Schechter. Vienna, 1887.

Ayinn, Sidney. "Kant and Judaism." *Jewish Quarterly Review* 59 (1988): 9–23.

Baeck, Leo. *The Essence of Judaism*. New York: Schocken, 1948.

Bamberger, Bernard. *The Search for Jewish Theology*. New York: Behrman House, 1978.

Barack-Fishman, Sylvia. *Negotiating Both Sides of the Hyphen: Coalescence, Compartmentalization, and American Jewish Values.* Cincinnati: Publications of the Judaic Studies Department at the University of Cincinnati, 1995.

Baron, Salo W. *A Social and Religious History of the Jews.* Vol. 13. New York: Columbia University Press, 1969.

———. *Social and Religious History of the Jews.* Vol. 15. New York: Columbia University Press, 1973.

Beit ha-Midrash. 6 vols. Edited by Adolph Jellenik. Jerusalem: Wahrmann, 1967.

Belliotti, Raymond Angelo. *What Is the Meaning of Human Life?* Atlanta: Rodopi, 2001.

Ben Asher, Jacob. *Arba'ah Turim.* 4 vols. New York: Grossman, n.d.

Ben Betzalel, Hayyim. *Sefer ha-Hayyim.* Jerusalem: Weinfeld, 1968.

Bentwich, Norman. *Solomon Schechter: A Biography.* Philadelphia: Jewish Publication Society, 1938.

Berkovits, Eliezer. *God, Man and History.* New York: Jonathan David, 1959.

Birnbaum, Philip. *High Holiday Prayerbook.* New York: Hebrew Publishing, 1951.

Blenkinsopp, Joseph. *A History of Prophecy in Israel.* Philadelphia: Westminster Press, 1983.

Bokser, Baruch M. *The Origins of the Seder.* Berkeley: University of California Press, 1984.

Bokser, Ben Zion, ed. and trans. *The Prayerbook.* New York: Hebrew Publishing, 1961.

Borowitz, Eugene. *Masks Jews Wear.* Port Washington, N.Y.: Sh'ma, 1980.

———. *A New Theology in the Making.* Philadelphia: Westminster Press, 1968.

———. *Renewing the Covenant: A Theology for Post-modern Jews.* Philadelphia: Jewish Publication Society, 1991.

Breslauer, Daniel. "Alternatives in Jewish Theology." *Judaism* 30 (Spring 1981): 233–45.

Brightman, Edgar S. *A Philosophy of Religion.* New York: Prentice Hall, 1940.

Buber, Martin. *Hasidism and Modern Man.* Translated by Maurice Friedman. New York: Horizon Press, 1958.

———. *I and Thou.* Translated by Ronald Smith. New York: Scribner's, 1958.

———. *Tales of the Hasidism: Early Masters.* Translated by Olga Marx. New York: Schocken, 1947.

———. *Tales of the Hasidim: Later Masters.* Translated by Olga Marx. New York: Schocken, 1948.

Campbell, Joseph, ed. *The Portable Jung.* New York: Penguin, 1971.

———. *The Power of Myth.* New York: Doubleday, 1988.

Camus, Albert. *The Myth of Sisyphus.* Translated by Justin O'Brien. New York: Knopf, 1955.

Carmi, T., ed. *The Penguin Book of Hebrew Verse*. New York: Penguin, 1981.

Cohen, Arthur A. *The Myth of a Judeo-Christian Tradition*. New York: Schocken, 1971.

———. *The Natural and the Supernatural Jew*. New York: McGraw-Hill, 1964.

Cohen, Arthur A, and Paul Mendes-Flohr, eds. *Contemporary Jewish Religious Thought*. New York: Scribner's, 1987.

Cohen, Morris Raphael. *Reason and Nature*. New York: Harcourt Brace, 1931.

Cohen, Steven. *American Modernity and Jewish Identity*. New York: Tavistock, 1983.

———. *Content or Continuity?* New York: American Jewish Committee, 1991.

Cohen, Steven, and Arnold Eisen. *The Jew Within*. Bloomington: Indiana University Press, 2000.

Cohon, Samuel S. *Jewish Theology*. Assen, Netherlands: Royal Vangorcum, 1971.

———. *Judaism: A Way of Life*. New York: Union of American Hebrew Congregations, 1948.

Copelston, Fredrick. *A History of Philosophy: Medieval Philosophy*. 2 vols. Garden City, N.Y.: Image Books, 1962.

Cottingham, John. *On the Meaning of Life*. London: Routledge, 2003.

David, Yonah, ed. *The Poems of Amittay* [in Hebrew]. Jerusalem: Achshav, 1975.

Davidson, Israel. *Otzar ha-Mashalim ve-ha-Pitgamim*. Jerusalem: Mosad ha-Rav Kook, 1969.

Di Vidas, Elijah. *Reshit Hokhmah*. 3 vols. Jerusalem: Or ha-Musar, 1984.

———. *Reshit Hokhmah*. Tel Aviv: Esther Press, n.d.

Dorff, Elliot N., and Louis E. Newman, eds. *Contemporary Jewish Theology*. New York: Oxford University Press, 1999.

Ebreo, Leone. *The Philosophy of Love*. Translated by F. Friedberg-Seeley and Jean H. Barnes. London: Soncino Press, 1937.

Edelheit, Joseph, ed. *The Life of Covenant*. Chicago: Spertus College of Judaica Press, 1986.

Edwards, Paul, ed. *The Encyclopedia of Philosophy*. 3 vols. New York: Macmillan, 1972.

———. "Meaning and Value of Life." In *The Encyclopedia of Philosophy*, edited by Paul Edwards, vol. 3. New York: Macmillan, 1972, 467–70.

Elbogen, Ismar. *Jewish Liturgy*. Translated by Raymond Schiendlin. Philadelphia: Jewish Publication Society, 1993.

Emet mei Kotzk Titzmah. Bnai Brak: Nezah, 1961.

Encyclopedia of Religion and Ethics. 12 vols. New York: Scribner's, 1908.

The Epic of Gilgamesh. Translated by N. K. Sanders. New York: Penguin Books, 1972.

Fackenheim, Emil. *Quest for Past and Future*. Boston: Beacon Press, 1968.

The Fathers According to Rabbi Nathan. Translated by Judah Goldin. New Haven, Conn.: Yale University Press, 1955.

Faur, Jose. *Golden Doves with Silver Dots*. Bloomington: Indiana University Press, 1986.

————. *In the Shadows of History*. Albany: State University of New York Press, 1992.

Fein, Leonard. *Where Are We?* New York: Harper and Row, 1988.

Fine, Lawrence. "*Tikkun*: A Lurianic Motif in Contemporary Jewish Thought." In *Ancient Israel to Modern Judaism*, edited by Jacob Neusner, et al. Atlanta: Scholars Press, 1989, vol. 4, 35–53.

Finkelstein, Louis, ed. *The Jews*. Philadelphia: Jewish Publication Society, 1928.

Frimer, Norman. "The A-theological Judaism of the American Community." *Judaism* 11 (Spring,1962): 144–54.

Gerondi, Jonah. *Sha'arey Teshuvah* [*Gates of Repentance*]. 2 vols. Edited and translated by Shraga Silverstein. New York: Feldheim, 1971.

Ginzberg, Louis. *The Legends of the Jews*. 7 vols. Philadelphia: Jewish Publication Society, 1968.

Glatt, Herman A. *He Spoke in Parables: The Life and Works of the Dubnow Maggid*. New York: Bithmar, 1957.

Glatzer, Nahum, ed. *Franz Rosenzweig: His Life and Thought*. New York: Schocken, 1970.

Gleuck, Nelson. *Hesed in the Bible*. New York: Ktav, 1975.

Goldschmidt, Daniel. *Mahazor Le-Yamim Nora'im—Yom Kippur*. New York: Leo Baeck Institute, 1970.

Goldstein, Sidney. "Profile of American Jewry: Insights from the 1990 Jewish Population Survey." *American Jewish Yearbook 1992*. Philadelphia: Jewish Publication Society, 1992, 77–173.

Goldy, Robert G. *The Emergence of Jewish Theology in America*. Bloomington: Indiana University Press, 1990.

Gordis, Robert. *The Book of God and Man*. Chicago: University of Chicago Press, 1965.

Green, Arthur. *Seek My Face, Speak My Name*. Northvale, N.J.: Jason Aronson, 1992.

————. *Tormented Master*. University: University of Alabama Press, 1979.

Guttman, Julius. "The Principles of Judaism." *Conservative Judaism* 14, no. 1 (Fall 1959): 1–23.

Halevi, Judah. *Kuzari*. Translated by Hartwig Hirschfield. New York: Schocken, 1964.

Halivni, David Weiss. *Midrash, Mishnah, Gemara*. Cambridge, Mass.: Harvard University Press, 1986.

Harris, Monford. "Interim Theology." *Judaism* 7 (Fall 1958): 302–8.

———. "The Passover Seder: On Entering the Order of History." *Judaism* 25 (Spring 1976): 167–74.

Hartman, Geoffrey, and Sanford Budick, eds. *Midrash and Literature*. London: Yale University Press, 1986.

Hertzberg, Arthur, ed. *The Zionist Idea*. New York: Atheneum, 1973.

Heschel, Abraham J. *The Earth Is the Lord's*. New York: Henry Schuman, 1950.

———. *God in Search of Man*. Philadelphia: Jewish Publication Society, 1955.

———. *The Insecurity of Freedom*. New York: Farrar, Straus and Giroux, 1966.

———. *Kotzk* [in Yiddish]. 2 vols. Tel Aviv: Menorah, 1973.

———. *Man Is Not Alone*. Philadelphia: Jewish Publication Society, 1951.

———. *Moral Grandeur and Spiritual Audacity*. New York: Farrar, Straus and Giroux, 1966.

———. *A Passion for Truth*. New York: Farrar, Straus and Giroux, 1973.

———. *The Prophets*. Philadelphia: Jewish Publication Society, 1962.

———. *Torah min ha-Shamayim*. 2 vols. London: Soncino Press, 1962, 1965.

———. *Who Is Man?* Stanford, Calif.: Stanford University Press, 1965.

Hesse, Herman. *Reflections*. Translated by Ralph Manheim. New York: Farrar, Straus and Giroux, 1974.

Hick, John, ed. *The Existence of God*. New York: Macmillan, 1964.

Hoffman, Lawrence, ed. *The Land of Israel*. Notre Dame, Ind.: Notre Dame University Press, 1986.

Horowitz, Isaiah. *Shnei Luhot ha-Brit*. 3 vols. Jerusalem: Edison, 1960.

Horowitz, Shabbtai Sheftel. *Shefa Tal*. Frankfurt, 1719.

Hume, David. *Dialogues Concerning Natural Religion*. New York: Hafner, 1966.

Ibn Gabbai, Meir. *Avodat ha-Kodesh*. Jerusalem: Levin-Epstein, 1954.

Ibn Gabirol, Solomon. *The Fountain of Life*. Translated by Alfred B. Jacob. Stanwood, Wash.: Sabian, 1987.

Ibn Pakudah, Bahya. *The Book of Direction to the Duties of the Heart*. Translated by Menahem M. Mansoor. London: Routledge and Kegan Paul, 1973.

———. *Duties of the Heart*. 2 vols. Translated by Moses Hyamson. Jerusalem: Boys Town, 1965.

Ibn Zimra, David. *Teshuvot ha-Radbaz*. 4 vols. Furth, 1781.

Idel, Moshe. "Infinities of Torah in Kabbalah." In *Midrash and Literature*, edited by Geoffrey Hartman and Sanford Budick. London: Yale University Press, 1986, 141–58.

———. *Kabbalah: New Perspectives*. New Haven, Conn.: Yale University Press, 1988.

Idel, Moshe. *Messianic Mystics.* New Haven, Conn.: Yale University Press, 1998.

Jacob Joseph of Polnoyye. *Toledot Yaakov Yoseif.* 2 vols. Jerusalem: Sifrei ha-Musar Va-Hasidut, 1960.

Jacobs, Louis. *Faith.* New York: Basic Books, 1968.

———. *Hasidic Thought.* New York: Behrman House, 1976.

———. *A Jewish Theology.* New York: Behrman House, 1973.

———. "Jews and Law." *Judaism* 37 (Spring 1988): 244–47.

———. *Principles of the Jewish Faith.* New York: Basic Books, 1964.

———. *Seeker of Unity.* New York: Basic Books, 1966.

John Paul II. *Fides et Ratio: On the Relationship between Faith and Reason.* Boston: Pauline Books, 1998.

Jonas, Hans. "Immortality and the Modern Temper." *Harvard Theological Review* 55 (January 1962): 3–20.

Jung, Carl. *Modern Man in Search of a Soul.* Translated by W. S. Dell and Cary F. Barnes. New York: Harcourt Brace, 1933.

Kadushin, Max. *Organic Thinking.* New York: Bloch, 1938.

———. *The Rabbinic Mind.* New York: Jewish Theological Seminary, 1952.

Kant, Immanuel. *Foundations of the Metaphysics of Morals.* Translated by Lewis Beck. Indianapolis: Library of Liberal Arts, 1959.

———. "What Is Enlightenment?" Translated by Lewis Beck. Indianapolis: Library of Liberal Arts, 1959.

Kaplan, Aryeh. *The Light Beyond: Adventures in Hasidic Thought.* New York: Maznaim, 1981.

Kaplan, Dana Evan, ed. *The Cambridge Companion to American Judaism.* New York: Cambridge University Press, 2005.

Karff, Samuel E., ed. *Hebrew Union College–Jewish Institute of Religion at One Hundred Years.* New York: Hebrew Union College Press, 1976.

Karo, Joseph. *Shulhan Arukh.* 4 vols. Reprint, Vilna: Romm, 1911.

Katz, Jacob. "The Possible Connection of Sabbateanism, Haskalah and Reform Judaism" [in Hebrew]. *Studies in Jewish and Religious Intellectual History,* edited by Siegfried Stein and Raphael Loewe. University: University of Alabama Press, 1979, 83–100.

Katz, Steven, ed. *Jewish Philosophers.* New York: Bloch, 1975.

Kaufman, William. *Contemporary Jewish Philosophies.* New York: Reconstructionist Press, 1976.

Kaufmann, Yehezkel. *Toledot ha-Emunah ha-Yisraelit.* 8 vols. Tel Aviv: Dvir, 1964.

Keats, John. *Selected Poetry and Letters.* New York: Holt, Rinehart and Winston, 1964.

Kellner, Menahem. *Dogma in Medieval Jewish Thought.* New York: Oxford University Press, 1986.

———. *Maimonides on Human Perfection.* Atlanta: Scholars Press, 1990.

————, ed. *The Pursuit of the Ideal: Jewish Writings of Steven Schwarzschild.* Albany: State University of New York Press, 1990.

Kelsen, Hans. "Causality and Retribution." *Journal of the Philosophy of Science* 8 (1941): 533–56.

Kierkegaard, Søren. *Training in Christianity.* Translated by Walter Lowrie. Princeton, N.J.: Princeton University Press, 1944.

Klausner, Joseph. *The Messianic Idea in Israel.* Translated by W. F. Stinespring. New York: Macmillan, 1955.

Knesset Yisrael. Warsaw: n.p., 1906.

Kohler, Kaufmann. *Jewish Theology: Systematically and Historically Considered.* 2nd ed. New York: Ktav, 1968.

Kohut, Heinz. *The Analysis of the Self.* New York: International Universities Press, 1971.

Kullman, Eugene. "Tikvah and Mitzvah." *Conservative Judaism* 10, no. 4 (Summer 1956): 34–36.

Kushner, Harold. *When All You've Ever Wanted Isn't Enough: The Search for a Life that Matters.* New York: Pocket Books, 1986.

Lazaroff, Alan. "Judaism as Art." *Judaism* 30 (Summer 1981): 353–63.

Lazarus, Moritz. *The Ethics of Judaism.* 2 vols. Translated by Henrietta Szold. Philadelphia: Jewish Publication Society, 1900.

Leshon Hasidim. Lwow, 1876.

Levi ben Gershon (Gersonides). *Commentary to the Torah* [in Hebrew]. Photostat ed. Venice, 1547.

————. *Milhamot ha-Shem.* Leipzig, 1866.

Levi Yitzhak of Berditchev. *Kedushat Levi.* Brooklyn: Derarendiger, 1966.

————. *Kedushat Levi.* Jerusalem: Mosad l'Hotzaat Sifrei ha-Musar ve-ha-Hasidut, 1958.

Levine, Hillel. "Dwarfs on the Shoulders of Giants: A Case Study on the Impact of Modernization on the Social Epistemology of Judaism." *Jewish Social Studies* 40 (Winter 1978): 68–72.

Liebman, Charles. *The Ambivalent American Jew.* Philadelphia: Jewish Publication Society, 1973.

Likkutim Yesharim. Lwow: n.p., 1863.

Lipman, Eugene. "Mipne Tikkun ha-Olam in the Talmud." In *The Life of Covenant,* edited by Joseph Edelheit. Chicago: Spertus College of Judaica Press, 1986, 97–112.

Loew, Judah. *Be'er ha-Golah.* New York: Judaica Press, 1969.

————. *Derekh Hayyim.* New York: Judaica Press, 1969.

————. *Hiddushei Aggadot.* 4 vols. New York: Judaica Press, 1969.

————. *Netivot Olam.* 2 vols. New York: Judaica Press, 1969.

————. *Netzah Yisrael.* New York: Judaica Press, 1969.

————. *Tiferet Yisrael.* New York: Judaica Press, 1969.

Loewe, Raphael, ed. *Studies in Rationalism, Judaism and Universalism.* New York: Humanities Press, 1966.

Luzzatto, Moses Hayyim. *Mesillat Yesharim—The Path of the Upright.* Translated by Mordecai M. Kaplan. Philadelphia: Jewish Publication Society, 1936.

Macquarrie, John. *Principles of Christian Theology.* New York: Scribner's, 1966.

Maimonides, Moses. *Commentary to the Mishnah* [in Hebrew]. Edited by Joseph Kapah. Jerusalem: Mosad ha-Rav Kook, 1963.

————. *The Eight Chapters of Maimonides on Ethics.* Edited and translated by Joseph Gorfinkle. New York: Columbia University Press, 1912.

————. *Guide of the Perplexed.* Translated by S. Pines. Chicago: University of Chicago Press, 1963.

————. *Iggarot.* Jerusalem: Mosad ha-Rav Kook, 1944.

————. *Mishneh Torah* [with commentaries]. 6 vols. Reprint: New York: Friedman, 1963.

————. *Moses Maimonides: The Commentary to Mishnah Abot.* Translated by Arthur David. New York: Bloch, 1968.

Margolis, Max. "The Theological Aspect of Reformed Judaism." *Yearbook of the Central Conference of American Rabbis* 13 (1903): 185–338.

Mayer, Egon, and, Barry Kosman. *2001 American Jewish Identity Survey.* New York: City University of New York, 2002.

Mekhilta de-Rabbi Yishmael. Edited by Hayyim Horovitz and Israel Rabin. Jerusalem: Wahrman, 1960.

Menahem Nahum of Chernobyl. *Ma'or Einayim.* Jerusalem: n.p., 1966.

Mendelssohn, Moses. *Jerusalem.* Translated by Alfred Jospe. New York: Schocken, 1969.

————. *Jerusalem.* Translated by Alan Arkush. Hanover, NH: Brandeis University Press, 1983.

Meyer, Michael. *Response to Modernity.* New York: Oxford University Press, 1988.

Midrash on Psalms [in Hebrew]. Edited by Solomon Buber. Vilna: Romm, 1891.

Midrash Rabbah [with commentaries]. 2 vols. Vilna: Romm, 1921.

Midrash Tanhuma. 2 vols. Edited by Solomon Buber. Vilna: Romm, 1885.

Midrash Tanhuma ha-Nidpas. Jerusalem: Levin-Epstein, 1964.

Mikra'ot Gedolot [Hebrew scripture with commentaries]. 5 vols. New York: Tanach, 1959.

Mishnah [with commentaries]. Jerusalem: Horeb, 1952.

Mor, Sagit. "*Tikkun Olam*: Its Early Meaning and Influence on Divorce Law during the Mishnaic Period" [in Hebrew]. *Moed* 15 (2005): 24–51.

Mordecai of Chernobyl. *Likkutei Torah.* New York: Noble Printing, 1954.

Moses Hayyim Ephraim of Sudlykow. *Degel Mahaneh Ephraim.* Jerusalem: Hadar, 1963.

Nahman of Bratzlav. *Likkutei Maharan.* 1866. Reprint: New York: Bratslaver, 1966.

Neusner, Jacob. "The Tasks of Theology in Judaism." *Journal of Religion* 59 (1979): 71–86.

———, ed. *To Grow in Wisdom: An Anthology of Abraham Joshua Heschel.* Lanham, Md.: Madison Books, 1990.

Neusner, Jacob, et al., eds. *Ancient Israel to Modern Judaism.* Atlanta: Scholars Press, 1989.

Palestinian Talmud [with commentaries]. Krotoschin, 1886.

Pascal, Blaise. *Pensees.* Translated by A. J. Krailsheimer. London: Penguin Books, 1966.

Pegis, Anton, ed. *Introduction to St. Thomas Aquinas.* New York: Modern Library, 1948.

Pesikta de-Rav Kahana. Edited by Solomon Buber. Lyck: Mekitzei Nirdamim, 1868.

Pesikta de-Rav Kahana. 2 vols. Edited by Bernard Mandelbaum. New York: Jewish Theological Seminary, 1962.

Pesikta Rabbati. Edited by Meir Friedmann. Vienna: Herausgebers, 1880.

Petuchowski, Jakob. "The Beauty of God." *The Life of Covenant,* edited by Joseph Edelheit. Chicago: Spertus College of Judaica Press, 1986, 125–30.

———. "The Question of Jewish Theology." *Judaism* 7 (Winter 1958): 49–55.

———. *The Theology of Haham David Nieto.* New York: Ktav, 1970.

Pines, Shlomo. "The Jewish Religion after the Destruction of Temple and State: The Views of Bodin and Spinoza." *Studies in Jewish Religious and Intellectual History,* edited by Siegfried Stein and Ralph Loewe. University: University of Alabama Press, 1979, 215–34.

Pirkei d'Rabbi Eliezer. Translated by Gerald Friedlander. London: n.p., 1916.

Pirkei d'Rabbi Eliezer. Warsaw: Bomberg, 1852.

———. *Pirkei d'Rabbi Eliezer.* New York: Ohm, 1946.

Ringrenn, Helmer. *Israelite Religion.* Philadelphia: Fortress Press, 1966.

Roof, Wade Clark. *A Generation of Seekers.* San Francisco: HarperSanFrancisco, 1993.

Rosenbloom, Noah. "Menasseh ben Israel and the Eternality of Punishment Issue." *American Academy for Jewish Research* 60 (1994): 241–62.

Rosenthal, Gilbert. "*Tikkun ha-Olam*: The Metamorphosis of a Concept." *Journal of Religion* 85 (April 2005): 214–40.

Rosenzweig, Franz. *On Jewish Learning.* New York: Schocken, 1955.

———. *The Star of Redemption.* Translated by William H. Hallo. New York: Holt, Rinehart and Winston, 1970.

Rotenstreich, Nathan. "Enlightenment: Between Kant and Mendelssohn." In *Studies in Jewish Religious and Intellectual History*, edited by Siegfried Stein and Raphael Loewe.University: University of Alabama Press, 1979, 263–79.

Roth, Cecil. *A Life of Menasseh ben Israel*. Philadelphia: Jewish Publication Society, 1934.

Rubenstein, Richard. *Power Struggle*. New York: Scribner's, 1974.

Ryle, Gilbert. *The Concept of Mind*. New York: Barnes and Noble, 1949.

Saadya Gaon. *The Book of Beliefs and Opinions*. Translated by Samuel Rosenblatt. New Haven, Conn.: Yale University Press, 1948.

Samuel of Uceda. *Midrash Shmuel*. Jerusalem: Brody-Katz, n.d.

Samuelson, Norbert. "Philosophical and Religious Authority in the Thought of Maimonides and Gersonides." *Central Conference of American Rabbis Journal* 16, no. 4 (October 1969): 31–43.

Schachter, Zalman. *Jewish with Feeling*. New York: Riverhead, 2005.

Schechter, Solomon. *Aspects of Rabbinic Theology*. New York: Macmillan, 1909.

———. *Seminary Addresses and Other Papers*. New York: Burning Bush Press, 1959.

———. *Studies in Judaism: A Selection*. New York: Meridian, 1958.

———. *Studies in Judaism: First Series*. Philadelphia: Jewish Publication Society, 1911.

———. *Studies in Judaism: Second Series*. Philadelphia: Jewish Publication Society, 1908.

———. *Studies in Judaism: Third Series*. Philadelphia: Jewish Publication Society, 1924.

Schneur Zalman of Liady. *Likkutei Amarim (Tanya)*. Brooklyn: Otzar ha-Hasidim, 1965.

Scholem, Gershom. *Major Trends in Jewish Mysticism*. New York: Schocken, 1941.

———. *The Messianic Idea in Judaism*. New York: Schocken, 1971.

———. *On Jews and Judaism in Crisis*. New York:, 1976.

———. *On the Kabbalah and Its Symbolism*. New York: Schocken, 1965.

———. *On the Mystical Shape of the Godhead*. Translated by Joachim Neugroschel. New York: Schocken, 1991.

———. *Shabbatai Sevi*. Translated by R. J. Zwi Werblowsky. Princeton, N.J.: Princeton University Press, 1973.

Seder Eliyahu Rabba ve-Seder Eliyahu Zuta. Edited by Meir Friedmann. Vienna: Ahiyasaf, 1904.

Sefer Ba'al Shem Tov al Nah ve-Aggadot ha-Shas. Jerusalem: Otzar Midrash, 1968.

Sefer ha-Bahir. Edited by Reuven Margaliot. Jerusalem: Mosad ha-Rav Kook, 1951.

Sefer Yetzirah. Jerusalem: Levin-Epstein, 1965.

Shakespeare, William. *The Arden Shakespeare: Complete Works*. London: Thomas Nelson and Sons, 1998.

Shapiro, David S. "The Doctrine of the Image of God and *Imitatio Dei*." *Judaism* 12 (Winter, 1963): 57–77.

Shapiro, Nathan Nata. *Megaleh Amukot—Ve-Ethanan*. Bnai Brak: n.p., 1992.

Sherwin, Byron L. "*Corpus Domini*: Traces of the New Testament in East European Hasidism?" *Heythrop Journal* 35 (1994): 267–80.

———. *In Partnership with God: Contemporary Jewish Law and Ethics*. Syracuse, N.Y.: Syracuse University Press, 1990.

———. *Kabbalah: An Introduction to Jewish Mysticism*. Lanham, Md.: Rowman and Littlefield, 2006.

———. "*Mai Hanukkah*: What Is Hanukkah?" *Central Conference of American Rabbis Journal* 50 (Fall 2003): 19–28.

———. *Mystical Theology and Social Dissent*. London: Oxford University Press, 1982.

———. *Studies in Jewish Theology: Reflections in the Mirror of Tradition*. London: Vallentine Mitchell, 2007.

———. "Thinking Judaism Through: Jewish Theology in America." *The Cambridge Companion to American Judaism*, edited by Dana E. Kaplan. New York: Cambridge University Press, 2005, 117–32.

———. *Toward a Jewish Theology*. Lewiston, N.Y.: Edwin Mellen Press, 1991.

Sherwin, Byron L., and Seymour J. Cohen. *How to Be a Jew: Ethical Teachings of Judaism*. Northvale, N.J.: Jason Aronson, 1992.

Shirman, H., ed. *Solomon ibn Gabirol: Selected Poems* [in Hebrew] Jerusalem: Schocken, 1964.

Siegel, Seymour. "The Unity of the Jewish People." *Conservative Judaism* 42, no. 3 (Spring 1990): 21–27.

Sifre. Edited by Louis Finkelstein. Berlin: Judischer Kulterband in Deutschland Abteilung Verlag, 1939.

Sifre on Deuteronomy. Edited by Meir Friedmann. Vienna, 1865.

Silberman, Lou M. "Theology and Philosophy." In *Hebrew Union College–Jewish Institute of Religion at One Hundred Years*, edited by Samuel E. Karff. New York: Hebrew Union College Press, 1976, 383–430.

Silver, Jeremy. *Maimonidean Criticism and the Maimonides Controversy*. Leiden: Brill, 1965.

Simeon Mendel of Guvarchov. *Sefer Ba'al Shem Tov*. 2 vols. Lodz, Poland: n.p., 1938.

Simon, Leon, ed. and trans. *Selected Essays of Ahad Ha-Am*. New York: Meridian, 1962.

Singer, Irving. *Meaning in Life*. New York: Free Press, 1992.

———. *The Pursuit of Love*. Baltimore: Johns Hopkins University Press, 1994.

Singer, Isaac Bashevis. *Gifts*. Philadelphia: Jewish Publication Society, 1985.

Slonimsky, Henry. *Essays*. Chicago: Quadrangle Books, 1967.

Soloveichik, Joseph B. *Halakhic Man*. Translated by Lawrence Kaplan. Philadelphia: Jewish Publication Society, 1983.

———. "Redemption, Prayer, *Talmud Torah*." *Tradition* 17 (1978), 55–72.

———. *Worship of the Heart*. New York: Ktav, 2003.

Stein, Siegfried, and Raphael Loewe, eds. *Studies in Jewish Religious and Intellectual History*. University: University of Alabama Press, 1979.

Susser, Bernard, and Charles Liebman. *Choosing Survival*. New York: Oxford University Press, 1999.

Talmud [with commentaries]. 20 vols. Vilna: Romm, 1895. English translation: *The Talmud*. 18 vols. Edited by Isadore Epstein. London: Soncino Press, 1935–61.

Taylor, Charles. *The Ethics of Authenticity*. Cambridge, Mass.: Harvard University Press, 1991.

Tempkin, Sefton. "Solomon Schechter and Max Heller." *Conservative Judaism* 16:1 (Winter 1962): 54–56.

Tishbi, Isaiah. "Al Makorei ha-Ma'amar Kudsha Brikh hu, Torah ve-Yisrael had Hu." *Kiryat Sefer* 50 (1975): 480–92, 668–74.

———. *Mishnat ha-Zohar*. 2 vols. Jerusalem: Mosad Bialik, 1957.

Tolstoy, Leo. *The Portable Tolstoy*. Edited by John Bayley. New York: Penguin Books, 1978.

Twerski, Abraham J. *Let Us Make Man*. New York: CIS Publishers, 1987.

Urbach, Ephraim. *The Sages*. Translated by Israel Abrahams. Cambridge, Mass.: Harvard University Press, 1987.

Vital, Hayyim. *Sefer Sha'arei Kedushah*. Jerusalem: Eshkol, n.d.

———. *Sha'ar ha-Gilgulim*. Jerusalem: Eshel, 1963.

Watts, Alan. *The Two Hands of God*. New York: Collier, 1969.

Weinryb, Bernard. *The Jews of Poland*. Philadelphia: Jewish Publication Society, 1973.

Wellhausen, Julius. *Prolegomena to the History of Ancient Israel*. New York: Meridian, 1957.

Wiesel, Elie. *Souls on Fire*. New York: Random House, 1972.

Wilson, Bryan. *Rationality*. New York: Harper and Row, 1971.

Wittgenstein, Ludwig. *Notebooks 1914–1916*. Translated by G. E. Anscome. New York: Harper and Brothers, 1961.

Wolf, Arnold J. "Repairing *Tikkun Olam*." *Judaism* 50 (Fall 2001): 479–82.

Wolfson, Harry A. "Notes of Proofs of the Existence of God." *Hebrew Union College Annual* 1 (1924): 575–96.

Woocher, Jonathan S. *Sacred Survival: The Civil Religion of American Jews*. Bloomington: Indiana University Press, 1986.

Yerushalmi, Yosef Hayim. *From Spanish Court to Italian Ghetto*. Seattle: University of Washington Press, 1971.

Yoetz of Rakatz. *Siah Sarfei Kodesh*. Lodz, Poland: n.p., 1931.

Zlotnick, Dov. "Al Makor ha-Mashal ha-Nanas ve-ha-Anak ve-Gilgulav." *Sinai* 77 (1975): 184–89.

———. "The Commentary of Rabbi Abraham Azulai to the Mishnah." *American Academy of Jewish Research Proceedings* 40 (1973), 147–68.

Zohar. Vilna: Romm, 1882.

Index